LEGO STAR WARS II
THE ORIGINAL TRILOGY

Prima Games
A Division of Random House, Inc.

3000 Lava Ridge Court
Roseville, CA 95661
(800) 733-3000
www.primagames.com

PRIMA OFFICIAL GAME GUIDE

Michael Littlefield

Prima Games
A Division of Random House, Inc.

3000 Lava Ridge Court, Ste. 100
Roseville, CA 95661
1-800-733-3000
www.primagames.com

Product Manager: Mario De Govia
Editor: Christy Seifert
Design and Layout: Winter Graphics North

ISBN: 0-7615-5411-4
Library of Congress Catalog Card Number: 2006928153
Printed in the United States of America

06 07 08 09 LL 10 9 8 7 6 5 4 3 2 1

CONTENTS

INTRODUCTION

GALAXY BASICS

STAR WARS CHARACTERS

TRANSPORTATION

MOS EISLEY CANTINA

WALKTHROUGH INTRODUCTION

EPISODE IV: A NEW HOPE

EPISODE V: THE EMPIRE STRIKES BACK

EPISODE VI: RETURN OF THE JEDI

BONUS FEATURES

INTRODUCTION

Right this very moment, in a toy box not too far, far away....

Once again, little LEGO *Star Wars*® figures fight an ongoing battle for freedom in the galaxy. For years the noble Jedi were the guardians of peace and justice throughout the galaxy until they were betrayed by one of their own and hunted to near extinction. With the Jedi nearly wiped out, the evil Empire grew in power until it ruthlessly controlled the galaxy. But all is not lost, for a few Jedi still remain scattered across the different worlds. With their ancient wisdom and teachings they may be able to assist the heroic Rebellion fight for freedom and restore justice throughout the galaxy.

It's time to experience the excitement and adventure of those brave Rebels. Be there as young Luke Skywalker first meets Obi-Wan Kenobi and begins his training in the Force to help him destroy the Empire's Death Star in Episode IV. Discover the true might of the dark side as Luke's true father is revealed and Han Solo is captured by Boba Fett in Episode V. And witness the brave fight of the Rebellion at a last stand against the Empire's reconstructed Death Star that will determine the fate of the galaxy in Episode VI.

Saving the galaxy from the iron fist of the Empire can be a dangerous and difficult task. This guide will help you on your adventure as it walks you step by step through the game's exciting episodes. With it you'll find important items scattered throughout the chapters, such as LEGO canisters and studs, power bricks, and gold bricks. This guide also gives you detailed information about every character and vehicle that you can use during your adventures. Discover all the fun and exciting areas of gameplay that LEGO® *Star Wars*® II: The Original Trilogy has to offer.

The Empire might have the upper hand to begin with, but with a band of valiant Rebels on your side and the Force, you just might have what it takes to save the galaxy and restore freedom to all who live there. May the Force be with you. Always.

GALAXY BASICS

Game Modes

LEGO *Star Wars* II has two different game modes in which you can play: Story mode and Freeplay mode. When you first start the game you must play in Story mode. This mode follows the plot of the original *Star Wars* trilogy. The characters that were in certain scenes in the movies are found in corresponding scenes in the game. You cannot deviate from that in Story mode. For example, in Episode IV *A New Hope*, Luke Skywalker, Han Solo, and Chewbacca went to the holding cells on the Death Star to find Princess Leia, so in the game's Story mode, you have to use those same characters to find her.

After you have completed a mission through Story mode, you may go back and play through it again in Freeplay mode. In this mode, you can return to any mission, and have the option of playing as any character from your character inventory. After you make your choice, the game randomly chooses a cast of other characters from your inventory. This cast of characters is always available for your use throughout the mission. You can switch to any of them at any time. The game chooses characters with the different abilities you might need in order to get to all the areas of a mission. Playing in Freeplay mode gives you the ability to use characters you weren't able to use in Story mode. You have the ability to change the scenes from the movie and can actually make Boba Fett fight himself during Episode V.

Special Abilities

Almost every character that you can use in the game has some special ability that will be very useful as you play. Some characters can use the Force to move or open objects, some can hover through the air over long distances, some have special tools or weapons you need, and some have greater jumping abilities to get to higher places. As you play, you will need to use all the special abilities of your team of LEGO characters to complete the game in Freeplay mode.

ASCENSION GUN

All characters who use some type of blaster weapon also carry an ascension gun with them. As you travel throughout the chapters of LEGO *Star Wars* II, be on the lookout for red circle swirls on the ground. Each swirl has a corresponding hook somewhere nearby. If you see

a hook on a level, you know that a red circle swirl is probably hidden

somewhere close. To use this special ability, stand on the red circle swirl and fire your ascension gun to go for a ride to a location that's otherwise inaccessible. The ascension gun lets you grapple up to hard-to-reach places, or it can be used to swing across dangerous areas.

THERMAL DETONATOR

One of the bounty hunter's most powerful special abilities is his thermal detonator. Toss this device at your target, and then move away. After a few seconds, the detonator explodes, destroying objects around it. Although your regular blaster fire just bounces off the shiny metal LEGO objects found around the galaxy, the thermal detonator blasts them to pieces. This weapon helps you uncover hidden goods and get to new places.

TRAVEL CHUTES

Throughout the missions, you will find small chutes in some walls. Most characters are too big to use the chutes, but a few are just small enough to fit. Use a small character, such as a Jawa or Ugnaught, to jump into the chute and travel to the chute's end. These chutes lead to places that are otherwise impossible to reach, and can reward you with many valuables.

HOVER

A few characters in the game have to ability to hover through the air for a certain amount of time. The astromech droid, R2-D2, and the bounty hunter, Boba Fett, both have this special ability. They can fly through the air across an area, but cannot ascend any higher than the level where they started. These characters are crucial to finding many hard-to-reach items and areas during your missions. If you see an object that is floating out in space just out of reach, send one of these characters to fly out and get it. The hover ability only lasts for a little while, though, so get what you want and return to safety before you drop from the sky.

INTRODUCTION

GALAXY BASICS

STAR WARS CHARACTERS

TRANSPORTATION

MOS EISLEY CANTINA

WALKTHROUGH INTRODUCTION

EPISODE IV: A NEW HOPE

EPISODE V: THE EMPIRE STRIKES BACK

EPISODE VI: RETURN OF THE JEDI

BONUS FEATURES

THE FORCE

Those in the galaxy who can still use the Force are few and far between since the Jedi became enemies of the Empire. For those characters who can still wield its power, the Force is a strong weapon and tool in the *Star Wars* universe. Those who use this power for good are known as the Jedi, and include characters such as Obi-Wan Kenobi and Luke Skywalker. Those who have turned to the dark side and use the Force for evil are known as the Sith. Darth Vader is a Sith Lord. The power of the Force works the same way, whether it is used for good or evil purposes.

Things or characters that can be influenced by the Force in the LEGO *Star Wars* universe begin to glow when you get close to them. This glow changes depending on the character who is wielding the Force. Light glow colors such as green and blue can be influenced using the good side of the Force. Something that is dark and has a red glow can only be affected by using the dark side of the Force. The Force can be used to activate switches, open compartments, move objects around, disable droids, and stop your enemies.

Objects that are affected by the Force are found all over the game. During some missions in Story mode, you might not have a Jedi by your side to use this special ability. Be sure to return to these levels later in Freeplay mode with characters who can use both the light and dark sides of the Force to fully explore the level.

DOUBLE JUMP

As you explore, you will find certain objects or areas that might be a little too high or too far away to reach. On these occasions, it's good to have a teammate who can use the Force. These characters can channel the Force to double jump to where they want to go. Use the double jump straight up in the air to nab a hard-to-reach blue stud, or double jump across an extra-large break in a walkway to get to the other side.

ACTIVATION PANELS

Throughout the game you will see many activation panels on walls and on equipment. Walk up to these panels and you'll see a picture of the character that you need in order to use it. Some panels have pictures of droids, such as C-3PO and R2-D2. All they have to do is walk up to the panel to access it. They might not be that good at fighting but these droids are invaluable for exploring entire areas of a map.

Other panels have a picture of a stormtrooper or bounty hunter and have a colored circle on the ground in front of them. Stand on the circle in front of the panel when you go to access the activation panel. These panels are used frequently in Freeplay mode and can lead to lots of hidden treasure.

Weapons

From Mos Eisley spaceport to Jabba's palace, the *Star Wars* galaxy is a rough place, so you'll need weapons to defend yourself. You can carry different weapons—from blasters to lightsabers—depending on who you are. Become familiar with each type of weapon and it will not only help keep you alive, but can also help you get to new and exciting places.

BLASTERS/BOWCASTER

Many characters use laser blasters as their main weapon. The different kinds of blaster weapons can shoot lasers to hit near and far enemies. Depending on the enemy's strength, it might take more than one shot to destroy him. The blaster is also an important tool to get through many of the levels. At times, you might see targets that require a shot from your gun in order for you to activate them. At other times, you might need your blaster or bowcaster to break items that other weapons can't reach.

 NOTE

When an enemy moves in close, you no longer need to fire your weapon at him. You automatically go into hand-to-hand combat mode; then you can slap your enemy down or hit him with the butt of your gun.

ENERGY GUN

Smaller creatures such as Jawas and Ugnaughts were never meant to be warriors. Instead, they thrive on working with droids and electronic devices. As such, they only carry energy guns, which have no effect on human characters. Energy guns can be used to short-circuit a droid and cause it to shut down temporarily. Never try to use this gun in battle because it will have no effect.

GALAXY BASICS

LIGHTSABER

Only the Jedi and the Sith can use a lightsaber. This weapon is very versatile and not as clumsy as a blaster. The lightsaber can be used to hit targets both near and far. When up close, use the lightsaber to hack and slash at your enemies to break them into little pieces. For an

even more powerful attack, perform a double jump before you attack: You will drive your lightsaber into the ground beneath you, causing damage to any enemies that are around.

The lightsaber can also be used for defensive purposes. Just hold up your weapon to make all incoming shots harmlessly bounce off it. You can also reflect enemy shots back at the shooter. After an enemy fires at you, wait for the blast to almost hit you. Just before it does, bring up your lightsaber to block the shot and deflect it back at the shooter. This is a great way to drop those far-away targets.

Items

The game has many items scattered about, just waiting for you to collect them. Some items make you rich, some unlock hidden extras, and some might just help keep you alive. Keep a sharp eye out for anything that you can add to your stash.

LEGO STUDS

Scattered about every level of LEGO Star Wars II are different colored LEGO studs. These can be found lying on the ground or hidden in secret compartments. Studs already on the ground stay there indefinitely until you touch them, but studs that spill out of a hidden area or from a

broken container only stay on the ground for a short period of time. Make sure you get them quickly before they disappear.

There are four colors of studs that you can collect, and each is worth a different amount: silver (10), gold (100), blue (1,000), and purple (10,000). The gold and silver studs are pretty common and are found almost everywhere. The more valuable blue and purple studs usually take some effort to find and collect.

Every stud you collect on a level helps fill up your yellow True Jedi Status meter at the top of the screen. Collect enough studs to fill up the meter to become a True Jedi. Completely fill up the True Jedi Status meter in both Story mode and Freeplay mode to get a gold brick for each.

Collecting LEGO studs not only fills up your True Jedi Status meter, but also allows you to buy more things at the cantina bar. Walk up to the bar to see what is for sale. You can buy helpful

tips, gold bricks, game extras, and even different characters for the game. Some characters and items cost a lot of studs, so be sure to search every part of a level to get more studs. Every little bit helps.

HEARTS

Scattered about the galaxy are large red hearts. For every heart you pick up, a heart in your health meter is replenished. If your health meter is already full, the hearts you gather will have no effect on you. Hearts can mostly be found with the many LEGO studs hidden

around each level. You can also find hidden hearts by dispatching enemies and other characters who roam the galaxy. Always try to keep your health meter full, so pick up any hearts on the ground before they disappear.

LEGO CANISTERS

Every level contains ten hidden LEGO canisters. These canisters are usually placed in areas that are fairly difficult to reach. Sometimes, you must find hidden objects scattered about a level in order to reveal a hidden canister. Sometimes, you have to move certain switches

using the Force. Some canisters are hidden behind breakable panels. And some LEGO canisters are locked away in rooms that only certain characters can get to in Freeplay mode. There are many different ways the canisters are hidden throughout the galaxy, so keep a sharp eye out for where they might be. If you collect all ten canisters on a level, you get a huge LEGO stud bonus added to your total. Find all the LEGO canisters in the galaxy to build vehicles out in the cantina parking lot.

RED POWER BRICKS

Every mission has a red power brick hidden somewhere on the level. Red power bricks are usually hidden pretty well and may require you to go back in Freeplay mode in order to find them. Finding power bricks unlocks extra features such as super lightsabers that you can

purchase at the cantina bar. After you find the red power brick on a level, you are rewarded with a gold brick as well.

2/99

GOLD BRICKS

A total of 99 gold bricks is scattered throughout the game, and there are different ways of earning them. Reaching True Jedi status in Story mode, True Jedi status in Freeplay mode, finding all the LEGO canisters on a level, and finding the red power brick are four ways you can earn a gold brick when playing through the missions. You can also purchase more bricks at the cantina bar, but they do get expensive. You must find ten gold bricks to open up the sixth mission in all three episodes. Outside the cantina is a huge question mark that you must fill by collecting 50 gold bricks.

Environment

The *Star Wars* galaxy is an extremely interactive environment. Objects made of LEGOs that you find along your adventure can usually be interacted with in one way or another. Some of these LEGO pieces can be destroyed by shooting them with blasters or chopping them up with a lightsaber. If a LEGO object seems impervious to destruction, it probably means that you can use the Force on it to either move it in some way or cause it to break apart. LEGO *Star Wars* II has a new feature: You can put LEGO pieces together to form a new object. Whenever you see a pile of LEGOs bouncing up and down slightly, that means they can be assembled. During your adventures, be sure to interact with everything in the environment to find hidden treasures.

Multiplayer

LEGO *Star Wars* II has the perfect design for playing with your friends. At anytime during the course of the game, another player can plug in a controller and take control of one of the other characters in your party. Now instead of fighting your enemies alone, you have a friend to help finish them off even quicker. And when the second player is ready to quit, all he or she has to do is pause the game and choose the option to drop out.

Everything you collect on your adventure together, from LEGO studs to LEGO canisters, goes into a community pot for all to share. The only issue everyone should be concerned about is keeping the health meter filled with enough hearts. This kind of sharing eliminates any unnecessary competition rivalry that might get one or both of you broken into pieces during a mission. Instead, have a positive, friendly competition and see how many enemies you can break apart.

STAR WARS CHARACTERS

There are at least 70 different characters you can choose to play during your LEGO *Star Wars* adventure. As you progress through the game, you will come across many strange and exotic characters. Some will be added to your list of playable characters. Others will become available to purchase at the bar using the LEGO studs you find. And the added feature of character creation lets you mix and match characters just to your liking. The cast of characters you buy and collect all have unique attributes and abilities. Some of these characters will get you into otherwise unreachable lands. Be sure to collect and purchase all the characters you can, because you never know when you might need their help getting through a mission.

NOTE

SELECTING TWO CHARACTERS IN FREEPLAY MODE INSTEAD OF ONE

Choose the first character you want to use in Freeplay mode. After you start the mission, take control of the other character and return to Mos Eisley cantina. Now the character you first picked is your companion. When you choose to play Freeplay mode again, you can choose another character that you want to use during the mission. For example, start a mission as Boba Fett and the game will select your other partner, say, Princess Leia. Take control of Princess Leia and return to the cantina. Now enter the Freeplay mission again. Boba Fett is automatically your partner, leaving you free to choose another character to take with you. This gives you the power to choose two characters that you want to use during a Freeplay mission.

CHARACTER TYPES

Jedi/Sith: Force attuned, double jump ability
Small characters: Chute travel ability
Activation panel droids: Accesses panels
Bounty hunters: Thermal detonators
Ghost characters: Impervious to damage
Blaster characters: Ascension gun ability

JEDI

OBI-WAN (BEN) KENOBI

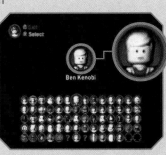

Old Ben Kenobi is the strange hermit who lives out in the desert by himself and who everybody talks about. What few people know is that he is one of the last surviving Jedi left in the galaxy. He even trained Luke's father in the ways of the Force. Now it falls on his shoulders to train the young Luke Skywalker and keep his fingers crossed! As a Jedi, Ben Kenobi doesn't need to use a blaster because he can use the Force.

YODA

Yoda is a master Jedi, having trained in the ways of the Force for hundreds of years. Being so old, Yoda is forced to walk with the assistance of a cane. When he does, he is very, very slow. But the Force is still strong in his old frame and it gives him the ability to double jump pretty far and cover more ground. The Force allows him to interact with objects scattered around the various worlds. And when danger comes, Yoda doesn't shy away, but instead readies his lightsaber to meet the challenge.

LUKE SKYWALKER (DAGOBAH)

Luke Skywalker goes to Dagobah a Rebel fighter and becomes a Jedi...for the most part. With Yoda on his back, Luke learns the ways of the Force—until he sees that his friends are in trouble on the Cloud City of Bespin. Then he has to leave. He might not be a full Jedi yet, but the ways of the Force are strong with this one. After Dagobah, he no longer uses a blaster. Rather, the lightsaber is his new weapon of choice. Luke can control the Force to manipulate objects found in the world around him.

INTRODUCTION
GALAXY BASICS
STAR WARS CHARACTERS
TRANSPORTATION
MOS EISLEY CANTINA
WALKTHROUGH INTRODUCTION
EPISODE IV: A NEW HOPE
EPISODE V: THE EMPIRE STRIKES BACK
EPISODE VI: RETURN OF THE JEDI
BONUS FEATURES

LUKE SKYWALKER (JEDI)

Luke Skywalker has come a long way since growing up on Tatooine. Back then he was just a moisture farm boy with big dreams of flying around space. Now he is a Jedi and the only hope to save the galaxy from the ruthless Empire. Dressed all in black like his father,

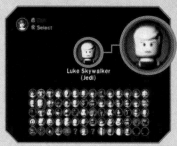

Anakin Skywalker, Luke can wield the Force not only to interact with objects in the environment but also to crush his enemies. The Force also gives him the special ability to double jump in the air, allowing him to get to places ordinary people can't get to. When he doesn't want to use the Force, Luke can unleash the fury of his lightsaber to deal out justice to those that stand in his way.

LUKE SKYWALKER (ENDOR)

Luke Skywalker goes to Endor to assist his friends in taking out the shield generator for the Death Star. Because Endor is completely covered with jungle growth, Luke must wear green camouflage to cover up his black Jedi clothes so he blends in a little better. Luke is well

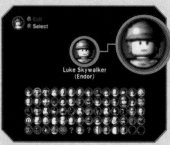

trained in the Force at this point and can use it to move objects or to hurt his enemies. The Force even grants him the ability to double jump to reach otherwise inaccessible places. When he gets to the business of fighting, he always has his lightsaber by his side.

SITH
DARTH VADER

One of the most feared people in the galaxy, Darth Vader is notorious for his cruelty. He enforces the will of the Galactic Empire with an iron fist, crushing any who oppose it. That means tracking down the Rebel Alliance that wishes to destroy the Empire. Vader

might be part of the establishment, but he is not a politician. He's an enforcer. He carries with him a red lightsaber to hack and slash his enemies. Vader also has mastery over the dark side of the Force. He can use this power to lift and choke his opponents to death. He can also use this power to interact with certain black objects found around the galaxy.

THE EMPEROR

Even more powerful than Vader is his master, Emperor Palpatine. The evil Sith Lord deceived the galaxy to acquire status of chancellor, then tricked Anakin Skywalker into betraying his fellow Jedi. This led to the collapse of the Galactic Republic and made Palpatine Emperor of

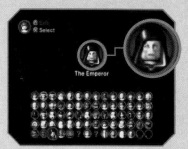

the galaxy. The Emperor is extremely powerful and can wield the dark side of the Force as well as anyone. When he has to fight, he pulls out his lightsaber to cut his opponents to ribbons. When his enemies get too close, the Emperor really gives them a shock when he zaps them with electrical currents that flow from his hands.

SMALL CHARACTERS
JAWA

These little guys are the scavengers of the deserts of Tatooine. They collect what others consider garbage and turn it into their own brand of treasure. Jawas like to pick up droids because they have a special knack for refurbishing droids and reselling them. Jawas are

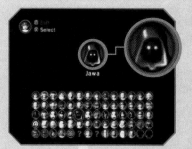

small creatures, and as such, are not meant to be fighters. The only weapon they carry is the energy gun they use to disable droids. But Jawas are useful to any mission because their small size lets them navigate travel chutes found all over the galaxy.

UGNAUGHT

The poor Ugnaught is one of the small creatures that toil away in the waste management section of Cloud City. Because these little guys are workers and not fighters, they don't carry any real weapons with them. All they have is a little energy gun. They can use these guns to

zap stray droids to cause them to short-circuit for a few seconds. Otherwise, the Ugnaught is helpless. But these little guys aren't totally worthless, because their small stature allows them to move through travel chutes found throughout the galaxy. These chutes are very important and can lead to great treasure.

WICKET

The forest moon of Endor is inhabited by small, furry creatures known as Ewoks. One of these creatures is Wicket; he makes first contact with the Rebels (who are trying to destroy the deflector shield generator protecting the half-completed Death Star). Wicket might

appear soft and cuddly, but he is a trained warrior who carries a slingshot with him to drop anyone that gets in his way. Because of his small stature, Wicket is able to get into travel chutes located around the galaxy. These chutes can lead to untold riches, making Wicket a valuable member of any team.

EWOK

The Ewoks are the small, fluffy creatures that inhabit the forest moon of Endor. Many people might assume a creature so soft and cute would make a great pet. But Ewoks are wild and unpredictable creatures. They have learned to survive with just the basic necessities.

They live in the trees and fight using slingshots. But don't discount the slingshot's effectiveness; it can take down any opponent. What makes these little guys so useful is their ability to move through the small travel chutes found around the galaxy, and thereby collect valuable items.

ACTIVATION PANEL DROIDS
R2-D2

This little astromech droid might not look like much, but R2-D2 is critical to the Rebel Alliance. Located on the different worlds around the universe are various kinds of Activation Panels. These panels require a certain character to operate them. Only R2-D2 can access

the panels with his picture on them and thus perform a task such as opening a door or raising a bridge.

   R2-D2 is also a very handy droid with lots of surprises. This astromech can hover in the air for long periods of time. This allows him to fly through the air to get to hard-to-reach areas or items. R2 also can short-circuit any droid and turn it into spare parts.

C-3PO

C-3PO is a protocol droid who seems like an endless fountain of knowledge. Unfortunately that's almost all he's good for. He can't use a weapon, he can't attack, he can't run, and he can't jump. But what he can do is access the activation panels that have a picture of a

protocol droid on them. For this one reason alone, C-3PO is invaluable to your success in the game. He can get you into new areas where you can find valuable treasure and items.

BOUNTY HUNTERS
GREEDO

Greedo is an old bounty hunter acquaintance of Han Solo. Unfortunately he's not a good acquaintance and has been contracted by Jabba the Hutt to bring Han in. It's lucky for Han Solo that Greedo isn't the brightest of creatures and is a little slow on the draw. But Greedo does
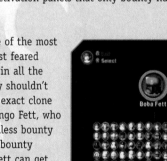
have a few things going for him. For one, he carries thermal detonators with him so that he can blow up shiny metal objects found around the galaxy. And because of his profession, he can access certain activation panels that only bounty hunters can use.

BOBA FETT

Boba Fett is one of the most popular and most feared bounty hunters in all the galaxy. And why shouldn't he be? He is an exact clone of his father, Jango Fett, who also was a merciless bounty hunter. Like all bounty hunters, Boba Fett can get into areas only accessible by

other bounty hunters. He also carries thermal detonators, which are the only weapons that can destroy the shiny metal LEGOs found around the galaxy. The things that set Boba Fett apart from the other bounty hunters are his more-powerful gun and his ability to fly. In a lot of cases, he can get to locations that only he and R2-D2 can reach.

IG-88

IG-88 isn't your typical droid like C-3PO or R2-D2. This is one droid you would not want to mess with. Don't let his tall, lanky metal frame fool you, IG-88 is an assassin droid bounty hunter that is programmed to break you into pieces with ease. Along with a powerful blaster rifle,

this droid also carries thermal detonators to blow up shiny metal objects found around the galaxy. And being a bounty hunter has other privileges as well, like getting into exclusive places where only bounty hunters are allowed.

BOSSK

Bossk is a cold-blooded bounty hunter, literally! This reptilian creature from Trandosha stops at nothing to catch his prize, even if it means traveling halfway across the galaxy. Bossk carries thermal detonators with him to destroy any shiny metal LEGOs found on

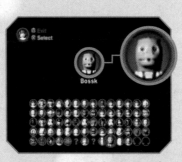

various planets. This can help you get to previously hard-to-reach areas where you can find untold treasure. And what would a bounty hunter be without a blaster rifle to earn a bounty?

DENGAR

Dengar might look like he just got out of the hospital with his wrapped-up head, but if he was there, it was just to check on his victims. Dengar is a ruthless human bounty hunter hired by the Empire to track down Han Solo and his friends. He carries a blaster rifle to drop

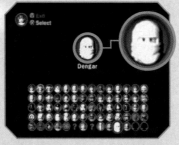

anyone who gets in his way. And because he is a bounty hunter, he also carries with him thermal detonators to destroy any shiny metal LEGOs he finds.

4-LOM

If you thought all droids were helpful to humans, think again. Being a droid is what makes 4-LOM such an effective dispatching machine. He doesn't let anything like feelings get in the way of earning his bounties. To catch his prey, he uses a powerful blaster rifle to drop

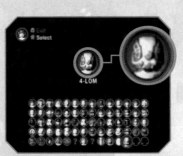

them in a hurry. And for those really tricky situations, he carries

thermal detonators to blow up anything from shiny metal LEGO pieces to a group of enemies. Being a droid might make him a good bounty hunter, but it also limits him from doing things that humanoid creatures can do, like pulling levers or riding in vehicles.

PRINCESS LEIA (BOUSHH)

In order to rescue Han Solo from the evil Jabba the Hutt, Princess Leia disguises herself as the bounty hunter Boushh. Since she looks like a bounty hunter, she also acts like one. She carries a blaster rifle with her to take out anyone who stands in her way to rescue her man, as

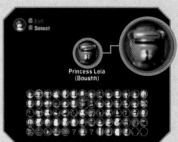

well as the dangerous thermal detonator. The thermal detonator is the only weapon that can destroy the shiny metal LEGOs found around the Star Wars universe. Looking like a bounty hunter also has other advantages: it gets Leia into locations that only bounty hunters can go.

GHOST CHARACTERS

BEN KENOBI (GHOST)

If you liked what Ben Kenobi could do in life, then you'll love what he can do in death. As in life, Ben the ghost can wield his lightsaber to chop up enemies and objects. He can use the Force to interact with the environment. But now, because he is a ghost, he can't be hurt. In fact,

enemies won't even try to hit him, which makes them easy targets. And if Ben Kenobi (Ghost) happens to fall off a ledge where a live person might die, he won't lose any of the studs you've collected. Use this character in areas where there is the possibility of taking a lot of damage.

YODA (GHOST)

Yoda was really old, so it was no surprise when he passed on. And really, death only made the little guy more powerful. In life he was the small, old, yet spunky Jedi Master who could use the Force to take on any opponent. And Yoda's lightsaber skills were among

the best. But as good as he was while living, he could still get hurt. But no more! Now, as a ghost, Yoda can go about his business of handing out beat-downs without any fear of repercussions. Use him when the going gets too rough and you don't want to take a lot of damage.

ANAKIN SKYWALKER (GHOST)

Luke Skywalker eventually got to see how his father really looked. Too bad his dad had to die for that to happen. What is bad news for Luke is good news for you because Anakin Skywalker (Ghost) has the same abilities as Ben Kenobi (Ghost). Anakin can use his

lightsaber to bust up people and objects, and he can use the Force on certain objects found around the galaxy. Most importantly, no one can hit him because he's already dead. That means no worrying about hearts or losing studs.

BLASTER CHARACTERS
PRINCESS LEIA

Beautiful Princess Leia claims that she is on a diplomatic mission for her home planet of Alderaan, but her Royal Highness has more up her sleeve than she lets on. She's secretly trying to help the Rebel Alliance. Leia might be a princess, but she knows how to defend herself. Not

only does she carry a blaster to shoot her enemies, but she also has an ascension gun to use whenever she stands on a red circle swirl so that she can reach new areas. And when she is fighting her enemies, she has the natural ability to dodge most incoming shots.

CAPTAIN ANTILLES

A trusty soldier dedicated to the Rebel Alliance, Captain Antilles risks his life to try to restore freedom and order to the galaxy. One of his duties is to make sure that Princess Leia doesn't come to any harm. To do this, he needs the help of his men, as well as his trusty blaster

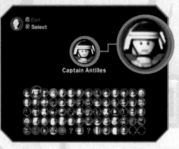

weapon. A direct shot or two should drop anyone who disobeys his orders. Captain Antilles can be invaluable on missions thanks to his ascension gun, which can be used to reach new areas to explore.

REBEL FRIEND

Devoted to the Rebel cause, the Rebel Friend will fight to the death to help the Alliance. Unfortunately, many friends of the Alliance have perished during their missions, but still the Rebels fight on with even more determination. The Rebel Friend carries a blaster with him to shoot anyone from

the Empire who tries to interfere with his objectives. He also carries an ascension gun so that he can grapple to hard-to-reach areas.

LUKE SKYWALKER (TATOOINE)

Just a simple boy who works on his uncle's moisture farm on the planet of Tatooine, Luke doesn't know much about the galaxy, or even his home world for that matter. But there is something special about him; his abilities suggest there is some kind of Force guiding him. Luke

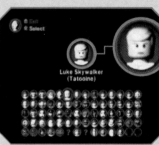

Skywalker might just be a farm boy at this point, but his life changes after he meets an old hermit out in the desert. Not yet knowing the true power of the Force, Luke must rely on a blaster to defend himself. He also has an ascension gun for grappling.

HAN SOLO

This fearless smuggler crisscrosses the galaxy to wherever the money opportunities take him. He might be an experienced smuggler, but he meets the challenge of his life when he accepts the charter to take Luke and Ben to Alderaan. It's lucky for everyone involved that

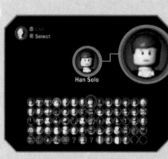

Han is an ace pilot and a great fighter. He has a tremendous aim with his blaster pistol, which can get him out of almost any jam.

CHEWBACCA

Chewbacca is a large, fur-covered Wookiee who is also Han Solo's best friend for life. No matter what adventures await Han, Chewy is always there to help. Chewbacca carries his trusted bowcaster to defeat anybody who messes with his friend. And because he has a blaster

weapon, he can also use an ascension gun whenever a red circle swirl is nearby. Chewy might prefer using his bowcaster, but if you make him mad close up, he can also jump on your stomach and rip your arms off!

INTRODUCTION
GALAXY BASICS
STAR WARS CHARACTERS
TRANSPORTATION
MOS EISLEY CANTINA
WALKTHROUGH INTRODUCTION
EPISODE IV: A NEW HOPE
EPISODE V: THE EMPIRE STRIKES BACK
EPISODE VI: RETURN OF THE JEDI
BONUS FEATURES

Han Solo (Stormtrooper)

Sneaking onto the Death Star is no easy task. The best way to do it is to disguise yourself as someone who works there, like a stormtrooper. Even though he looks like a stormtrooper, Han is still Han. He's great with a blaster rifle and can use an ascension gun to grapple from place to place. He should expect a paycheck from the Empire for his services.

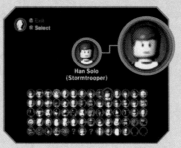

Luke Skywalker (Stormtrooper)

Luke Skywalker is with Han Solo when they have to sneak aboard the Death Star. Stealing uniforms from some unconscious Imperials is the best way to do that. With a helmet on, they can pass for ordinary stormtroopers, even if Luke is a little short. Luke doesn't yet realize the true power of the Force at this point in the story, and must rely on his blaster and ascension gun to help him through his adventures.

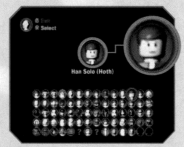

Han Solo (Hoth)

After the destruction of the first Death Star the Rebels go into hiding on the icy planet of Hoth. This frozen planet would have been the perfect hiding place if not for one little probe droid. Han Solo (Hoth) must escape through the underground tunnels to find the *Millennium Falcon* parked at the landing pads. As he journeys to his ship, he uses his trusty blaster to drop all the enemy troopers who rush at him. If he needs to grapple anywhere, he always has his ascension gun with him.

Princess Leia (Hoth)

Princess Leia is in the secret Rebel base on Hoth when the Empire attacks. As the Rebels quickly flee the planet, she and Han Solo run through the underground corridors in search of the *Millennium Falcon*. Han might want to protect the princess, but she is more than capable of protecting herself, because she can fire her blaster as well as any man.

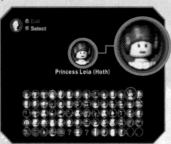

Lando Calrissian

Lando Calrissian is an old friend of Han Solo, which makes it all the more tragic that he was forced by the Empire to betray Han. But you can't count Lando out because he is ready to do whatever it takes to rescue his old buddy. Anyone who tries to stop him gets a full helping from his blaster rifle. Lando might be in charge of all of Cloud City, but when Princess Leia is close, he always has time to put the moves on her and kiss her hand. Play on, player!

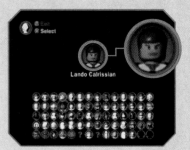

Princess Leia (Bespin)

The journey to Bespin doesn't go according to plan when the Rebel friends are greeted by Darth Vader and then Han is frozen in carbonite. But Leia is a tough lady who does whatever it takes to get her man back, even if it means risking her own life. In order to fight her way to Han, she must be ready to drop anyone who tries to stop her. For that reason, Leia has a blaster rifle that's perfect for stopping enemies in their tracks. She also carries an ascension gun in case she needs to grapple to hard-to-reach ledges.

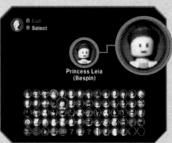

Luke Skywalker (Bespin)

Luke Skywalker is forced to cut short his Jedi training with Yoda in order to rescue his friends from the dark clutches of Darth Vader. It is on Bespin that Luke discovers that Vader was really Anakin Skywalker, his father. To top it all off, daddy cuts off Luke's hand! It's not really a good day for poor Luke, but maybe one day he'll get his revenge. This Luke is able to use the Force to do his will, and also carries his trusty lightsaber with him when the time comes to exact his vengeance.

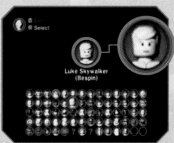

Lando (Palace Guard)

As part of the rescue plan to get Han Solo out of Jabba's palace, Lando Calrissian disguises himself as one of the Palace guards. But don't be fooled by the funny-looking helmet that he wears, because it's still the same old womanizing Lando. He still has a blaster rifle with him for when the time is right to use it. Because he carries a blaster rifle, he can also use an ascension gun.

HAN SOLO (SKIFF)

Another rescue attempt that doesn't really go according to plan. Sure, the Rebels released him from the carbonite, but Jabba was on to them the whole time. Now Jabba wants to toss the band of friends into the Great Pit of Carkoon! But Han is a survivor and doesn't let little things like

that get him down; he always has a smirk on his face. As always, he has his trusty blaster by his side. When it's not in use, watch Han spin his gun when returning it to his holster.

PRINCESS LEIA (SLAVE)

Following a failed attempt to rescue Han Solo, Princess Leia becomes a slave to Jabba the Hutt and is forced to wear a golden bikini. Not one to let that get her down, Leia knows how to shake it and will do a little dance for you whenever you want her to. But don't think this

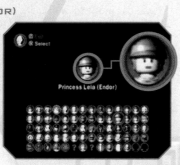

Princess Leia is all sugar and spice; she still carries a blaster rifle with her and can take down the best of them. Talk about dressed to kill!

PRINCESS LEIA (ENDOR)

Endor is a lush green world covered in nothing but forest. To blend in with the surroundings, Princess Leia must dress all in green. Unfortunately for her, one of the locals finds that extremely attractive. With her camoflage on, Leia can better sneak around the

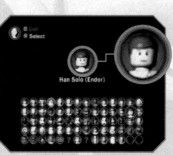

jungle without getting noticed. If she is spotted, she always has a blaster rifle to drop anyone who might try to do her harm.

HAN SOLO (ENDOR)

Wherever you find Princess Leia, you are pretty likely to find Han Solo as well, and Endor is no exception. Like the rest of the Rebels, Han is dressed all in green to blend into the forest. The camouflage helps him to sneak around by making him harder to see. He can sneak

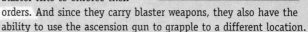

up close to his enemies and put a blaster shot right in their gut.

STORMTROOPER

The stormtrooper is the trusted foot soldier of the Imperial forces. Stormtroopers always seem to be the first into battle and the first to drop dead. Yet these nameless and faceless soldiers fight on because of their belief, or fear, in the Empire and the Emperor. Guided by their higher-ups,

they enforce fear amongst local populations using any means necessary, which is one reason they carry blaster rifles. Their use of the ascension gun helps them get to many otherwise inaccessible places.

IMPERIAL SHUTTLE PILOT

The Imperial shuttle pilot is the one responsible for getting important government figures from one place to another. With such an important job this pilot must know how to defend himself and his cargo. To do that he carries a blaster rifle to fire at any one who gets too close. Along with

the rifle, he also carries an ascension gun in case he needs to get to places that would otherwise be unreachable. When not performing an Imperial duty, he waits at attention for his next set of orders.

TUSKEN RAIDER

The Tusken Raiders, also known as Sand People, roam the desert dunes of Tatooine terrorizing everyone. Sand People grunt and howl before they attack, and attack they will, because they are aggressive and have no remorse. They will try to take out anyone they see. To do this they use their long-

range rifles to snipe unsuspecting victims. If someone gets too close, Sand People club the attacker with the butts of their guns.

SANDTROOPER

The sandtrooper looks almost identical to the stormtrooper, except that he has an orange shoulder pad and carries a backpack. These Imperial troops also act the same as stormtroopers. Both are dedicated to serving the Empire and both carry a blaster rifle to enforce their

orders. And since they carry blaster weapons, they also have the ability to use the ascension gun to grapple to a different location.

INTRODUCTION

GALAXY BASICS

STAR WARS CHARACTERS

TRANSPORTATION

MOS EISLEY CANTINA

WALKTHROUGH INTRODUCTION

iv EPISODE IV: A NEW HOPE

v EPISODE V: THE EMPIRE STRIKES BACK

vi EPISODE VI: RETURN OF THE JEDI

BONUS FEATURES

15

BEACH TROOPER

All work and no play make stormtroopers very unhappy. So even the Empire lets the troops have a little rest and relaxation. These beach troopers might be chilling in just their swim trunks and helmets, but they are still ready to enforce the rule of the Empire. That is why they always carry their blaster rifles with them. With their weapon and ascension gun always within easy reach, these beach troopers continue to do their jobs in between margaritas.

DEATH STAR TROOPER

The Death Star trooper is another member of the Empire's army who can be found, you guessed it, on the Death Star! They run the day-to-day operations on the giant dispatching machine. In addition to running the Death Star, they are also responsible for its defense. If you encounter these guys in your adventure, remember that they are tough and require two direct hits to defeat them. And watch out for their blaster, which can shoot a hole right through you.

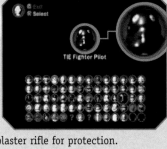

TIE FIGHTER PILOT

The TIE fighter pilots need to be brave in order to fly those TIE fighters around space. Not only are they brave, but they are also really tough fighters. If you meet one in battle, you'll have to hit him a few times before you can take him out. When not shooting people out of space, the TIE fighter pilot carries a blaster rifle for protection.

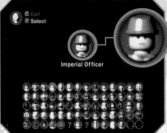

IMPERIAL OFFICER

The Imperial officer is part of the large Empire army and likes to stand at attention whenever he's not engaged in an activity. He's more suited to directing his men than to fighting. He only carries a blaster pistol and an ascension gun with him, but they get the job done. As an officer, he is a little harder to defeat, so when you encounter him in battle you'll have to hit him two times to take him down.

GRAND MOFF TARKIN

Grand Moff Tarkin is Emperor Palpatine's right-hand man. He might not know much about the Force, but he does know about politics. He is so powerful in the Empire that he oversees the operations of the planet-destroying Death Star. Too bad for him. But just because he's in politics doesn't mean Grand Moff Tarkin can't fight. He carries a blaster pistol with him just in case someone disagrees with his views.

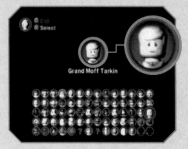

HAN SOLO (HOOD)

The frozen planet of Hoth can be a cold place. It's lucky Han has a nice, furry coat with a thick hood to keep him warm. Although warm, the hood doesn't offer Han any extra protection so be careful when fighting. To protect himself, Han still carries a blaster pistol to knock out anyone foolish enough to try to stop him. Along with the blaster rifle, he also has his ascension gun so he can grapple from red circle swirls found around the galaxy.

REBEL TROOPER (HOTH)

Decked out in his snow gear, this Rebel trooper bravely stands ready to engage the attacking Imperial fleet on Hoth. Too bad his blaster rifle is no match for the AT-AT walkers that Vader throws at the Rebels. His weapon might not be effective at taking down those large vehicles, but it gets the job done against any living creature.

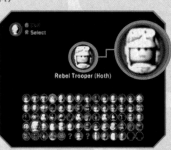

REBEL PILOT

Flying for the greater good of the Rebel Alliance motivates these pilots when they fight the Empire. They have dedicated their lives to helping bring freedom back to the galaxy. When not buzzing around the sky, these Rebel pilots walk around sporting bright orange jumpsuits with white flight helmets. They might not be in their ships, but they can still do some damage with their blaster weapons when push comes to shove.

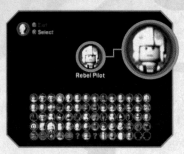

SNOWTROOPER

Since the temperature on Hoth is so cold, the Imperial troops sent in to attack the Rebel forces must be specially outfitted. That's where the snowtroopers come in. They wear extra-long masks to protect them from the elements. They might look a little different from the regular stormtroopers, but they are just as effective. They carry the same standard-issue blaster rifles to defeat enemies of the Empire and to keep the rest of the population in line. They even carry ascension guns in case they need to grapple to out-of-the-way locations.

LUKE SKYWALKER (HOTH)

Luke Skywalker might have had a taste of the Force from Ben Kenobi while back on Tatooine, but he is still no Jedi. While on Hoth, Luke has no mastery of the Force and can't wield his lightsaber. But Luke is no pushover; he is armed with a powerful blaster rifle. He can use this weapon to mow down any enemies. Along with his blaster rifle, Luke also carries an ascension gun so that he can grapple to far-away ledges.

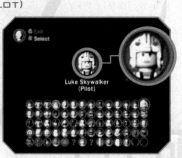

LUKE SKYWALKER (PILOT)

Luke Skywalker is known for being an excellent pilot. Most of his great flying skills and instincts come from the fact that the Force is strong with him, even if he can't quite use it's full power. For now, he wears his bright orange jumpsuit while he flies his snowspeeder at attacking enemies. When he's out of his craft, Luke is still dangerous with his trusty blaster rifle.

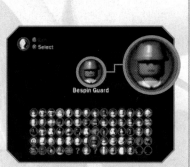

BESPIN GUARD

Cloud City is a big place—too big for just Lando Calrissian to watch over. That's why he employs Bespin guards. These guards carry blaster weapons with them to watch over the city and make sure everything is secure. If things start to go downhill, the Bespin guards are more than willing to step up and defend Bespin from any threats. And since they carry a blaster weapon, they can also use an ascension gun anywhere there's a red circle swirl.

PRINCESS LEIA (PRISONER)

Princess Leia might have been a prisoner on the Death Star, but that doesn't mean she's helpless. After the destruction of her home world of Alderaan, a fire burns brightly in her gut. She wants nothing more than to end the Empire's ruthless reign of terror. To do this, she needs a weapon, and it just so happens that she has a blaster rifle to get the job done.

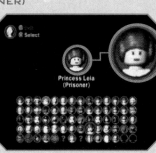

PALACE GUARD

Jabba's palace is not the safest place. Being a Hutt means being surrounded by some of the worst scum in the galaxy. That's why he employs palace guards for extra security. They're not too special to look at, but they do carry a blaster rifle with them and will use it to blast anyone they consider to be a threat.

SKIFF GUARD

The skiff guards patrol the tiny skiffs that accompany Jabba's large barge on excursions into the deserts of Tatooine. These guys have wrinkly leathery faces from being out under the twin suns of Tatooine all day. But it's a job, and that's the price they have to pay. While escorting prisoners to be dropped in the Sarlacc pit to be digested over a thousand years, these guards carry blaster rifles for protection. They are a little slow on the draw, but their aim is true.

ADMIRAL ACKBAR

Although you might think to see this bright orange squid-like creature swimming in the ocean, he is actually a high-ranking military official in the Rebel Alliance. He commands one of the greatest fleets the Rebels has and is in charge of the final attack on the reconstructed Death Star. Even though he holds a high position of authority, Admiral Ackbar still knows how to get his hands dirty. When in battle, he drops enemies with his blaster pistol. He can even use an ascension gun to get to out-of-reach spots.

REBEL TROOPER

A true and trusted friend to the Rebel Alliance is the Rebel trooper. These men are always on the front lines and are always the first to die for their cause. They might not get any glory like Luke or Han, but they are just as important in the Rebel fight to restore freedom and peace to the galaxy. These troopers are always prepared for battle with their blaster rifles close by, just in case the Empire rears its ugly head.

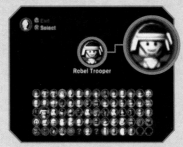

OTHER CHARACTERS

GONK DROID

The gonk droid can be a dangerous droid if you get caught using one in battle. It's extremely slow and has no means of defending itself or accomplishing tasks. If you find yourself about to play as this character be sure to change right away.

LOBOT

On the Cloud City of Bespin, Lobot is Lando Calrissian's right-hand man and does his every bidding—even if it means going against the powerful Empire. Unfortunately for Lobot, he is not much for shoot-outs, and doesn't carry any kind of blaster weapon. If he does find himself in a fight, at least he has his hand-to-hand combat skills. He throws right and left uppercuts before tossing in a headbutt for good measure. He fights dirty!

IMPERIAL SPY

The Imperial spy is great for calling in backup and ratting out the location of wanted Rebels. But when it comes to fighting, the Imperial spy is less ideal. He has absolutely no means to defend himself, so selecting another character might be more helpful during your adventures.

GAMORREAN GUARD

The Gamorrean guard might not be the sharpest knife in the drawer, but he is the biggest. That's probably why Jabba has them employed to protect his palace. They are large porcine creatures that carry around big axes. These powerful axes can take out some enemies with one stroke, be used in a lunging attack, and even block incoming attacks. But the Gamorrean guards aren't all work and no play. Whenever a jukebox has been assembled, they rock out and play air guitar on their weapons.

BIB FORTUNA

Bib Fortuna is the special advisor to Jabba the Hutt. Wherever you find Jabba, you'll find Bib Fortuna. Other than helping Jabba, though, Fortuna can't really do a whole lot. He doesn't carry a weapon, so his fighting skills are limited. Up close, he can throw a punch or two, but chances are he'll be dead by then from a long-range blaster shot.

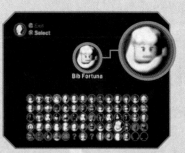

IMPERIAL GUARD

Wearing their bright red uniforms, the Imperial Guard are loyal guards sworn to protect the Emperor. Since they are mostly used for defense, they don't have a lot of offensive power. They carry a staff that they can swing at enemies who are really close, but don't try a jump attack or you'll wind up on your face. If an enemy tries to shoot you from far away, use the staff to deflect the shots right back at him.

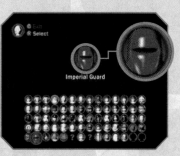

CREATE A CHARACTER

The last two spots in the characters selection screen are reserved for two characters that you create. You could have a lightsaber-wielding Jawa warrior wearing a bikini. Or you could have Ben Kenobi with a Princess Leia hairdo, sporting a bowcaster. Whatever character you wish to make, you can play him or her in the game's Freeplay mode.

TRANSPORTATION

During your adventures through the LEGO *Star Wars* II universe, you're going to need transportation. Luckily there is plenty to go around, whether you need to fly around in space to attack the Death Star or speed across the snow in a snowspeeder. There are many kinds of transportation, so you can always find a vehicle that fits your needs. These are the vehicles you can play during the main chapters of the game, such as "Rebel Attack" and "Hoth Battle."

Spacecraft and Speeders

X-WING
An important craft in the Rebel Alliance's fleet, the X-wing has proven itself effective in battle. It has plenty of speed and firepower to take on almost any challenge.

Y-WING
The Y-wing can almost always be seen entering space battles with the X-wing. The Y-wing is a little more bulky and a little slower than other craft, but it can still get the job done. But if you can, choose another ship that will fly a little smoother than this one.

SNOWSPEEDER
The snowspeeder is excellent for maneuvering around the icy planet of Hoth. It is small and quick, making it a hard target for enemy fighters. But the best thing about the snowspeeder, which makes it invaluable, is its tow cable. It can use this cable to wrap up enemy AT-AT walkers and pick up rolling bombs to smash into things.

MILLENNIUM FALCON
Han Solo's famed spaceship is known throughout the galaxy for its speed. It's a large craft, making it an easier target, but it has excellent offensive capabilities. When firing, the *Falcon* can hit things in front, to the side, and even behind it. When you're playing this ship, no enemy ship is safe.

TIE FIGHTER
The TIE fighter is the standard ship in the Imperial fleet. These fighters are usually the first to enter any fray. Quick and nimble, these little TIE fighters make worthy adversaries and can take on almost any other spacecraft.

TIE INTERCEPTOR
The TIE interceptor is one of the fastest ships in the Imperial fleet; it can hit a target quickly and escape without taking too much damage. Whenever you get the chance to play one of these ships, be sure to do so.

TIE FIGHTER (DARTH VADER)
Being as powerful as he is in the Imperial ranks, Vader has his own custom-made TIE fighter. It is similar in design to the standard TIE fighter, but has bent wing panels. Vader's craft has good speed and firepower, making it a good option to have when you're trying to blast your enemies out of the air.

TIE BOMBER
The TIE bomber is the largest of all the Twin Ion Engine spacecraft in the Imperial fleet. As such, it is a little slower than the others. The bomber's design allows it to haul around large payloads like torpedoes. Try to avoid flying with the bomber if at all possible, because it makes an all-too-easy target.

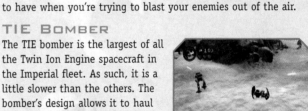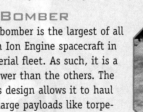

IMPERIAL SHUTTLE
The Imperial shuttle was not designed to be an offensive powerhouse. It is designed to transport important people from place to place. It is large, slow, and has a weak firing system. Avoid using this ship when you go to battle.

TIE ADVANCED
Another form of the standard TIE fighter the TIE Advanced has similar features. It has pretty good speed and effective offensive capabilities. If you fly one of these in battle, you won't be sorry.

INTRODUCTION

GALAXY BASICS

STAR WARS CHARACTERS

TRANSPORTATION

MOS EISLEY CANTINA

WALKTHROUGH INTRODUCTION

iv EPISODE IV: A NEW HOPE

v EPISODE V: THE EMPIRE STRIKES BACK

vi EPISODE VI: RETURN OF THE JEDI

BONUS FEATURES

MOS EISLEY *CANTINA*

Your new LEGO *Star Wars* adventure begins at the Mos Eisley Cantina. It is just the place for intergalactic travelers to unwind. You are Princess Leia, royalty on the planet Alderaan, and secretly a Rebel spy fighting against the Empire. By your side is trusted Captain Antilles, who is there to serve and protect. The Mos Eisley Cantina on the planet Tatooine is a nice place to find disreputables when you're looking for somebody to do a dirty job. Unfortunately, with so many shady characters boozing it up, there is always some trouble here and fights break out often. Try to keep a low profile, but if someone comes after you, break him into little pieces.

The cantina is the only way to get from place to place, and episode to episode, in the universe. As you walk around the circular cantina, you see many doors. Not all of these doors are open at the game's beginning, but the more you play and the more missions you complete, the more doors open up for you to explore. Three extra-wide doors with Roman numerals over them stand along the outer walls; they lead to different episodes. Smaller doors with blue arrows over them lead to the dusty parking lot outside. There is even a bonus room with a picture of Jabba the Hutt above it, waiting to be unlocked by the best of the best.

As you play through the game and discover more characters along your journey, they begin to frequent the cantina. When you start the game, the place is pretty dead, but after you complete eight or nine missions, the cantina gets kind of crowded. These new bar patrons are at your disposal; you can switch to them at any time to add them to your party. Some characters at the cantina just want to be left alone, however, and you can't switch to them.

The Cantina is a great place to find new characters to use on your adventures.

Before you decide to start your first mission in Episode IV, it's a good idea to explore the cantina area. The main cantina room is circular, so if you follow the outer wall you will always end up where you started. As you move about, you'll see many things to do in this place. You can blast all the chairs in the cantina to find hidden studs and hearts. When a Jedi is added to your party, you can use the Force on the blue lights around the place to find even more hidden treasure.

When you're finally ready to fight the evil Galactic Empire and save the universe, move through the large door marked "IV." Each door with a Roman numeral leads to the corresponding episode room. This room contains seven smaller doors, each one leading to a different chapter of the story. The first five chapters you can play consecutively, but the sixth room of every episode can only be played after you collect ten gold bricks. These bricks pile up in front of where the sixth door should be. When you have ten, you can assemble the pile to make a doorway that you enter to start the chapter. The seventh door is a bonus room that you can play after you complete the first six missions of that episode. These chapter rooms are where most of the action takes place, so move into the first one and start your journey.

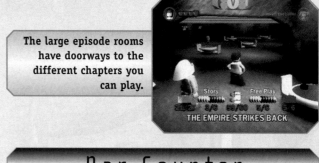

The large episode rooms have doorways to the different chapters you can play.

THE EMPIRE STRIKES BACK

Bar Counter

At the main bar in the Mos Eisley Cantina, the not-so-friendly bartender is waiting to sell you his goods. Along the wall behind the bar you can buy hints, characters, extras, or even gold bricks. The hints give you bonus information about the game and won't cost you very many studs. The characters option lets you buy characters and vehicles that you won't otherwise be able to get by playing the game. If you want that old Grand Moff Tarkin on your side, you'll have to pay the studs for him. The extras option lets you buy bonus features, such as giving everyone a disguise or getting super lightsabers. Some of the extras only become available for purchase after you find the corresponding power brick as you play the game. The last thing you can buy at the bar are the gold bricks that help you get into secret and hard-to-get-to places. The items at the bar range in price from one hundred studs to hundreds of thousands of studs. Be sure to spend your studs wisely because things can get expensive.

The bartender drives a hard bargain on some of his wares, but you have to pay since his is the only shop around.

Create a Character Area

It's alive! New to LEGO *Star Wars* II is the character creation area where you get to create and name your very own unique character. Just to the right of the bar are two large tanks with characters inside. These are the building blocks for your new creation. Press up or down to choose what part of the character you want to change: the head, body, hands, weapon, etc. When you have selected the part you want to change, press to the left or right to change the color or style of that object. Options include different hats, hairstyles, faces, weapons, colors of clothes, etc. You can customize these characters any way you like, depending on the options you have available.

Put Luke's head on top of Vader's body so he can carry on the family tradition. Or put Grand Moff Tarkin's head on top of Princess Leia's bikini-clad body. Or put a Jawa head on top of a Tusken Raider body with the hair of Princess Leia, and have him hold a lightsaber. Mix and match the parts to come up with your own fun and exciting creations. If you are having trouble thinking of things to do, use the random option and the game will create a character for you. After you have the character you want, give your creation a name. After you create your two unique characters, you can always go back and make more changes.

That is one Jawa the Tusken Raiders wouldn't want to mess with!

Who knew Greedo could look so good in a bikini?

Cantina Parking

Inside the cantina, the small doors with blue arrows over them lead outside to the parking lot. Go outside and run around the circular cantina, shooting all the containers you find to get lots of hidden studs. There's not much else outside at the beginning of the game, but that changes as you play. As you complete missions, you'll collect LEGO canisters hidden in the chapters. Each canister is a part for a vehicle that is put together out in the cantina parking lot in one of the 18 parking spaces that correspond to the different chapters. As you play, you can check the parking spaces and see what you've built so far. Collect all ten canisters in a chapter to complete the vehicle for that chapter. On the outside wall of the cantina, you will also find the impression of a large question mark. You have to fill it with 60 gold bricks to find a new area to explore. On the other side of the parking lot, another pile of gold bricks starts to collect as you play through the game. Collect 81 bricks to find out what that one reveals as well.

The more canisters you collect, the more vehicles you can build outside.

CAUTION

The cantina is on an island. Don't run too far to the south or you will fall off and die.

INTRODUCTION

GALAXY BASICS

STAR WARS CHARACTERS

TRANSPORTATION

MOS EISLEY CANTINA

WALKTHROUGH INTRODUCTION

EPISODE IV: A NEW HOPE

EPISODE V: THE EMPIRE STRIKES BACK

EPISODE VI: RETURN OF THE JEDI

BONUS FEATURES

21

WALKTHROUGH
INTRODUCTION

Now that you have all the information you need about what to do and how to do it, it is time for you to begin your adventure. LEGO *Star Wars* II begins in Episode IV with a princess who is secretly trying to smuggle plans for the Empire's Death Star to the Rebel Alliance. As the rest of the episode unfolds, you will find an old, mysterious Jedi to befriend, smugglers to hire, and a princess to save. A farm boy will grow from a whiny kid to an ace fighter pilot who is just beginning to understand the true power of the Force.

After you complete the first chapter of Episode IV, more worlds and characters open up for you in Episode V and Episode VI. In Episode V, the Empire will hunt down the Rebels to exact revenge for the destruction of the Death Star. Luke will meet a new Jedi Master to help with his training, Han will be betrayed by an old friend on Cloud City, and Luke will discover what really happened to his father. But just when things look bleak, Episode VI will reunite our heroes as they travel across the galaxy from the deserts of Tatooine all the way to the forest moon of Endor. Luke will become a true Jedi and he will need all the help he can get as the Rebels try to defeat the evil Empire once and for all.

The Empire has complete control of the galaxy, so your adventure is going to be dangerous and difficult. You have to be ready for anything. Abilities such as the Force, thermal detonators, ascension guns, and flying will help you in your journey.

Be sure to return to each Episode later and play in Freeplay mode, after you unlock new characters with new abilities. These can help you to reach unexplored areas, defeat your enemies, and discover hidden treasures.

Jump into the adventure and follow the information in this guide. You might just help the overmatched Rebellion defeat Vader and the evil Empire.

EPISODE IV
A NEW HOPE

Chapter 1: Secret Plans

STORY CHARACTERS

Princess Leia
Captain Antilles
Rebel Trooper

R2-D2
C-3PO

It is a period of civil war. Rebel spaceships, striking from a hidden base, have won their first victory against the evil Galactic Empire.

During the battle, Rebel spies managed to steal secret plans to the Empire's ultimate weapon, the Death Star, an armored space station with enough power to destroy an entire planet.

Pursued by the Empire's sinister agents, Princess Leia races home aboard her starship. She is custodian of the stolen plans that can save her people and restore freedom to the galaxy....

Just when the Rebels are about to get away, the dreaded Empire shows up with one of its massive ships.

C-3PO looks as confused as ever about what's going on in the galaxy. It's a good thing he has R2-D2 with him for help.

After a brief fight with the Rebels, Darth Vader and his stormtroopers are able to board Princess Leia's spacecraft.

Smuggling stolen plans is no easy business for Princess Leia. That sort of job is best left to professional smugglers. Maybe she'll meet one someday, but for now, it's her responsibility to get the plans somewhere safe. They must certainly be kept out of the hands of Darth Vader and his stormtroopers, who just boarded her vessel. Time to dump the evidence!

It's lucky for Leia that she doesn't have to do this on her own; trusted Captain Antilles is right by her side. Before you get moving, explore the room you are in. In front of you are two large piles of LEGOs that are bouncing on the ground. Put them together to form the control panels nearby. After you complete each panel, LEGO studs spill onto the floor. Collect all the studs you find. This also opens the door in the distance.

Putting together the loose LEGO pieces to form the control panels not only produces hidden LEGO studs, but it also opens the door in the distance.

FREEPLAY AREA

A metal grate covers holes on both sides of the room. Have a bounty hunter use a thermal detonator to destroy each one and collect the goodies that spill out.

NOTE

LEGO pieces bouncing on the ground indicate that they can be assembled to form an object.

TIP

LEGO studs and hearts that spill onto the floor from secret locations only appear for a little while. Run around the area and collect as many as you can before they disappear.

INTRODUCTION
GALAXY BASICS
STAR WARS CHARACTERS
TRANSPORTATION
MOS EISLEY CANTINA
WALKTHROUGH INTRODUCTION
iv EPISODE IV: A NEW HOPE
V EPISODE V: THE EMPIRE STRIKES BACK
vi EPISODE VI: RETURN OF THE JEDI
BONUS FEATURES

Before you charge through the open door, finish exploring the room. Move to the right and collect the studs on the ground. While you're there, blast open the equipment you find for some more hidden LEGO studs. Move to the other side of the room and destroy more equipment for other goodies. When the floor is clear, pull the switch on the wall for a few more studs. On your way out, blast the equipment to the right of the door and collect anything that spills out.

The next room has more of those gray equipment pieces for you to destroy. Shoot at the wall panels that have red and yellow lights and a blue sparkle to them. Shoot the top and bottom of each panel and collect the studs that litter the ground. Pull the lever to one side of the door, while Antilles pulls the other lever next to you at the same time.

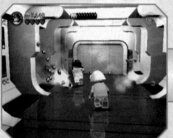

Destroy the wall panels to reveal a boatload of studs.

In the next hall, Rebels guard the left passage and a dark room at the end of the hall to the right. Before you go past the Rebels, destroy the wall panels in front of you and down the right hall. As you knock out those panels, pick up the LEGO studs that spill out before they disappear. Grab the valuable blue stud that is across the hall, opposite the door. After the wall panels are gone, you see that one of them was hiding a lever. Pull the secret lever to get a new look for Princess Leia. Unfortunately, Captain Antilles likes his hat just fine and won't put on a new one.

FREEPLAY AREA

The room down the right hall closes when you get close and can only be opened using the dark side of the Force. Use Vader's Force to destroy the door and go inside. Grab the LEGO canister from the ground and smash all the containers in sight. Collect the treasure on the ground, then use the Force to open the small compartments along the wall to find more goodies.

Go toward the small group of Rebels guarding the hall. When you get to them, a door opens in the distance and stormtroopers pour into the hall. Help those Rebels and blast any white-masked goon that charges you. As you fire, stay close to the Rebels and use them for cover from incoming blaster fire so that you don't take damage. After you cut through the enemy ranks, the Rebels rush down the hall to the open door. With the coast clear, you can

follow behind them and destroy more wall panels and equipment in the hall for hidden loot. A door in the left wall can only be opened by C-3PO, so you'll have to come back later to open it.

Advance down the rest of the hall and into the next room. When you get there, go to the red circle swirl against the side wall and use your ascension gun to get to the walkway above you. Follow that walkway to another red circle swirl where you can grapple to the ledge above you. At the top, assemble the loose LEGO pieces to form machinery to extend a bridge between both pieces to the wall's other side. Follow the new bridge through the doorway on the other side.

Use your Rebel friends as cover while you fight your enemies because that's what friends are for.

FREEPLAY AREA

The bounty hunter's thermal detonator is the only thing that can destroy the shiny piece of metal machinery on the bottom floor. Blowing the machinery up opens a hole in the floor into which you can drop. When you're under the floor, grab all the studs you find as well as a LEGO canister for your collection.

On the other side of the room, across from the shiny machinery, is a small chute in the wall. Use a small character, such as a Jawa, to travel through the chute to an area under the floor. Collect all the studs in the bottom area; then re-enter the chute to return back to the main floor.

When you get to the top of the bridge at the top of the walkways, go over the right wall. Use the Force to assemble two platforms attached to the wall above you. Jump to the top platform, and from there, jump to get another LEGO canister for your collection.

After you move through the doorway, you're greeted by a long hall and...Darth Vader! Luckily, he is at the hall's far end. An invisible force field prevents you from getting too close, but he sends his goons in to try to take you out. Blast the fools who rush you, as well as the equipment that lines the hall. When the coast is clear, pull the four levers on the sides of the hall. Stop and shoot any more guards who charge you before you finish pulling the levers.

Pulling the levers causes explosive equipment to be placed on both sides of Vader. In between dropping the stormtroopers who rush you, fire at the equipment next to Vader. A hit to each piece of equipment turns it them more and more orange. After the equipment takes enough blaster hits from you, it explodes and Vader is gone. Take out any surviving enemies and collect any loose studs on the ground. Before you move through to the end of the hall, grab the two blue studs on the ground nearby.

The next room has many containers on the ground for you to shoot. Loose studs spill onto the ground. A container to the far right has one of three special LEGOs for you to collect. Shoot the wall panels for more goodies. Don't forget to shoot the top and bottom halves of the wall.

After you pull the levers to place the explosive equipment next to Vader, fire at the equipment to clear the hall's end.

FREEPLAY AREA

A door to the right of the room is for bounty hunters only. After you get inside, use the Force to open all the small compartments along the hall and collect the studs that spill out. Follow the corridor to the north and destroy the containers along the way. Before you head down a hall to the right, make your way to the straight hall's end. When you get to the end, small ramps raise up on both sides of you. Run up the ramps and into the small alcove on each side. You'll toss two LEGO pieces out into the hall. Assemble the loose pieces to form a doorway nearby. Enter the new doorway and grab the LEGO canister inside.

Return to the hall you passed earlier and run inside. Don't forget to use the Force to open the small compartments on the hall's sides. Shoot the first container to find the second special LEGO in this area. Down the hall is a shiny piece of metal, so use your bounty hunter to blast it to pieces, leaving only some loose LEGOs behind. Assemble these pieces to form a little car you can drive around for fun.

A door in the left wall is locked, and the hall at the end is blocked with a force field. Have C-3PO access the activation panel to get rid of the force field. Destroy the first container you see. You'll find the third special LEGO piece you need. A LEGO canister appears back in the hall where you assembled the door in the wall. Collect it. Smash more containers in the hall and use the Force on more side compartments to find more hidden items.

Follow the hall to the room at the end. Inside the room is a special growing area. Use the Force to turn on the sprinklers

around the room to make the plants grow. Smash the plants to get some hidden studs to add to your stash. Smashing the plants to the right of the entrance leaves a red Power Brick for you to grab. Breaking the plants in the back of the room leaves some LEGO pieces behind. Put the pieces together, then use the Force to turn them into a truck you can drive. To the right of the back growing station is a blue stud to grab and shiny metal objects to blow up using a thermal detonator. Grab the studs the metal debris leaves behind, then jump into the vehicle you made and drive it to where you first entered the secret area.

After you clean the room of LEGO studs, move into the next room where there is more fighting. Assist the Rebels in taking out the two waves of stormtroopers so you can explore the hall in peace. After you secure the area, destroy the containers and wall panels for some hidden studs. Destroy the items before joining the Rebels down the hall.

FREEPLAY AREA

A door to the right of the hall is for stormtroopers only. This door takes you to the hall you went to using the bounty hunter, so don't bother going there again.

When you get to the Rebels at the hall's intersection, go to the dead end on the left. Pull the levers on the wall to open the window and reveal pretty flowers along with some hidden studs. On the ground are some glowing red tiles. Run across them to turn them all green and cause some valuable LEGO studs to drop from the ceiling.

Across the hall is another closed window and what sounds like heavy breathing and cracking. What could that be? Run across the glowing red tiles on the ground in front of the window to turn them all green. This causes studs to rain from overhead. After you gather the studs, pull the lever on the wall to open the window. The heavy breathing you heard was Darth Vader and that cracking sound was him using the Force to turn some poor Rebel into pieces!

There's nothing you can do from here, so move down the hall past the Rebel troopers. As you move, blast open any containers you find, as well as all the wall panels. Collect any spilled studs and continue through the doorway at the hall's end.

Run across the red glowing floor panels to turn them all green. You get a surprise that falls from the ceiling.

The next room has plenty to do. On one side of the room is a locked door, and on the other side are small black gates. Move along the gates, blasting them as you go to collect a massive amount of studs. At the end of the line of gates is a valuable blue stud for your collection. Move around the area and destroy the containers for more loot.

On the ground near the room's center are checkerboard patterns and boxes with yellow and black striping. Push the boxes along the floor until they fall into the nearby red slots. When both boxes have been pushed into their appropriate slots, the locked door opens and three stormtroopers rush in to greet you. Drop them with your blaster.

Push the boxes along the floor until they fall into the red slots nearby.

Here are two different kinds of droids. They might come in handy some day.

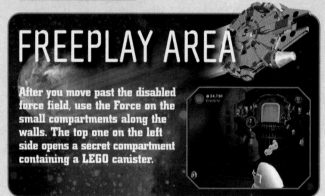

FREEPLAY AREA

After you move past the disabled force field, use the Force on the small compartments along the walls. The top one on the left side opens a secret compartment containing a LEGO canister.

FREEPLAY AREA

In between the small black gates you destroyed are small blue posts. Use the Force on these posts to uncover hidden loot. Move to the wall on the right and use the Force to stack the boxes. Jump from the top box to the ledge on the wall. Add another LEGO canister to your collection. Drop to the floor and use the Force on the LEGOs sticking out of the wall to form a ramp and get more LEGO studs.

The door you recently opened leads to a hall where you find C-3PO on one side of a red force field, and R2-D2 on the other side. It's lucky for you this protocol droid is just the droid to get you through this. Switch to C-3PO and activate the door panel to the right to make the force field disappear. When the barrier is gone, Princess Leia shoves a disk into R2-D2 and runs off. Those must be the valuable Death Star plans that Vader is looking for.

It is up to the rest of the gang to get those plans to safety. Before you go any farther, go near the level's beginning and use C-3PO to open the locked door with his picture next to it. Inside is a small room that has containers for you to smash. Collect the goodies inside, then return to where you found the droids.

Move to the end of the hall and collect studs on the ground as you go. Switch to R2-D2 and activate the door panel to unlock the door. Ignore the gun battle going on in the distance for now, and concentrate on shooting the containers and gates around the room to collect valuable studs. When the room is free of studs, run to the center of the room and use Captain Antilles to jump into the crane. Now you have control over a giant blue claw in the back of the room. Use the crane to pick up each stormtrooper and drop him over the side of the ledge into the darkness.

Now that the Rebel doesn't have anyone shooting at him, he can lower a bridge connecting the two sides of the room. After the walkway is lowered, wait in the crane for C-3PO to get to the other side. Use the crane to pick him up and drop him in front of the door on the room's other side. With C-3PO safely across, run to join him. Blast any containers along the way. The container to the far left leaves behind a red circle swirl for you to use at another time. Jump across the small chasm near the door to get to the ledge in front of it. Use C-3PO to open the door.

Use the crane to pick up the bad guys and drop them over the edge.

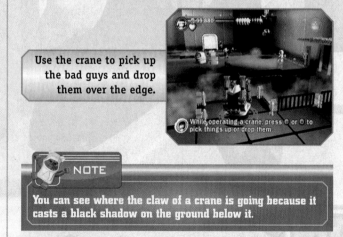

NOTE

You can see where the claw of a crane is going because it casts a black shadow on the ground below it.

FREEPLAY AREA

Use the Force to turn the small blue posts in between the black gates. When you do this, hidden goodies spill onto the floor. Switch to a bounty hunter and blast the shiny metal to pieces with a thermal detonator. Collect the studs on the floor. In the back of the room, use the red circle swirl to grapple to the ledge above. From there, use R2-D2 to float across to the other ledges and collect valuable studs.

The doorway leads to another long hall where you see some Rebel troops being taken prisoner. It's lucky for them you showed up just in time. Stay behind your friends and blast the enemies at the end of the hall. Continue to stay close to your buddies as you fight off multiple waves of enemy troops. When the threat is gone, move down the hall, destroying wall panels as you go. A panel near the center not only gives you studs, but also contains the first of three special LEGO pieces you must find.

In the next section of hall, more Imperial troops run out to greet you, so blast them to pieces. The walkway leading to the rest of the passage has a small break in it. Stand next to the edge and put the scattered LEGO pieces together to form a small bridge. Cross to the other side, destroying containers and collecting studs as you go.

FREEPLAY AREA

Only a stormtrooper can open the locked door in the hall. After you're inside, blast the containers on the ground to find studs and the second special LEGO piece you need to find in this area. Assemble the LEGOs against the back wall to create two activation panels that only C-3PO can use. Access the panels, through the window you see poor Imperial troopers getting sucked out into space. How long can they hold their breath?

Follow the rest of the hall as it bends and destroy more containers containing studs. Another break in the path means that you can assemble more loose LEGOs on the ground to form another walkway. On the other side, are three doors. Use R2-D2 to open the door on the right. Behind it are Rebel prisoners and a wall lever for Captain Antilles to pull.

FREEPLAY AREA

Throw a thermal detonator at the shiny piece of metal in the hall. You'll find the third special LEGO piece in that area. Finding all three pieces causes a LEGO canister to form at the end of the hall. Grab it.

With the prisoners free, use R2-D2 to open the center door where there are...two stormtroopers in a hot tub! Geez, it's hard to find good help these days! Use Captain Antilles to blast them before they have time to grab their weapons. With the coast clear, pull the lever behind the hot tub. After you pull this second lever, a wall panel C-3PO can access becomes available near the last door. Use R2-D2 to move through the last open door. Have him access the panel in the back of the room to get into the escape pod.

FREEPLAY AREA

After you blast the bathing stormtroopers, use the Force on the hot tub controls to break them apart. This makes a LEGO canister appear over the water. Grab it.

The droids barely make it to an escape pod with the Death Star plans.

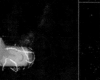

R2-D2 doesn't make it far before Jawas capture him and put him into their sandcrawler vehicle.

Why can't these droids just get along? Once on Tatooine, they decide to go separate ways.

Well, look who it is. Reunited again.

Chapter 2: Through the Jundland Wastes

STORY CHARACTERS

Luke Skywalker (Tatooine)

Ben Kenobi

R2-D2

C-3PO

Darth Vader searches in vain for the secret rebel plans on Princess Leia's starship. The droid, R2-D2, has escaped with the Death Star blueprints to the planet Tatooine below.

But R2-D2, along with his companion C-3PO, has been captured by Jawas—small scavenger creatures who trade in mechanical scrap.

Young Luke Skywalker, unaware of the great destiny that lies before him, is looking for droids to help with work on his uncle's moisture farm. As he approaches the Jawas' sandcrawler, his life is about to change forever....

Luke thinks he's buying ordinary droids for his uncle. Unfortunately, they go missing in the night.

On the search for the missing droids, Luke runs into...Tusken Raiders! Uh-oh. That looks like trouble.

It's lucky for Luke that Ben Kenobi was in the neighborhood to save the day.

Maybe going looking for the droids alone wasn't such a smart idea—especially since so many dangerous Tusken Raiders are lurking about. It's just a good thing that old Ben Kenobi was out and about to save young Luke's life. Now they must get out of the area and find safety away from those Sand People.

From your starting location, run to the wall to the right and pick up loose studs on the ground, including a valuable blue one. Next, head to the left and assemble the pile of LEGO bricks into a nice little castle. After your work is complete, break it apart for some hidden loot. Continue along the wall to the left and bust open all the containers and equipment you find. Pick up the spilled studs on the ground as you go. Use Ben Kenobi to climb the rock ledge along the cliff wall in the back. Follow the ledge along the cliff. Double jump when you get to the end to reach another ledge farther to the right. There, you find a prized blue stud for your collection.

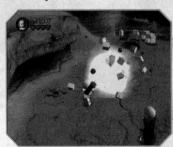

The desert might be a dangerous place, but it has plenty of things for you to break to find hidden studs.

NOTE

Giant orange rodents wander the desert. They're harmless, but can sometimes provide a heart if you take them down.

By now you're sure to have made your presence known to the local Tusken Raiders. They come jumping down from the cliffs to chase you off their lands, so use your lightsaber to cut them down. When you get a moment of peace, break the fence boards surrounding the Sand People's riding beasts to discover some hidden loot. Jump on the back of one of the riding beasts. From there, you can jump to the cliff ledge behind you. Grab all the studs you find before dropping to the ground to fight more Tusken Raiders.

As you fight the Sand People, make your way to the right until you get to a deep chasm blocking your path. Use Luke's blaster to drop the fools on the cliff wall in the distance, then shoot the LEGO pile in the cliff wall on the left. Not only will you get to collect LEGO studs that spill out, but you also can jump on the rock over the LEGO pile you destroyed to get to a bridge that crosses the chasm.

If you want to get across the chasm, you'll have to shoot out the LEGO bricks in the cliff wall.

iv

FREEPLAY AREA

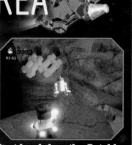

Before you jump on the rock bridge you created, follow the chasm to the right until you can see some large, shiny LEGO bricks in the distance. Use R2-D2 to fly across the chasm and land next to the bricks. Switch to the bounty hunter, and toss a thermal detonator on the left side of the pile. Quickly move as far to the right as you can go until the detonator goes off and the pile blocking your path is gone.

Run to the right side of the area and smash all the equipment you see to find hidden studs. Next, use the Force on the large boxes to stack all three on top of each other. Double jump your way to the top, and from there, double jump to the rock pillar nearby. Switch to R2, and fly to the large rock platform to the left. Grab the studs on the ground, then get behind the cart and push it forward. When the cart goes over the edge, it follows some tracks on the ground and crashes into some boards in the mountainside.

Before you go chasing after the cart, run to the hillside on the left and smash the white containers on the ground. Hidden in the hillside is a small chute. Switch to a small character, like a Jawa, and enter the chute. This takes you to the top of the hill, where you can slide back down the hill, collecting studs as you go. Repeat going to the top of the hill and sliding down as often as necessary to collect all the studs.

Now follow the trail to the north in the direction that the runaway cart went. On your way, use the Force on a shovel in the dirt, causing it to dig up some LEGOs. Assemble them into a droid and collect the studs that spill out. Continue north, smashing more containers as you go. When you see another shovel, use the Force on it to dig up some hidden studs. Follow the tracks north and into the hillside, where you can collect a red power brick.

Use the Force on a pile of LEGOs just outside the cave with the power brick and turn them into a solid mass. Jump on this creation, then to the pathway above. The main trail heads to the right, but head left first until the path drops off. Switch to R2-D2, and fly across the chasm to the rock ledge in the distance. Once you get there, add some studs and a LEGO canister to your stash.

Now return to the area where you first jumped to the upper pathway and smash the equipment on the ground. Use the Force on the doors of the huts nearby to create a platform on the side wall. Jump on each platform, and then to the top of each hut, to grab a valuable stud. Continue to follow the path to the right and smash all the containers and pots on the ground, grabbing all the studs that spill out. One of the pots to the right of the large red well leaves behind a crank. Reattach the crank back to the well, then use the Force to turn the crank. The bucket goes down and brings back up water and valuable studs.

As you cross the bridge, be sure to pick up the blue stud in your path. On the other side, you'll find some LEGO pieces to assemble to make a red circle swirl pad. As you put the thing together, more Sand People charge at you, so blast them as soon as you complete the construction. When the area is clear, use the ascension gun to get to the ledge above and collect more studs.

FREEPLAY AREA

After you get to the ledge using the ascension gun, use R2-D2 or Boba Fett and fly to a ledge across the canyon to the left. Using a small character, like a Jawa, enter the chute in the wall; it takes you to a tunnel far below. Follow the short tunnel and collect the studs and the LEGO canister that are hidden down there. Use the chute to get back to the ledge above, where you can return to the main trail.

FREEPLAY AREA

Some large LEGO pieces are blocking a trail in the left hillside. Use the dark side of the Force to shatter them and collect the studs that spill out. Run into the trail behind the pieces you destroyed and use the Force on a pile of LEGOs to the left. These turn into a bomb, so back away and wait for it to detonate. Jump into the alcove created by the blast and use your lightsaber on some boards. Next, use the Force to move the LEGO pieces on the ground and turn them into another bomb on the cliff wall. This creates another alcove for you to jump to. From there, you can double jump to a ledge on the right for some studs and a LEGO canister to add to your collection. Before you return to the main trail, use the Force on the white LEGO pieces on the ground to raise the dead.

Move farther down the canyon, collecting more studs along the way. Soon you come to some strange-looking plants along the right wall. Destroy the plants and the pipes nearby and grab the resulting loot, including a blue stud. Tusken Raiders try to rush your position, so blast them as they approach.

Move to the alcove in the rock wall to the left, collecting the blue stud along the way. Then break all the equipment you find for even more goodies. Some nearby boulders have some LEGO parts next to them. Ben Kenobi can use the Force to stack them on top of each other on the boulders. After you have three stacks, go ahead and break the LEGO pieces you just stacked for some hidden studs. Before you move on, collect the studs behind the boulders as well.

INTRODUCTION
GALAXY BASICS
STAR WARS CHARACTERS
TRANSPORTATION
MOS EISLEY CANTINA
WALKTHROUGH INTRODUCTION
iv EPISODE IV: A NEW HOPE
v EPISODE V: THE EMPIRE STRIKES BACK
vi EPISODE VI: RETURN OF THE JEDI
BONUS FEATURES

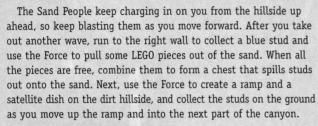

The Sand People keep charging in on you from the hillside up ahead, so keep blasting them as you move forward. After you take out another wave, run to the right wall to collect a blue stud and use the Force to pull some LEGO pieces out of the sand. When all the pieces are free, combine them to form a chest that spills studs out onto the sand. Next, use the Force to create a ramp and a satellite dish on the dirt hillside, and collect the studs on the ground as you move up the ramp and into the next part of the canyon.

Destroy the vegetation for some valuable goodies.

Use the Force to create a walkway up the dirt hillside so you can keep moving.

After you enter the next canyon, run to the right to find a pile of LEGO bricks. Before you do anything, shoot the Tusken Raiders in the distance who keep firing at you. When they're dead, run past the LEGO pile to the cliff wall and follow it to the right. The wall leads you to more studs, including a valuable blue stud. Continue to collect studs around the area, then return to the pile of pieces and assemble them to make a movable box.

First, push the box to the right so that Ben Kenobi can double jump from its top to the nearby ledge to collect some loot. With the loot in hand, drop down and continue to push the box to the very end of the checkerboard pattern. Use the box to jump to the ledge above, and then to another ledge to the left.

Push the box to the other side of the area so you can reach the ledge above.

CAUTION

If you try to walk through the mud that blocks your path instead of jumping to the ledge above, you will die instantly.

Follow the ledge back to the canyon floor, where you find more LEGO pieces to put together. Once assembled, they form a platform with a red circle swirl. Use your ascension gun to get from there to a hidden ledge above, where you can collect a blue stud. Drop down and follow the canyon to a large opening and a Jawa sandcrawler.

Follow the right cliff wall until you find a shovel in the sand. Use the Force on it to dig up some hidden LEGOs. Assemble the LEGOs and you'll create a droid and uncover loads of studs. Destroy the droid you created, then advance up the ledges in the right cliff wall, collecting studs along the way until you get to the blue stud at the top. From there, you can jump to the dirt ramp in front of you and reach another blue stud for your collection.

Scale the cliff wall for some valuable studs.

Back on the ground next to the dirt ramp, you'll find lots of things to destroy. Blast all the equipment and containers you find and collect the studs that spill out. Just be careful not to stand too close to the pieces with the orange markings (in the back, near the sandcrawler) because they are explosive. If you're standing too near when they explode, you'll lose health. Some LEGOs litter the ground. Each pile can be turned into a fully functioning droid and some studs to add to your pocket. For some more bonus loot, you can drop the newly created droids.

With that area clear move to left, where you'll find two large blocks that Ben Kenobi can stack using the Force. When the blocks are stacked, go under the sandcrawler and shoot the brown grates to reveal some blue studs. Now keep going to the left and put together the LEGO bricks on the ground to create a red circle swirl pad. Before you grapple up, run to the right to break more equipment and collect more studs along the left wall.

The equipment in the back is explosive, so be careful not to stand too close when you blast it.

Return to the red circle swirl pad and have Ben Kenobi use the Force to lower a platform above. Luke can then grapple to the new platform and pull the lever there to lower another platform that Ben can use to get to the same location. After Ben gets up there, have him use the Force again to lower another platform above. Double jump your way to the new platform and pull the lever you find. This lever activates a small elevator to the right. You need to jump onto it to get to the top of the vehicle.

EPISODE IV
A NEW HOPE

At the top, pull the levers near the elevator. This activates the suction entrance under the sandcrawler. With the entrance activated, move to the left and follow the inside wall to find a blue stud. Next, move to the right and smash the four pieces of equipment on the roof and collect the loot that is exposed. Don't stand on the piece of equipment that is closest to the levers you pulled because a chute located under it could send you back to the ground. Now, move to the edge of the sandcrawler to the right of the roof chute you just discovered and jump over the edge. Push the controls toward the vehicle, and you should land among a pile of studs. Fall to the ground, then move under the sandcrawler and under the entrance chute.

Make your way from platform to platform to get to the top of the sandcrawler.

Jump over the edge of the vehicle so you can land on a ledge full of studs.

TIP

If you have trouble getting the studs on the side of the sandcrawler, you can always go back to the area's entrance and ride it back. From its top, you can jump to the ledge with the studs.

FREEPLAY AREA

When you are on the top of the sandcrawler, you'll see that its left side is covered with shiny circular LEGO pieces. Use a thermal detonator to blast them to pieces and collect the studs that are left behind. After you destroy all the pieces, you will find two hidden floor switches on the ground. Step on one, and your buddy will step on the other. When you press both switches at the same time, a chute rises in the middle of the sandcrawler. Using a small character, crawl through the chute to get into the side of the vehicle. Grab a LEGO canister for your collection. Use the chute again to return to the top.

When you are inside the sandcrawler, it is time to get to work. Follow the path to the right until you see a pile of LEGOs on the floor. Put them together to form on the wall an activation panel, which only a protocol droid can use. Continue down the hall and blast the explosive gray and orange containers in the corner. Collect the loose studs on the ground, then blast the flashing red wall panels for even more loot. Under those containers are some loose pieces you can put together to create a droid. Once it is assembled, LEGO studs scatter on the floor.

FREEPLAY AREA

A black grate on the floor is glowing red. Use the dark side of the Force to shatter it and reveal a tunnel below. Jump inside and follow the tunnel to collect some valuable studs. Use the Force on the grate at the end to destroy it so you can get back to the floor above.

The next hallway is lined with red bars covering yellow wheel cranks. Destroy each bar, then use the Force to turn each wheel. After each wheel is turned, a compartment above spills studs onto the floor; collect them all. After the last wheel is cranked, two containers down the hall open, exposing blue studs.

Run into the next room to discover a room full of droids. The first thing to do is to blast all the red flashing wall panels and explosive containers in the area, and be sure to collect all the loot that spills out. Next, move around the room and put together all the LEGO piles you find to create more droids and collect more studs. When the room is clear, move to the back wall and pull the lever on the wall. A moveable box is transported to your right. Push the box along the path and into the red slot on the right side of the room. Back up as soon as the box is inserted into the red slot in the floor because it will explode, opening the door behind it. When the door is open, you can climb in and get a blue stud.

Return to the lever on the wall and activate it to get another moveable box. This time, push the box to the left side of the room where you have three more doors to open. Repeat the same technique you used the first time and open all three doors. You'll collect more blue studs and set R2-D2 free. When the room is stud free, use R2 to access the activation panel at the room's center. This opens the door to an elevator leading up.

Break the red bars and use the Force to turn the yellow wheels so you can get some blue studs.

Push the moveable boxes into the red floor slots to blow open the door and free R2-D2.

Move into the next room and blast the grate in the wall to the right of the doorway through which you entered. Grab the blue stud inside. Under the grate, you'll find three caps on the ground. Remove each one by using the Force and collect the goodies that pour out. Next, look to the left of door and blast open the explosive containers for more hidden studs.

At the room's center are some rows of circles on the ground. Step on each one to turn them green and cause some levers to appear at the end of the row. Pull the levers. The gate at the center of the room opens. To the left of the left lever you'll find more caps on the ground. Use the Force to open them and collect what's inside before you leave.

Step on the floor switches to activate some levers nearby.

FREEPLAY AREA

Use the dark side of the Force on the black grate on the ground to break it apart. Jump in the hole in the ground and follow the tunnel you find to get some valuable studs. Move back to floor level and use the Force on the black equipment on the left wall. When the equipment shatters, it reveals a chute in the wall. Use a small character to jump in the chute. It takes you to a small gated room nearby. As soon as you enter, the gate locking you in opens up and your partner runs in. Step on the floor switches on the right to make them turn green. Another gate opens right next to you.

Move through the gate and onto a ledge overlooking a stream of lava gushing out of the wall. Use the Force to turn the valve against the left wall. Use the Force again to break the equipment against the wall to stop the gushing stream of lava. When the lava stops flowing, use R2 to fly to the platform on the other side of the room to the north. Grab the LEGO canister and blast the panels on the wall. Next, use the Force to break the caps on the ground for some well-deserved studs.

The next room has C-3PO in a cage and a giant green turnstile at the center. Push the turnstile with your body. You'll see a black suction tube move over the first cage. The suction tube is directly over a cage when the light at the top of the cage turns green. Once the light turns green, an activation panel opens up to the left of the cages. R2-D2 can then activate the panel, and the droid in the cage under the suction tube will be sucked up. It then slides down a chute to the left of the room and is free of its cage. Push the turnstile until the suction tube is directly over C-3PO, then R2-D2 can use the activation panel nearby to suck him out.

A door to the left with the picture of a protocol droid on the activation panel leads to the way out, but you have business to take care of first. Move around the room and collect all the studs you find, including blue studs behind the support beams that look like X's. To the right of the exit door are some more caps on the floor that can be removed using the Force.

Turn the green turnstile until the light on C-3PO's cage turns green.

Before you leave, head back to the area where you first entered the sandcrawler and assembled the activation panel with the picture of a protocol droid on it. Use C-3PO to open the door. Inside, blast the explosive containers in the back of the room. Collect all the studs on the ground, then have R2-D2 use the activation panel to the left of the door through which you came. This causes the piece of machinery in the alcove to be moved into the room.

From there, use the Force to move the grate on the side of the room and create a pile of LEGO pieces on the floor. Assemble the pieces to form a yellow tank that fits together with the other piece of machinery you just moved. When everything is complete, use the Force on the new object and a load of valuable blue studs spews forth for you. After you collect the studs, move to the back of the room and use the Force on the antenna on the floor to attach it to the television. Then use the Force on the cups on the table and the chairs around it to reveal more hidden treasures. After you collect all of your loot, go back to the locked door you left behind.

Put all the pieces together the right way and you have a big payday.

Use C-3PO to access the activation panel and move into the next room. Shoot the explosive containers and the red flashing wall panels to uncover some valuables to collect. Use the Force to pull down some stairs on the left wall so C-3PO can climb up and access the panel there. Doing so releases some studs and some loose LEGO pieces. Put the pieces together to form a droid. On the other side of the room, you'll find more pieces to assemble into another droid. Finally use the Force to destroy the four small beams in the back of the room. Destroying these opens the door for you to get out.

Those small beams are the only things keeping you from the outside world.

Once outside, head down the Jawa ramp to the dirt trail. You don't get far before Tusken Raiders show up to stop you. Blast away until all of them are dead, then run up the dirt ledge on the left, collecting studs as you go. When you get to the end, double jump to reach the next ledge and a blue stud. With the loot in hand, drop to the trail below and destroy the rock pile against the trail's left side. Run into the short cave hidden behind the rocks to find some blue studs. Exit the cave and blast the equipment you find for more treasure.

The next area has plenty of deadly mud pits that can take you out if you get too close. Luckily, these Tusken Raiders have the ability to dry out the mud. After you drop from the ledge, take out any enemies in the area and run to the cliff wall on the right. Over there, C-3PO can activate a machine to suck the water out of the ground, making it safe to walk across.

Use the nearby machine to suck the water out of the dangerous mud.

After the water has been sucked out of the mud and into a nearby container, you can walk safely across the ground. Now break open the container with the water to cause some plants to grow. Use Ben Kenobi to double jump from the top of the plants onto the nearby ledge for some hard-to-reach studs. Return to the ground and use the Force to bust those plants out of the ground, revealing hidden loot.

Check the nearby cave for loot, then put the pile of LEGOs together to form a ramp that C-3PO can ascend. At the top of the ramp you made, use the Force to move a hook to the ledge above, then put the pile of LEGO bricks together to form a red circle swirl pad. Use Luke's ascension gun to grapple to the top for some much-deserved studs and a well-earned LEGO canister.

Use the Force to pull up plants and find hidden items.

After collecting the studs, drop to the ground where you'll find another machine that sucks the water from the mud. After C-3PO activates the machine, the ground is safe to cross. Bust open the water tank, and the plants spring to life. Use the Force to demolish those plants and turn them into studs and LEGO bricks. After you collect the studs, put the LEGO pieces together to form a platform. The dirt ramp nearby has two pieces of equipment on it that you must move using the Force. After you move them, you can use the Force to put the platform you created on top. From there you can jump on the platform and onto the rock bridge for some well-deserved goodies. Drop down from the dirt bridge you were on and run up the ramp from which you pulled those LEGO pieces.

Stack the LEGO pieces you find using the Force so you can jump to the ledge above.

FREEPLAY AREA

To the left of the ramp out of here, you'll find some ledges in the cliff wall. Blast the pile of debris along the nearby wall, then use your bounty hunter's thermal detonator to destroy the equipment on the back wall. The blast reveals a chute in the cliff wall. Use R2-D2 to fly over the bubbling mud on the ground to get to the ledge on the other side. Enter the chute with a Jawa that takes you to a ledge above. Collect the valuable studs there, then follow the ledges to the right to get safely back to the ground level.

FREEPLAY AREA

On the left side of the mud pits, you'll find some black scaffolding. Use the dark side of the Force to destroy the equipment and cause the rocks above it to come crashing down. Shoot the Tusken Raiders that come charging down the rocks. After the threat is gone, climb the rock steps to find a trail leading to a small oasis at the top.

When you get to the oasis, jump on the back of one of the large beasts you find. Ride it over to the large red button on the ground to turn it green. As soon as it changes color, jump down from the beast and step on the smaller red button on the ground to change it to green. When both buttons are green at the same time, the equipment in the middle of the nearby pond opens up.

Run to the right of the large button and use the Force on the shovel to dig up the ground. This reveals a large seed. Use the Force on it to create a large palm tree. Head to the north and smash all the pottery on the ground to uncover hidden studs. Move to the left of the broken pots, and use the Force to move another shovel to dig out another seed. Use the Force to turn this seed into a palm tree. Continue to make you way around the water and smash more pots. Use the Force on all the seeds you find to turn them into more palm trees. Be sure to collect all the studs that spill out. After you collect the studs on the ground, use your double jump to climb the ledges in the back to collect even more valuable studs.

It's time to keep moving. Head up the dirt ramp that goes under the rock bridge you were on earlier. Once you get to the other side, shoot the Tusken Raiders that start shooting at you. When the threat of getting shot is over, use the Force to move a pile of LEGOs from the right cliff wall to make steps up ahead. Run up the stairs you just made and grab the studs on the ledge you find.

Next to the stairs are some large, dark brown rocks. Double jump until you get to the top of the second rock, and from there, to the ledge where you can collect some goodies. While you're over there, use the Force to move some LEGOs in the cliff wall over to the other side of the canyon to create a bridge. Backtrack the way you came, then head for the newly formed bridge. As you cross, jump into the cave in the cliff wall over the bridge for a valuable blue stud.

Get over to the ledge so you can move the LEGOs in the cliff wall with the Force.

After you cross the bridge, more Sand People appear for you to take down. Blast them, then jump up the stone steps to the right. When you get to the top, push the moveable box all the way to the end until it falls to the ground and breaks apart. Drop down to the canyon floor and smash the containers for hidden loot, then double jump up the left canyon wall to reach a ledge with some more goodies for you to grab.

Drop to the canyon floor again and use the Force to turn that broken box into a small bridge. From there, C-3PO can access the equipment to suck the water out of the mud. When the area is safe to cross, smash open the water containers to cause some plants to grow. Use the top of the far-left plant to double jump to the ledge above. Collect all the studs from that ledge, then double jump to the ledge in the distance that has the blue stud on it. With your pockets full of studs, return to the dried mud pit and use the plants on the right side to get to the ledge above them. When you are done collecting studs, return to the plants and use the Force to bust them open for more treasure.

Use the tall plants to get to hard-to-reach ledges.

FREEPLAY AREA

At the ledge with the moveable box, float across the canyon to a ledge on the left. When you get there, collect all the valuable studs you see. Fly to the south until you land on top of the skinny stone pillar. Your weight causes it to sink down with you on it. When it stops sinking, you can collect a LEGO canister in the hillside, then double jump to return to the main trail above your head.

Move to the next canyon beyond the dried mud pit. You'll find two seeds on the ground. Use the Force to turn them into palm trees, then cut them back down and collect the studs. Head farther into the canyon and break any container you see to find some more valuables. Blast all the LEGO dirt piles along the way and explore the shallow caves hidden behind the piles to find some blue studs. At the end of the canyon, climb the dirt ledge on the right side until you arrive at the top. There, use the Force to open some containers for more studs. Drop to the floor and run to the end of the canyon.

EPISODE IV
A NEW HOPE

INTRODUCTION

GALAXY BASICS

STAR WARS CHARACTERS

TRANSPORTATION

MOS EISLEY CANTINA

WALKTHROUGH INTRODUCTION

EPISODE IV: A NEW HOPE

EPISODE V: THE EMPIRE STRIKES BACK

EPISODE VI: RETURN OF THE JEDI

BONUS FEATURES

You are now on the shore of a dangerous mud lake. Run to the top of the screen and break the equipment you find. Next, run to the bottom of the screen and use the Force to turn some more white caps for some hidden goodies. When the shore is clear, fix the landspeeder by putting the loose LEGO pieces back together. Use Ben Kenobi to jump in and take a ride north. The first island you reach has another broken landspeeder. Jump to the island and fix it up. Before you jump back in your landspeeder, collect any studs you see.

Fix up the landspeeder so you can cross this dangerous mud lake.

FREEPLAY AREA

On the islands out in the mud lake, you'll find some shiny metal containers. Use your bounty hunter to throw a thermal detonator at them and break them into tiny pieces. Collect the studs hidden inside.

With that island clear, jump in the landspeeder and drive to a small chunk of land to the northeast. Grab the studs on the ground, then head north to another island. Smash the containers and grab the studs. Then put the pile of LEGOs together. Use the Force to assemble the remaining pieces to form a minishuttle that flies off after it's assembled. Now head to the last island to the west. Assemble the LEGOs on the ground to form a red circle swirl pad. Use your ascension gun to grapple to the rock pillar in the distance. Jump down along the tops of the pillars and grab all the studs you find, as well as a LEGO canister. Get back to your landspeeder and return to the shore where you left your friends.

Take your landspeeder across the mud to the other side, where you'll find a small wooden dock. Next to the dock is a pile of LEGO pieces that, once assembled, form a lever. Pull the lever after you make it. A bridge rises out of the mud for your friends to cross. This side of the mud has a small dwelling in the center and lots of things to do.

Grapple to the top of the rock pillars to get some hard-to-reach treasures.

When your friends cross the bridge, move toward the dwelling nearby to find that some stormtroopers beat you there. Use your weapon and quickly dispose of those stormtroopers. Now, smash all the equipment you find around the lake for some studs. Go past the front of the dwelling. Use the Force to move the shovel you find and dig up some buried pieces. When all the pieces are dug up, put them together to make a treasure chest that spews forth many valuables.

Next, move to the right of the treasure chest, past the giant lizard, and on to the hanging laundry. Blast everything hanging from the line and collect anything that falls to the ground. Next to the laundry is an activation panel for R2-D2 to access. This causes the sprinklers in the nearby fence to turn on and some plants to grow. Jump into the fence area and assemble the LEGO pile into a lawnmower that Ben can move using the Force. As the mower moves around, studs are exposed on the ground. After the lawnmower is done, destroy everything in sight—the plants, mower, and fence. Behind the place where the fence used to be are some white caps on which Ben can use the Force to uncover more studs.

Go back to the giant lizard you passed earlier and hop on its back. Ride the beast back to the side of the dwelling where you can dismount. Dismounting off the animal boosts you into the air so that you can land on the roof. There you can collect many valuable blue studs. Drop to the ground and step on one of the four red switches on the ground. Your friends will step on the others. This activates a lever on the side of the dwelling. Pull that lever to open the nearby door that you can use to enter the abode.

Ride the giant lizard (the dewback)over to the building so you can jump down from its back and onto the roof.

Hey, it's Princess Leia's message.

It's not the size of your lightsaber that matters, Luke, it's how you use it.

C-3PO probably thinks Luke might need a little more practice with his new weapon.

LEGO STAR WARS II
THE ORIGINAL TRILOGY

STORY CHARACTERS

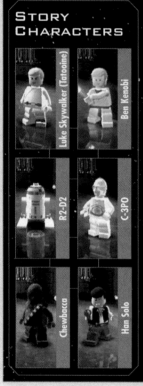

Luke Skywalker (Tatooine)

Ben Kenobi

R2-D2

C-3PO

Chewbacca

Han Solo

In search of a pilot who can take them to the distant planet of Alderaan, Luke Skywalker and old Ben Kenobi journey by landspeeder to Mos Eisley spaceport.

Here, among the most dangerous and reckless elements of Tatooine society, they hope to find someone brave or foolhardy enough to help in their quest to deliver R2-D2's secret data to the Rebel Alliance. But Imperial forces are everywhere....

There's Mos Eisley. For a despicable, retched place, it never looked so good.

Ben Kenobi is a master of the Force. He assures the stormtroooper that these aren't the droids he's looking for.

Does Luke have a license to drive that thing? Let's hope the Jawa he hit doesn't sue.

Mos Eisley isn't a nice place. It's not someplace you would normally take a young moisture-farm boy. But desperate times call for desperate measures. The droid and his secret plans must get to Alderaan, and that means finding a ship and an ace pilot to get you there. You have no time to waste because the Empire knows the plans are on Tatooine somewhere and it will stop at nothing until it finds them.

It's dangerous to stay out in the open too long, so get going and find your pilot. Run to the left and smash the container in the corner, then follow the back wall all the way to the right. Break open the containers to the left of the locked door and collect the loot that spills out. With your trusty double jump, get on the awnings overhead for a valuable blue stud. Drop to the ground and bust open some debris under the awning with your lightsaber for more loot.

Mos Eisley has long streets with many nooks and crannies to explore.

FREEPLAY AREA

When you see some shiny metal equipment on the streets of Mos Eisley, switch to your bounty hunter. Throw a thermal detonator at the equipment to break it into tiny pieces. Then collect the valuable studs that spill out.

EPISODE IV
A NEW HOPE

FREEPLAY AREA

A door in the right wall is locked, so switch to a sandtrooper and open it using the access panel. Run into the room beyond the doorway and grab all the studs on the ground. On the right side of the room is a small spa, and on the room's left side are two showers. Use the Force to pull both levers for each shower. After you pull the fourth lever, the water in the spa on the other side of the room drains out. When the water is gone, a LEGO canister appears for you to collect.

 TIP

Sandtroopers are crawling all over the city, and they will shoot at you when you least expect it. Always take them down first, before going about your looting business.

CAUTION

Plenty of sandtroopers with itchy trigger fingers are ready to shoot you on sight. Avoid hitting the local authorities wearing the tan uniforms while you fight sandtroopers, or you'll have them trying to blast you as well.

To the left of the awnings, you'll find more debris to chop up. Hidden underneath are not only studs but one of three large carrots hidden along the street. Use the Force to stack the green LEGOs next to the carrot to turn them into a potted cactus that young Luke's blaster can quickly destroy. Run up the stairs nearby. You're now in a double score zone filled with studs to collect. Follow the path upstairs to the left and double jump over the gap in the bridge to get to the other side and more goodies.

FREEPLAY AREA

On the other side of the bridge is an activation panel that you can only access with a bounty hunter. Switch to Greedo and use the panel. The door in front of you opens and LEGO pieces spill onto the dusty road below. Drop down and assemble the pieces to create a large fan on the ground.

Return to the bottom of the stairs you just climbed and assemble the loose LEGO bricks at the bottom for some hidden studs. Bust open the debris behind your creation to scatter some orange pieces into the street. Use the Force on these pieces to make pretty flowers sprout from the dirt. Collect the studs as you make your way across the street to a small white door. Use the Force to open the cans to the right of the door, then destroy them with your lightsaber for even more loot.

Next to the cans is a covered awning with studs on top. The awning can be reached with a simple double jump. Under the covering, use the Force to move the blue LEGOs out of the basket and onto the street. Use Luke's blaster to destroy the line of bricks you just made, as well as the debris to the left of the basket. To the right of the awning you'll find more containers to crack open and more studs on the ground to the right of those containers.

Collect the studs on the ground before they disappear.

Head across the street to a yellow awning with a yellow stud on top. Double jump to get the treasure up there, then put together the pile of LEGOs nearby to create a box. Use the Force to move the box up the street. You can use the Force again on another nearby box so that the two are stacked on top of each other. Climb the boxes and jump to the building nearby for two blue studs. From the top of the building, jump to the black tent on the left. Get the gold stud, and slide to the ground below.

When you get back to the ground, enter the large hut nearby to gather the goodies lying on the ground. Smash the dark gray container to the left of the hut. Next, use the Force to scatter the blue LEGOs in the bowl on the ground onto the dusty street. Use the Force again to turn each LEGO into a pretty plant and many studs. Climb the stairs in back of the bowl and collect all the goodies on the roof at the top.

Stack the boxes so you can get to the building nearby and some blue studs.

FREEPLAY AREA

While you're on the roof, switch to a dark side character and make your way to the black grate. Use the dark side of the Force to smash the grate open and collect the valuable studs that spill out. Jump through the hole that the grate left to fall into the small building where you collect a LEGO canister. Run out the doorway to return to the road.

Return to the base of the stairs and quickly run across the street. Smash the large container at the corner of the building. Inside is the second large carrot that you must find on this street. Use the Force to raise it out of the ground, then grab the blue stud on the ground under the building. In between the pretty plants and the giant carrot is a giant vent hidden under the sand. Return to the starting area and drive the landspeeder over to that location. The wind created by the landspeeder will clear away the dust so that you can jump on the exposed vent and ride the draft into the air for a blue stud.

With the stud in hand, follow the buildings along the left as you head north until you get to some small garbage cans. Use the Force to open each one, and then again to pull the LEGO contents out and onto the street. Put the pieces together to create a door with an activation panel showing the picture of an astromech droid. Use R2-D2 to open the door and grab the red power brick inside. When you have the brick, destroy all the cans outside the door. Follow the road to the north collecting all the studs you find along the way.

Putting the loose LEGO pieces together builds a door with a hidden power brick inside.

Run back to the set of stairs you were on earlier (on the opposite side of the road). Head north and smash the can next to the building. Inside is the last hidden carrot. After you find this third carrot, a LEGO canister appears high above the broken bridge you jumped across earlier.

FREEPLAY AREA

When you see the canister, run back to the large fan you assembled on the road underneath the broken bridge. Jump on the fan and the wind will push you into the air. You can add the canister to your stash.

Continue to move north down the street and smash the containers in the corner. After you collect the contents that spill out, use the Force to create a bicycle out of the loose LEGOs that are on the ground. Run up the stairs nearby to get to the roof where you find a small chute in the wall and more studs on the ground. Jump on the brown awning and slide back down to the ground. Use the Force on the stairs you just climbed to turn them into a ramp against the wall ahead.

Run to the base of the ramp and blast open the containers you find. Next, ascend the ramp and take out all the sandtroopers trying to drop you with their blasters. The ramp takes you to the building roof and many studs. Follow a ledge at the top to the left, past an activation panel, until you get to a wall. Double jump to get to the top of the wall, and follow the rest of the ledge down the street, collecting studs as you go. After everything has been collected, jump to the street and walk C-3PO to the activation panel you just passed on the ledge. This opens a gate below you so you can move down the street.

Run along the ledge over the city to find hidden loot.

FREEPLAY AREA

After you climb the stairs to get to the roof, switch to a Jawa and enter the chute in the wall. This takes you to a ledge high above the city. Grab the valuable studs you see, then drop back down to the roof you came from.

FREEPLAY AREA

A door on the ledge over the main exit can only be opened using a sandtrooper. This door just leads to a ledge in the next area, which you can reach using an AT-ST.

iv

EPISODE IV *A NEW HOPE*

When you get to the next part of the city, blast the containers to the left for some hidden goods. Continue north along the city wall until you see a part of the city that is blocked off with debris. Since you can't get through there just yet, follow the city wall to the left collecting studs as you go. Enter the white door for some loot, then use the Force on the garbage cans outside before you smash them to bits. Collect any treasure that falls to the ground.

Continue to follow the city wall until you get to three boxes on the ground, then take out all the sandtroopers that move in to greet you. When the coast is clear, use the Force to stack the boxes up ahead. Scale the stack until you can jump to the roof of the building. Add a LEGO canister to your collection. Return to the ground. Use the Force to clean out the garbage cans, then smash them to bits for even more studs. Search the room behind the white doorway nearby to collect some hidden loot, then smash a container next to your stack of boxes for a valuable blue stud.

Stacking the boxes with the Force will help you get to the roof.

FREEPLAY AREA

The next part of Mos Eisley has plenty of shiny metal equipment for you to blow up using your thermal detonators. After you explode the equipment along the right wall near the giant rocket, some LEGO pieces are left behind. Assemble these loose pieces to form a turnstile. Push the green side of the turnstile all the way around until some white LEGOs fall from above. Assemble this new set of pieces to form a red circle pad. Use the pad to grapple to a ledge high above. From there, double jump in the air to get a LEGO canister for your collection.

Smashing that last container left some pieces on the ground for you to assemble. Putting them together forms a ramp up the step. Walk C-3PO up the ramp to the door in front so he can use the activation panel. Inside are a lot of loose LEGO pieces that Ben Kenobi can quickly put together to form the head of something. Be sure to grab the valuable blue studs that appear after construction is complete.

Smash the two large containers on the left to reveal some studs and more LEGOs. Put the two piles together to form the feet of something. Continue along the wall to the left. The road leading down the street is blocked with more debris. Since you can't go that way for now, use R2-D2 to open the door to the left of the debris. With the door open, Ben Kenobi can pull the objects out using the Force. These objects land next to some more loose LEGOs that you need to assemble.

Now, on the dusty streets of Mos Eisley, you have all the parts to construct your very own AT-ST walker. Before you do anything though, move along the left wall and use the Force to empty all the trash cans you find, then use your lightsaber to smash them apart. Grab all the studs along the way, including a valuable blue one. Now it's time to construct the parts you left on the ground. Use the Force to move the feet, then the legs, then the base, and finally the head. Congratulations—you've made an AT-ST!

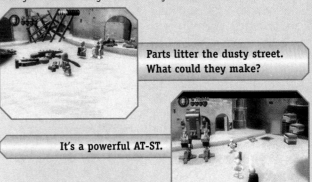

Parts litter the dusty street. What could they make?

It's a powerful AT-ST.

You don't get very long to celebrate your construction because a sandtrooper runs out of a nearby building and hops into your AT-ST. Use the Force on the vehicle to bring that sandtrooper to the ground where you can cut him down with your lightsaber. Now that the walker is free again, jump in. Ignore the blocked street next to you and head back to where you first entered this street and saw the first blocked road.

Move the At-ST to the building next to the roadblock and jump to the roof. Put together the loose LEGO bricks you find to create two turret guns. After the guns are complete, collect the studs on the ground and jump into the turret to take control of it. As soon as you do, some giant rodent creatures come out of the holes in front of you. Blast them with your gun. Drop ten of these critters, and a LEGO canister appears on the roof. Nab it.

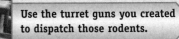

Use the turret guns you created to dispatch those rodents.

FREEPLAY AREA

A door to the right of the turret guns can only be opened by a sandtrooper, but that door just leads back to the first part of Mos Eisley and nothing new.

INTRODUCTION
GALAXY BASICS
STAR WARS CHARACTERS
TRANSPORTATION
MOS EISLEY CANTINA
WALKTHROUGH INTRODUCTION
iv EPISODE IV: A NEW HOPE
v EPISODE V: THE EMPIRE STRIKES BACK
vi EPISODE VI: RETURN OF THE JEDI
BONUS FEATURES

Drop to the ground and return to your AT-ST. If another sand-trooper got in while you were away, use the Force again to get him out and dispose of him. It's time to test out the power of this vehicle and blast the roadblock, but don't stand too close or you'll take damage. After the roadblock is blown to pieces, collect the studs on the ground and shoot the sandtroopers in the courtyard on the other side.

You found a double score zone! With the sandtroopers gone, get out of the AT-ST and assemble some loose LEGOs near the entrance to the courtyard. Blast your construction, then follow the right wall around the courtyard. Collect all the studs in the area: They can be found on awnings, in doorways, or on ledges that you have to double jump to reach. For even more hidden loot, be sure to break all the containers you find as well. As you follow the court-yard wall back to the entrance, you'll see some blue brushes lead-ing to a landspeeder washer.

Test it out. Run back to the starting area and grab your landspeeder again. Avoid enemy trouble and drive it back to the courtyard. Park it on the gray pad on the ground directly in front of the blue brushes. As soon as the speeder is on the pad, a lever appears to the left of the washer. Pull it. This activates the landspeeder wash, scrubbing your vehicle till it's shiny and new.

Wash your vehicle in the super duper landspeeder washer.

Get back inside the AT-ST and return to the other roadblock where you first assembled the AT-ST. Blast the second roadblock to bits and head down the street. There are many things to pick up down on the street level, but stay in your walker. Blast the enemy soldiers on the ground as you keep moving. When the street bends to the right, you come face to face with another AT-ST. Blast it with your lasers until you knock the other driver out of the cockpit. Then shoot him so he can't get back in.

Continue to move around this part of the street after the roadblock, picking up floating studs out of the air. Be sure to shoot the antennae on buildings for even more loot. If another trooper gets in the other AT-ST be sure to stop what you're doing and knock this powerful enemy out of commission before you move on. Continue collecting goods in the area until you walk all the way back to the roadblock.

Now that everything up high has been handled, you can search the ground. Near the former roadblock, you'll find a blue stud on top of an awning and some more studs scattered on the ground. Destroy the LEGOs along the walls for even more loot. As you head farther down the street, use the Force to open garbage cans and destroy containers along the way. Follow the bend in the road to the right, where you can smash more LEGO pieces and containers for hidden loot. Be sure to collect the blue stud tucked away in the corner along the right wall. Once the area is stud free, advance through the opening in the wall to the cantina.

Use the AT-ST to get the hard-to-reach studs.

Smash the containers near the exit door for some valuable loot.

The room you enter has devices to keep droids out. Since you want your buddies to follow you, you have to eliminate the devices. Use Luke's blaster to destroy each one. Head into the room and collect all the studs on the ground. The next door in the room is closed, so simply step on one of the four red floor buttons. When the rest of your party steps on the other buttons, the door opens to you.

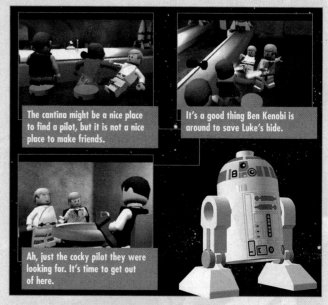

The cantina might be a nice place to find a pilot, but it is not a nice place to make friends.

It's a good thing Ben Kenobi is around to save Luke's hide.

Ah, just the cocky pilot they were looking for. It's time to get out of here.

Luke and Ben Kenobi take off for the ship, so it's time for Han and Chewbacca to join them. Before you leave the cantina, scour the area for loose studs, including a blue one behind the table to the right of your starting location. Another can be found to the far right of the bar. Be sure to blast all the chairs for even more hidden loot. After you've had enough creature watching and have soaked up enough ambiance, it's time to join the others, so go to the door where the large green arrow is pointing.

The large green arrows points you in the right direction... out of the dirty cantina.

FREEPLAY AREA

An alcove near the entrance of the cantina has a small chute in the wall. Use one of your small characters, like a Jawa, to climb inside. The chute takes you to a room to the right where you add another LEGO canister to your stash. Pull the levers on the back wall to remove the force field blocking you from the rest of the cantina.

FREEPLAY AREA

The cantina contains many Force-sensitive items. Use the Force on all the light fixtures, cups, and bar stools to reveal hidden goods. Follow the main bar to both ends to find some equipment on which you can use the Force to reveal even more hidden goodies.

Once outside, shoot the four large containers to find many valuable hearts and studs. One of the containers even has one of three new vegetables hidden around this part of town. Search the nearby doorway for a valuable blue stud and collect more items along the wall. Shoot the debris under the awning to find even more treasure. When the courtyard has been cleared, step on the red circle swirl and grapple up.

On the roof, you find a sandtrooper and the Imperial spy who ratted you out. The spy runs off, but you can blast the sandtrooper. Next, put the loose LEGOs together to form a red circle swirl pad, then collect all the studs on the ground. Follow the spy through the doorway and blast the antenna on the other side for more goods. Return to the circle swirl and grapple to the next rooftop to blast more antenna. Collect all the goods on the ground, including a blue stud.

Run through the open doorway and move from rooftop to rooftop until you get to the red circle swirl platform and can grapple to the building across the street. Pull the lever on the wall and when a box rolls off the conveyer belt nearby, push it over the edge of the platform. Before you drop down from the end of the ledge, jump on the ledge nearby so you can collect a blue stud.

Push the box to the ground before you get the goodies in the area.

FREEPLAY AREA

Use Greedo to open the door with the activation panel showing the picture of a bounty hunter. Run through the door and down the stairs to another rooftop with some studs to collect. Follow the roof to the left, and jump across the gap to a small ledge with more studs to grab. Drop to the dirty road below and start smashing LEGO debris to find LEGO studs. A doorway to the right can only be opened by C-3PO, but it just leads to a road you're going to use later, so don't bother entering now. Open the rest of the doors in the area to find the hidden loot behind them.

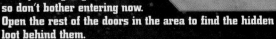

Follow the main road to the left and smash the large container against the wall. Find the second of three large vegetables around the area. Move into the alcove to the left of the vegetable and smash all the debris for more treasure. Move down the path, smashing equipment and checking doorways for more loot. When you get to the end of the path, double jump to reach the roof on the right. Use your bounty hunter's thermal detonator and blow up the shiny metal object. Collect the blue stud that drops, and then jump to the top of the tan dome to the right for another blue stud.

Drop to the ground and head to the wall to the north. Use the Force to turn the wheels on the wall and raise the small gates in the wall. This causes studs to sprout from the ground, so run around the area and pick them up before they disappear. After the studs stop appearing, run behind the open gate and grab the LEGO canister that was hidden there. Run to the left wall. You'll find some large black gates. Use the dark side of the Force to shatter each one and collect all the valuables that are left behind. The gates lead to another part of Mos Eisley that you will visit later so don't walk through them now. Instead, return to the area's entrance and double jump to the ledge on the left wall. From there, double jump to the roof on the right. Ascend the stairs to the door that only a bounty hunter can open, which you opened earlier.

When you get back to the road, scour the walls and doorways for loose studs in the small courtyard. Smash all the containers, garbage cans, and debris you find to uncover more treasure. Be sure to blast the debris hidden under the awning as well. Return to the box you pushed to the ground and push it along the checkerboard path.

As you push the box along the path, be sure to stop and collect LEGO studs from along the walls and in the doorways. Also, blast the debris and garbage cans along the way for even more hidden goods. Continue to push the box all the way along the path until you get to the closed gate. Shoot the box. It explodes, blasting open the gate and showering the path with studs.

INTRODUCTION

GALAXY BASICS

STAR WARS CHARACTERS

TRANSPORTATION

MOS EISLEY CANTINA

WALKTHROUGH INTRODUCTION

EPISODE IV: A NEW HOPE

EPISODE V: THE EMPIRE STRIKES BACK

EPISODE VI: RETURN OF THE JEDI

BONUS FEATURES

Push the heavy box along the path until you get to the closed gate.

NOTE

If you accidentally break the box you dropped to the ground, you can always return to the rooftop it came from and pull the lever again to get a new one.

FREEPLAY AREA

The door on the right wall can only be opened by C-3PO. This door just leads to the area that you entered earlier using your bounty hunter.

The courtyard on the other side of the door is swarming with stormtroopers, and you see the Imperial spy escape through the area. Using Han Solo, quickly run to the base of the stairs after the door and drop any enemies that try to stop you. From the base of the stairs, start shooting into the courtyard. You might not be able to see the enemies in the distance, but shots from your blaster will find them. As you fire, your auto defense ability will keep you from taking any shots yourself.

Once the courtyard is enemy free, move along the left wall, shooting garbage cans and collecting studs as you go. The next wall is lined with huge doors you can blast apart. Collect the goods hidden behind the doors, then blast the brown seeds on the ground. LEGO studs explode from the ground and little plants sprout up.

FREEPLAY AREA

Use the dark side of the Force to destroy each plant. As soon as the plant disappears, LEGO studs sprout from the ground. Grab them.

Follow the next wall and collect more studs on the ground and in the doorway. Blast open the container you see to find another large vegetable in this area. In the doorway to the right of the vegetable are more seeds that you can shoot to uncover buried valuables. Also to the right of the vegetables is the entrance to a movie theater. Hey look, LEGO *Star Wars* is playing at 8:30! Unfortunately, there's no time to watch a movie now, so follow the last wall of the courtyard and grab the blue stud on the ground. Push the box on the ground to the end of the checkerboard path. Jump from the top of the box to the ledge above.

Run to the courtyard's center and get on one of the riding beasts that are standing around. Ride it to the corner of the courtyard next to the movie theater. Jump off its back and into the air to get a valuable blue stud. When the beast is ready again, jump on its back and ride it to the large vegetable on the ground. Jump off the beast's back to land on the roof above. There, you can grab a blue stud and pull the lever on the wall to get a new hat. When you have the new fashion in hand, jump to the ground and ride the beast to the wall that had the giant doors. Jump from the beast to the roof, where you can check the doorways and floor for anything of value. Run through the archway and down the stairs to get to the next area.

Yee-Haw! Ride that beast to get to the rooftops above.

FREEPLAY AREA

If you found the third large vegetable in the area, then a LEGO canister appears back in the area where you pushed the box down to the road. Backtrack along the checkered path and get back to the ledge where you pulled the lever to get a new box. From there, jump on the ledge along the wall. Follow the ledge to the end. Add that canister to your collection.

EPISODE IV
A NEW HOPE

FREEPLAY AREA

They're showing a great movie but the door is locked. Luckily R2-D2 can access the activation panel and open the door. Go inside. You are in a double score zone. Start smashing all the chairs in the place and grab the studs that drop to the ground. After the chairs are gone, smash the four lights pointing at the curtain in the back of the theater. After the lights are gone, the curtains are pulled. This reveals a jumbled picture on the screen. Use the Force to fix the picture and start the movie. It's black-and-white footage of some of your favorite LEGO movies.

Double Score Zone!

When the movie is over, it goes back to the red LEGO logo. Show your appreciation for the film and blast the screen. As the screen breaks into pieces, collect all the studs that spill out because you'll nab lot of blue ones in the mix. Also, hidden behind the screen is another LEGO canister for your collection. After you completely destroy the screen and grab everything in the area, you can leave the theater.

FREEPLAY AREA

The shiny metal equipment in the area can only be destroyed using the thermal detonator of a bounty hunter. Destroy the equipment and grab the blue studs that were hidden underneath.

You finally get to the hanger where Luke, Ben Kenobi, and the *Millennium Falcon* have been waiting for you. Unfortunately, that Imperial spy has led the sandtroopers right to you. He runs for cover along the walkway over the hanger as the sandtroopers swarm in to blast you. Stay near the entrance to the hanger and start blasting the fools that rush you. While you shoot your enemies, let your auto defenses protect you from incoming fire.

After the last enemy falls, the spy runs to another safe spot and sends in more troops. Take this wave of enemies out just like the first. After the second wave is destroyed, the persistent spy calls in even more reinforcements—right before he slips to the ground. Blast this third wave of sandtroopers, including the spy on the ground. After the last sandtrooper is toast, the entry platform to the *Falcon* opens on the left side. Enter the ship.

Stay near the entrance of the hanger while you blast those sandtroopers.

Luke finally gets to leave that dusty old planet. Will he ever return?

Grand Moff Tarken threatens to destroy Princess Leia's home world Alderaan.

Oops...it doesn't look like Grand Moff Tarken makes idle threats.

INTRODUCTION
GALAXY BASICS
STAR WARS CHARACTERS
TRANSPORTATION
MOS EISLEY CANTINA
WALKTHROUGH INTRODUCTION
iv EPISODE IV: A NEW HOPE
v EPISODE V: THE EMPIRE STRIKES BACK
vi EPISODE VI: RETURN OF THE JEDI
BONUS FEATURES

STORY CHARACTERS

Luke Skywalker (Stormtrooper)

Ben Kenobi

R2-D2

C-3PO

Chewbacca

Han Solo (Stormtrooper)

Imprisoned in the Death Star, Princess Leia still refuses to reveal the location of the Rebel base to the evil Darth Vader.

Meanwhile, Luke Skywalker and Obi-Wan Kenobi have commissioned Han Solo to take them to Leia's home planet of Alderaan. Escaping from Imperial forces on Tatooine, they make the jump through hyperspace.

But Alderaan has disappeared, its population the victims of Darth Vader's impatience—and in Alderaan's place, they find only the deadly shadow of the Death Star....

Hyperspace is the only way to travel.

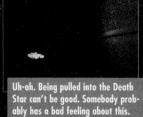

Uh-oh. Being pulled into the Death Star can't be good. Somebody probably has a bad feeling about this.

Those stormtrooper disguises worked like a charm.

Finding the planet Alderaan blown into a billion pieces was a little disappointing. And then, being pulled into the Death Star didn't really make things any better. But all is not lost, because your stormtrooper disguises worked: Nobody knows you're here. Now maybe you can snoop around and find out what is going on around here.

After you start, blast all the containers in the room and collect the studs that spill on the floor. The wall to the north is lined with destructible panels and long blue lights. Blast them to little bits to spill treasures on the ground and reveal a little nook inside. Use the Force on the machine in there to get some valuable blue studs. After you collect everything, use the Force on the door in the right wall to turn it into a TIE fighter. When the door is gone, two stormtroopers charge in, so quickly take them down.

The machine hidden behind the wall has many goodies inside.

Enter the hallway and destroy the containers you see. Collect the loot that litters the floor. Move through the open door in the right wall, and use one of the human characters to jump into the crane's controls. In the distance, you can see the hangar where the *Millennium Falcon* is being guarded. Move the crane's claw around until you see its black shadow rest on the unsuspecting guard below

it. Drop the claw and pick up the guard. Then move the claw and the captured guard over the opening in the hangar's center and drop the guard to his death. Toss ten guards away all in the same manner, and a LEGO canister appears below. Direct the crane's claw over the canister and pick it up to add it to your collection.

Move back to the hall and pull the lever on the left wall to get a stormtrooper helmet. With your new disguise, you can use the activation panel to open the door at the end of the hall. After you enter the room, blast the guards standing near the windows to the right. Run to the left of the doorway and collect a blue stud, then assemble the loose LEGOs nearby into a mini Star Destroyer.

Destroy the nearby containers, then move around the room to find more loose LEGO pieces on the floor. Assembled, they form a set of controls with a picture of R2-D2 on the activation panel. Move past this for now, and blast the colored lights on the wall the guards were standing near to find some hidden loot. Have C-3PO use the activation panel to the right of the windows to open the nearby door. Enter and grab the LEGO canister inside. Now use R2-D2 to access the panel you passed earlier and you see a picture of Princess Leia. Obi-Wan moves off to take care of some business and the droids hide, leaving Luke, Han, and Chewy to find the princess.

The LEGO canister appears after you dispose of ten guards.

INTRODUCTION

GALAXY BASICS

STAR WARS CHARACTERS

TRANSPORTATION

MOS EISLEY DANTINA

WALKTHROUGH INTRODUCTION

iv EPISODE IV: A NEW HOPE

v EPISODE V: THE EMPIRE STRIKES BACK

vi EPISODE VI: RETURN OF THE JEDI

BONUS FEATURES

After C-3PO opens the door, the canister inside is all yours.

Run into the next hallway that opened up to the left of the control panel. Blast the guards in the distance before they see you. When the coast is clear, move down the hall. Destroy containers and the orange and gray pillars along the wall to reveal valuable studs inside. The end of the hall could drop you down to your death, so head into the doorway in the left wall.

FREEPLAY AREA

The gap in the hallway is no problem for R2. Just hover in the air and fly across to the other side. Grab the blue stud on the ground. Blast the orange and gray pillar on the wall and the stormtroopers who emerge from the doorway in the left wall. Before you go charging down the hall, move into the room from which those stormtroopers came and grab the LEGO canister inside.

Now return to the hallway and head north. Shoot the guards in the distance, then destroy any containers you see. Along the way, you can see a canister on a ledge above the hallway. At this point, move to the edge of the hall to the right where it drops down to nothing. Switch to R2-D2 and fly across the room to the right until you get to a small ledge. From there, use a character with an ascension gun to grapple to the ledge above. A small chute in the wall is perfect for a Jawa to travel through. This takes you to the ledge above the hallway you came from, as well as a LEGO canister that you can grab. Once the canister is in your stash, drop down to the hallway and continue to head north.

Run through the doorway and shoot the stormtroopers you meet on the next walkway. When the coast is clear, move to the semicircular platform attached to the walkway. Use the Force to pull some metal covers off the wall to reveal some levers. Pull each lever. A LEGO canister appears above you. Follow the semicircular platform to the right and use your ascension gun when you get to the red circle swirl pad on the ground. This lets you grapple up to grab the canister.

Drop down to the walkway again and continue to follow it to the left and through the next doorway. In the next hall, shoot the container you see as well as the guard in the back-right corner. When more troopers rush in from the left doorway, blast them as well. Use the dark side of the

Force to move the gate blocking the end of the hallway and turn it into small platforms along the right wall. Double jump up the platforms you created until you get to the top one. From there, double jump in the air to collect another LEGO canister.

Drop down to the right corner where you shot the first stormtrooper and grab the blue stud. Use R2-D2 to hover back to the main walkway. The doorway ahead and the doorway in the left wall from which the stormtroopers came both lead to areas you don't want to go just yet. Backtrack to the chasm that you used R2 to get across and run into the doorway in the left wall.

In the next hall you come under attack again by Imperial troops, so take them out quickly. Move down the hall and blast the orange and gray side pillars to find the blue studs underneath. A door in the right wall has a blue stud to collect. There's also a LEGO canister behind some glass, which prevents you from getting it for now, so continue moving down the hall. Shoot more guards in the hall and pull the lever on the right wall to put on another stormtrooper mask.

Follow the hall to a walkway where you find more stormtroopers. Shoot them as they come out of the elevators in the right wall. The stormtroopers keep coming until you break the security camera over each elevator, so destroy the cameras. Now keep moving along the walkway. At the walkway's end, you can see Ben Kenobi fighting with more stormtroopers across a chasm in the distance. Ben's enemies are your enemies, so fire at those Imperials. After the last one drops, Ben uses the Force to create a LEGO bridge for you to cross.

Ben Kenobi looks like he is in trouble, so you had better help him out.

FREEPLAY AREA

A door in the left wall has an activation panel next to it. Use R2 to access the panel and open the door. Go through the door and you find yourself on a small ledge high in the air. Use R2 to fly over to the ledge on the left and grab some studs. Use an ascension gun on the red circle swirl pad to grapple to another ledge overhead. Grab the red power brick, then jump back to the right to land on the small ledge you started on. Move back through the door to return to the hallway.

FREEPLAY AREA

Get into any of the elevators on the wall and have R2-D2 access the panel inside. The elevator takes you up to a small room with four hat machines on the wall. Collect the studs on the ground, then pull the levers on the machines if you want a new look. Now, just hop in one of the elevators and ride it back down.

While Ben does his thing, cross the bridge he created and pick up the studs on the other side. Blast any containers you find and follow the walkway to a lever on the right wall. It gives you a new helmet. Across from the lever, some enemy stormtroopers use a grappling hook to get over the fence. These troops are tough and require two shots to take them down. Use your friends as cover and drop the enemies quickly, then blast the hook they are using to get up so that no more can enter the area. When the area is secure, pull the lever to put on your mask.

Run down the rest of the walkway until you get to a block in the road. Shoot at the blockade until it explodes. Run past the doorway in the right wall and continue down the hall, blasting orange and gray pillars while collecting all the studs on the ground. At the end of the hall, run through the door on the right. Shoot the guards in black when you get to the next area, as well as the hook on the fence that they are using to grapple. Run to the right of the door, and with your stormtrooper mask on, access the activation panel on the wall to open the door. When the door is open, smash any containers in the area and collect all the studs before moving along.

Blast the blockade so you can continue.

Pass through the doorway and run across the narrow walkway. At the circular platform in the middle of the area, assemble the loose LEGOs to make a turnstile. Push the green side of your creation to move that narrow walkway you crossed over to a platform against the back wall. Run to the newly discovered platform and use your ascension gun to reach the platform above you. If you don't have a stormtrooper helmet yet, you can get one here. Now grapple to a higher ledge and blast the guards on the ledge to the right. Jump to that ledge and fall off its right side; you land on a ledge with a door you can enter.

FREEPLAY AREA

When you get to the top ledge above the doorway to the right, switch to R2-D2. Fly across the room over to a ledge on the right and pick up another LEGO canister to add to your stash.

Move through the door to find a room full of enemy troops. Run to the left and drop the two stormtroopers there. When they're gone, focus on the troops on the other side of the room without having to worry about anyone shooting at your back. When the coast is clear, run around the room shooting out the red and green blinking monitors and collecting the studs along the walls. After the last monitor is history, a new one opens up showing a scary march of stormtroopers. A LEGO canister appears below it; add it to your collection. Assemble the nearby pile of LEGOs to form an activation panel for the door. While wearing your stormtrooper helmet, access the panel to open the door.

FREEPLAY AREA

Use the dark side of the Force on the equipment in the room's center to make it spin around and around. It spins so fast, it eventually breaks apart.

Blast the guards on the other side of the door and assemble the loose LEGOs on the left side of the hall. Run down the hall, blasting orange and gray pillars, as well as any container you find. More guards are posted in the next area, so blast them when they get in range. Also, blast more containers on the floor.

When the area is clear, open the first elevator while still wearing your stormtrooper mask. This takes you to the lounge where stormtroopers go to relax and take hot baths with each other. They may be wearing nothing but swimsuits and helmets, but these stormtroopers are packing, so quickly shoot them dead. Once the bathing area is free of enemies, run to the back wall. Three panels will open up when you get close, exposing a lever behind each one. Pull each lever to take a nice shower before you leave via the elevator you came up.

EPISODE IV
A NEW HOPE

INTRODUCTION

GALAXY BASICS

STAR WARS CHARACTERS

TRANSPORTATION

MOS EISLEY CANTINA

WALKTHROUGH INTRODUCTION

EPISODE IV: A NEW HOPE

EPISODE V: THE EMPIRE STRIKES BACK

EPISODE VI: RETURN OF THE JEDI

BONUS FEATURES

Blast these stormtroopers to pieces before they shoot you.

FREEPLAY AREA

Use the Force to stack the boxes at the end of the walkway. After everything is stacked, double jump to the top of the boxes, then double jump again into the alcove above. Push the box you find to the right until it drops down a chute in the ground. The box drops to the end of the chute where it breaks a gate in the wall. With the gate gone, you can drop down to the walkway and grab the LEGO canister that was behind it.

After you get off the elevator, run to the left and enter the elevator to ride it down. As soon as you enter the next room, start blasting the guards inside. As you fire, more guards enter the room from the elevators in the back. Keep shooting until all the enemies are gone. Above each elevator is a security camera. Fire at these cameras a few times until they break into tiny pieces. More guards will use the elevators to enter the room until each camera is destroyed.

Now move through the room shooting containers and collecting studs. Move to the room's center and put the loose LEGOs together to form the control panel. Collect all the goods that spill to the floor before you pull the levers on the equipment you just put together. This opens a door in front of you.

Destroy those security cameras over the elevators to stop the guards from storming in.

Before you go charging down the corridor behind the door you opened, jump into one of the elevators. Both elevators take you to a room with the controls to a couple of turret guns on the outside of the Death Star. Jump into the controls of a turret and start firing at the TIE fighters flying around outside. Shoot in their general direction and don't let up. After you destroy ten craft, a boatload of blue studs drops on the floor between the two guns. Quickly grab them before they disappear.

Ride an elevator back to the room you came from and head into the corridor leading into the prison block. Guards at the back of the corridor charge at you, so fire as they approach until they fall to pieces. While the coast is clear, pull a lever on the right side of

the hall; one of your friends will pull the other, opening the door between the two of you. Run inside the cell to collect the valuables on the floor. Return to the corridor and shoot more guards charging you. Pull the levers across from those you just pulled and clean out the inside of the cell.

In between pulling levers and cleaning out cells, always be sure to shoot the guards as they charge you. Now, head down the corridor to the next set of levers. Pull the levers on the left wall and enter the cell. Assemble the LEGOs on the ground to put together the skeleton of some poor prisoner who never tasted freedom again. At least he left you studs to collect.

Use the turret guns to drop those TIE fighters like flies.

Always stop to shoot the oncoming guards before you move to inspect the next cell.

Go to the next set of levers and pull the ones on the left wall for some studs. Pull the levers on the right wall to find the cell holding Princess Leia. The last set of levers down the corridor can only be opened by R2-D2. The elevator at the very end leads you back to the turret gun you controlled earlier, so go into the cell with Leia. Step on one of the floor switches in front of her. One of your friends will step on the other to disable the force field and set her free.

FREEPLAY AREA

Use the Force on the wall panel to cause a few studs to shake loose.

47

FREEPLAY AREA

Move to the end of the corridor where you find two doors that only R2 can open. Have R2-D2 access the activation panel on the right door and go inside the room to grab some valuable studs. Access the panel on the left wall and move through the open door. Grab the studs and a LEGO canister to add them to your collection.

Those guards are closing in fast and you can't hold them off forever.

Luckily, Leia takes control and blasts open the garbage shoot.

Chewy doesn't want to go, but a nice bone might entice him. Good boy!

Chapter 5: Death Star Escape

STORY CHARACTERS

Luke Skywalker (Tatooine) / Ben Kenobi

Chewbacca / Han Solo

R2-D2 / C-3PO

Luke Skywalker, Han Solo, and Chewbacca have rescued Princess Leia from the clutches of Darth Vader and his Imperial forces—but they must now find a way out of the Death Star.

Aided by the droid R2-D2, who can interface remotely with the Death Star control systems, they battle their way to the *Millennium Falcon*.

Meanwhile, the Jedi Knight Obi-Wan Kenobi moves closer to his final destiny:...

Down the chute and into...

...garbage! If Han Solo is upset about that, wait until the walls start to close in to flatten the garbage and them.

Luckily, R2-D2 can stop the garbage compactor before it turns Luke and his friends into mush.

EPISODE IV A NEW HOPE

INTRODUCTION

GALAXY BASICS

STAR WARS CHARACTERS

TRANSPORTATION

MOS EISLEY CANTINA

WALKTHROUGH INTRODUCTION

iv EPISODE IV: A NEW HOPE

v EPISODE V: THE EMPIRE STRIKES BACK

vi EPISODE VI: RETURN OF THE JEDI

BONUS FEATURES

The rescue mission hasn't gone according to plan. The heroes were almost done in by blaster fire, then they ended up in the garbage, and then the walls almost crushed them. It's a good thing R2 was able to stop the trash compactor in time. The stormtroopers haven't caught them yet, so the rescue mission is still on. It's time to find a way out of the trash.

To start, assemble the LEGOs near the back wall to form a small platform. From there, pull the lever on the wall, opening the door in the wall for you to use as an exit. Follow the corridor as it bends to the right, shooting guards and collecting studs along the way. Use the lever on the left wall to get a stormtrooper helmet as you go.

Pull the lever on the wall to get out of that dump.

FREEPLAY AREA

Use C-3PO to access the activation panel near the door on the left wall. Run through the doorway and you are in another garbage compactor. Assemble the LEGOs near the left wall to create a large box. After completing it, use the Force to open the box. You'll find a red power brick to add to your collection. Run to the right and assemble some more loose pieces to create a little bonfire. Now run around the garbage and collect all the studs hidden under the surface of the debris. Check near the room's center for a valuable blue stud. After the room is clear, you can exit by the same door you entered.

FREEPLAY AREA

To the right of the helmet dispenser is a shiny metal grate on the wall. Use your bounty hunter and toss a thermal detonator at it. After the grate explodes, grab the LEGO canister that was hidden behind it.

Follow the corridor to the next room, then run along the upper walkway to the wall in the back. Pull the lever twice to move a hook along the ceiling. A red circle swirl pad appears on the ground behind you. Use your ascension gun at the circle to swing to a floating platform over the room. Grab the studs you find, then

drop to the floor. Many stormtroopers are waiting for you, so you'll have to shoot quickly and take them all down.

Move around the edges of the room, collecting studs as you blast open all the containers. On the left wall is a blue piece of machinery that you can push to the north until it won't go any farther. Now push it to the right until you cover up the red flashing button on the floor. This connects the piece of machinery to the red and green turnstile next to it. Now push the green side of the turnstile to raise part of the blue machinery. Run to the right and use the red circle swirl to grapple back to the walkway you were on when you first entered the area.

Move the blue machinery over the red flashing button to create a platform.

Run to the lever on the back wall again and pull it one more time to move the hook along the ceiling. This causes the red circle swirl to move to the other side of the upper walkway. Find the swirl and use it to grapple to the machinery on the other side of the room. Be sure to press forward as you swing so you don't come up short. From atop the blue machinery, jump to the walkway in front of you and grab all the studs you see. Along the wall in the back of the walkway is another lever for you to pull. Out comes a box to push along the floor to the left until you can't push it any farther. When it stops, push it over the edge of the walkway where it crashes through the floor at the bottom.

Drop into the hole in the floor and jump into the little cart you find there. Ride the cart out of the hole you created to the center of the room. Leading to the back wall are a series of red and green lights. Line up your cart with the lights and ride across them as quickly as you can. If you do it fast enough, all the light switches are activated and a walkway extends along the upper back wall. Return to the corridor by which you entered the room and put on a stormtrooper mask, if you don't already have one. From the starting walkway, use your ascension gun to get to the blue platform you raised earlier, and then jump to the walkway on the other side of the room. Follow the walkway to the back wall where you can access the activation panel to open the door.

FREEPLAY AREA

A small chute is in the wall down where you found the drivable cart. Switch to a Jawa and go inside. It takes you to a small room where you can add a LEGO canister to your stash.

> **Quickly drive your little cart along the lights on the floor.**

When you get to the next room, blast the guards on the left before they can shoot you. Along the right wall, some happy stormtroopers are washing the outside window. Jump into the window washing controls next to the large window and move the controls to the left and right to move those window washers around. That causes them to clean the entire window, and once it's clean, it shatters. A mini-kit canister appears on the ground. Grab the canister, then shoot the window washers who rush in to give you a beating.

Run down the next corridor and put the LEGO pieces together next to the closed door. After the assembly is complete, pull the lever to open the door. There you find some stormtrooper waiting for you. Blast them to pieces, then pull the levers on the wall. This opens the next door where you find more guards waiting to take you down. Turn those guys into spare parts, then push the blue box along the path all the way into the slot in the wall of the next room. After the blue box is secure in the wall, pull the wall lever to open the next door. Run down the next corridor, collecting blue, gold, and silver studs as you go, and shooting any guards that rush you.

> **Give those window washers a hand and move them around the large window to thoroughly clean it.**

FREEPLAY AREA

A black grate in the right wall can only be influenced by using the dark side of the Force. Use Vader to bust the grate open, then grab the LEGO canister that was hidden behind it.

Follow the walkway along the wall in the next room until you arrive at a drop-off and three levers on the wall. Pull the levers. A blue platform starts to rotate out of the wall. Jump on it as it swings around so you can jump to the other side of the walkway. Shoot the guards on the other side and run to the red circle swirl on the ground. Grapple to the platform above and pull the lever. Doing so causes a box to drop to the walkway below you.

Drop down to the broken box and assemble the loose LEGOs to start an elevator moving up and down along the wall. Ride the elevator to the top-left walkway and pull the lever at the end to get a stormtrooper helmet. Ride up to the next ledge on the right and collect some valuable studs. Now ride the elevator all the way to the top where you can use your stormtrooper disguise to access the activation panel and open the door.

> **Push the box to the ground so that you have the pieces to get the elevator going.**

CAUTION

Stormtroopers keep pouring into the area, so destroy them as soon as you spot them to avoid taking any damage.

FREEPLAY AREA

To the right of the stormtrooper activation panel are some pieces of equipment sticking out of the wall. Use the Force to turn them into a ledge. Jump on top of the ledge, and then double jump into the air to add another LEGO canister to your inventory.

Follow the corridor as it wraps around to the right. Keep your blaster ready and shoot all the guards that get in your way. Move up the ramp and through the door at the end to wind up on a tiny ledge leading to nowhere. Quickly pull the levers on the sides of the doors to prevent any guards from sneaking up behind you. Guards on a platform in the distance start shooting at you, so stand behind your friends for cover. Assemble the LEGOs on the ground to create a red circle swirl and grapple across the chasm in the middle of the room to a small ledge across the way.

Run into the nearby hallway and pull the lever in the back to get a new stormtrooper helmet. Return to the platform and assemble the LEGOs to make a new circle swirl platform. From there you can grapple to another platform to the north. As soon as you land, shoot the stormtroopers on another ledge to the north. Wearing your stormtrooper helmet, open the door using the activation panel and go through.

50

EPISODE IV
A NEW HOPE

With the door closed behind you, quickly assemble the circle swirl pad so you can swing to the other side of the room.

Follow the hall until you get to a large corridor and can see a stormtrooper running away to the north. First, walk to the south until you get to an open window. Jump to the small ledge on the left to grab a LEGO canister for your collection. Return to the corridor and blast the orange pillar on the left wall to find one of three special bricks hidden around the area.

The door to the north opens as you come near, revealing another part of the corridor. Destroy all the orange and gray pillars. You'll find another special LEGO piece behind the pillar on the left wall. Shoot the controls to the right of the next door to open it and you'll see that stormtrooper still running scared in the distance. Shoot the orange and gray pillar along the right wall and you'll find the third and final special LEGO piece, causing a LEGO canister to form next to the wall. Add it to your collection.

Jump out the window to find the hidden canister.

Continue moving down the hall, collecting studs as you go. When you get to the locked door, blast the controls to the right to open them. You might regret doing this because you find a whole army of stormtroopers on the other side. Stay in the corridor and start firing. With your natural ability to avoid enemy fire you should be able to whittle away the enemy ranks. Next, fire at the guards along the upper walkway in the back of the room. When they are gone, pull the levers on both sides of the room to shut the doors and block more enemies from entering.

While the doors are temporarily closed, run to the back left of the room and put the LEGO pieces together to form a closed door in the wall. Collect all the loose valuables on the ground in the back of the room, then blast the new door you created to get out of there. Follow the hallway until you get to the left side of the hangar.

You might have a bad feeling about this.

FREEPLAY AREA

Use the Force to move the large boxes in the back of the room and stack them, one on top of the other. Double jump to the top of the stack, and from there, jump to the walkway along the back of the room. Follow the walkway to the left where you can add another LEGO canister to your collection.

Grab the studs to the right of the hangar entrance and pull the lever on the wall. This causes a grate in the floor near you to break and powerful steam to come out. Break all the containers you see and collect all the studs as you move to the right side of the hangar. Assemble the LEGO pieces on the right wall to form a door latch. Push this latch to the north to slide the door open. Inside, you find your droids and a LEGO canister. Destroy all the containers on the right side of the hangar and grab all the studs on the ground as you head to the back wall.

Along the back wall you'll find a blue piece of equipment. Jump onto the ledge it rests on and push it to the right. When it gets to the end, it bursts into pieces that you can use to build a red circle swirl pad. Grapple to the ledge above and pull the lever. This raises a platform below the floor in the center of the room. That's where the *Millennium Falcon* is parked. Jump down to the pad you created and get your gun ready. Stay close to the pad and drop all the stormtroopers who rush in to shoot you.

Push that blue piece of equipment all the way to the right.

CAUTION

Don't touch the pink force field in the center of the hangar or you die.

Follow the back wall to the left of where you found that blue piece of equipment to find an activation panel. Use R2-D2 to access the panel, and the *Falcon* is raised a little bit higher in the center of the hangar. Once again, get near the circle swirl pad and blast the new wave of enemy troops that try to take you down.

Move to the left wall of the hangar and have R2-D2 access the panel on the wall. This raises a platform nearby with a little cart on in. Jump in the cart and ride it to the room's center where you see the red and green lights on the floor. Line up your cart in front of the first light, next to the guardrail separating the lights from the pink force field. When you are in position, race your cart

51

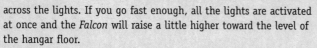

across the lights. If you go fast enough, all the lights are activated at once and the *Falcon* will raise a little higher toward the level of the hangar floor.

Another wave of stormtroopers comes in to stop you. Jump out of the cart and use your friends as cover while you take the stormtroopers out one by one. Run back to the entrance of the hangar and walk C-3PO onto the steam coming out of the ground. This boosts him to the ledge above where he can access the activation panel on the wall. This raises the *Millennium Falcon* all the way to the floor of the hangar and turns off the pink force field that covered the top of it. Walk to the right of the ledge and fall over the side where there is a break in the railing. Switch to a character with a blaster and shoot at all the incoming stormtroopers. After the last one falls dead, head to the left of the *Millennium Falcon* and run up the ramp leading inside.

Use the guardrail next to the lights to steer in a straight line across them.

The steam lifts C-3PO to the ledge above.

FREEPLAY AREA

Switch to a stormtrooper and access the activation panel in the left corner of the hangar. A large door in the wall opens up, revealing lots of LEGO pieces. Assemble the pieces to form a giant trophy and collect the studs that spill out. After you have your moment of glory, switch to a bounty hunter and toss a thermal detonator at the trophy to turn it into scrap metal. Pick up the studs it leaves behind.

Hey, Obi-Wan is fighting Darth Vader.

Ben—no!

Time to hightail it out of here.

FREEPLAY AREA

After you ride the steam to the ledge above the hangar, jump on the railing to the left. From there, double jump to the ledge on the wall to the left, where you can collect a blue stud for your collection. Return to the ledge you came from and run to the right. Switch to a bounty hunter and use the activation panel to open the door. As soon as the door opens, many stormtroopers run out, along with Vader himself! Switch to a Jedi and chop up the Imperial troops while protecting yourself from their fire. When the coast is clear, run into the room behind the door and grab the LEGO canister to add it to your stash. Use your stormtrooper to access the activation panel in the back wall. Watch the clock on the back of the wall.

EPISODE IV
A NEW HOPE

INTRODUCTION

GALAXY BASICS

STAR WARS CHARACTERS

TRANSPORTATION

MOS EISLEY CANTINA

WALKTHROUGH INTRODUCTION

iv EPISODE IV: A NEW HOPE

v EPISODE V: THE EMPIRE STRIKES BACK

vi EPISODE VI: RETURN OF THE JEDI

BONUS FEATURES

Chapter 6: Rebel Attack

STORY CHARACTERS

X-wing

With the Death Star plans in their hands at last, the Rebel Alliance plans a desperate assault on the Imperial space station.

But a hidden homing beacon attached to the Millennium Falcon has led Darth Vader to the Rebel's secret base on the moon of Yavin 4.

The moon will soon be in range of the mighty Death Star's superlaser. Now, a small band of fearless pilots bear with them the hopes of an entire galaxy....

The *Millennium Falcon* and crew make their way to the moon of Yavin 4.

The stolen Death Star plans show that there is a way to destroy it, although it will be close to impossible.

Luke and the other X-wing pilots fly into space to meet the Death Star and fulfill their destinies.

It was no easy matter getting the Death Star plans to the Rebel Alliance on the moon of Yavin 4. Unfortunately, the Empire was able to track the *Millennium Falcon* right to the secret base. With the Death Star closing in, the Rebels were able to analyze the plans and find that there is a fatal flaw in the Death Star design. This could be the only chance to destroy the Death Star and put a major hurt on the Empire. It's time for Luke and his friends to fly their spacecraft to try to save the rest of their Rebel friends.

Once you descend to the surface of the Death Star, you start in a safe area away from enemy fire. Shoot the blue panels on the walls, as well as the one on the surface to uncover hidden studs and hearts. In the back of the area is a pink force field preventing you from flying any farther. On the left side of the force field is a purple bomb dispenser. Fly over the dispenser to pick up a purple bomb that will trail behind your craft. When you have your bomb in tow, fly toward the center of the force field until you see a purple reticle appear on the ground over the force field controls. Fire your bomb in the general direction of the purple target. When you score a direct hit, the force field disappears.

Fire the purple bombs at the force field controls.

> **NOTE**
>
> You can have three bombs trailing your ship at one time. When you die, the bombs you are carrying will respawn with you.

> **TIP**
>
> You don't have to aim very well to hit the force field controls with your bombs. As soon as you see a reticle appear, you can fire your bomb. It will bounce around the area before homing in on its target.

Unfortunately, the other areas of the mission have enemy TIE fighters that fly in to shoot you down. The good news is that their guns don't fire very far and you are faster than they are. This helps you avoid getting hit. While you dodge enemy blasts, head to the center of the area and shoot the satellite dishes on the ground. Doing so breaks the chute between them from which the TIE fighters emerge. Now head to the right wall and blast the turret guns trying to shoot you and collect the studs they leave behind.

Next, fly to the left wall near the force field you destroyed earlier. When you get close, a red-and-green turnstile rises from the surface. Shoot the green side to swivel the turnstile. A LEGO canister rises from the surface directly in front of it. Shoot the canister to add it to your collection. Fly around the area shooting all the blue panels to collect extra studs.

Shoot the green blades of the turnstile to get your first canister.

TIP

TIE fighters scurry over the surface of the Death Star like mean little rats. Even though there is an endless supply of them, it is important to drop any that get in your way. Their shots don't go very far, but try not to engage them head-on or you will take damage. If you find some fighters behind you, loop your X-wing back around to come up behind the enemy ships so you can safely blast them to pieces. Shooting down TIE fighters is also a good way to collect hearts to fill up your heart meter.

Fly to the north and over the small groove in the Death Star. On the other side, quickly destroy the turret and collect the valuables it leaves behind. Fly to the far right wall to find another turret. Blast the gun to pieces, then shoot the blue panels behind it to reveal a small alcove. Fly inside to collect another LEGO canister.

To the north of the canister you'll find more purple force field controls. Fly to the area's center to pick up some purple bombs and fire them at the purple reticles that appear over the force field controls. After each control to the force field is destroyed, collect the treasures that it leaves behind. After the last control is gone, the force field at the top of the screen disappears and you can blast the gray-and-blue wall behind it. Be sure to destroy all the blue walls and floor panels before you continue.

Shoot the blue panels behind the turret gun to get another hidden canister.

FREEPLAY AREA

The red gate in the right wall can only be opened by a TIE fighter, which you'll be able to use later. Once your ship is inside the small enclosure, blast the two turret guns trying to shoot you down. After the last one is destroyed, a LEGO canister appears in the center of the area for you to collect.

Enter the next area and fly to the right to destroy the two turret guns trying to drop you. To the north, the path splits, so follow the left path for now. As you fly, shoot all the blue panels you find and a row of three turrets along the right wall. After you destroy the turrets, you find another bomb dispenser. Collect as many bombs as you can. You'll need them shortly.

Farther up the path, you'll find a couple of satellite dishes on the ground; destroy them. To the left of the satellite dishes is a wall that can only be opened by a TIE fighter. But if you fly to the right of the wall, a turnstile rises out of the surface. Fire at the green side to spin the turnstile until a LEGO canister rises next to it. Shoot and collect it.

Shoot the turnstile next to the blocked path to get another canister.

FREEPLAY AREA

Use a TIE interceptor to open the red gate in the left wall and enter the secret area. A series of green lights snakes along the floor toward the back of the area. Starting from the rear, quickly fly over the first four lights as they bend to the left and pass through some pillars. Fly over another light as you curve to the right to fly between another set of pillars. Follow the last section of lights around that last pillar to the left. If you move quickly enough over all the lights to have them all lit up at once, a LEGO canister appears in the back of the room as your reward.

The main path heads to the north, but you still have business to attend to near the right. Over there, you find more force field control panels at which you can launch you bombs. Before you get to those panels, blast the turret guns in the area. When you need more bombs, fly to a dispenser directly south. Once the controls are destroyed, continue to fly south, destroying satellite dishes and blue panels as you go until you see another locked gate in the right wall. The path south loops back to where you were before, so fly back north to the force field controls you just destroyed.

EPISODE IV
A NEW HOPE

FREEPLAY AREA

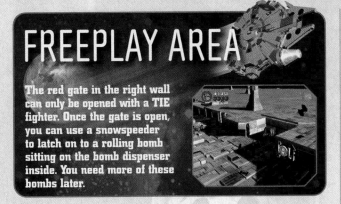

The red gate in the right wall can only be opened with a TIE fighter. Once the gate is open, you can use a snowspeeder to latch on to a rolling bomb sitting on the bomb dispenser inside. You need more of these bombs later.

Head back toward the destroyed controls, then follow the path north over a canal and into the next area. Fly your X-wing to the right wall and destroy the turrets shooting at you. Next, fire at the blue wall panels to the right of the locked red gate. Fly into the alcove behind the panel to add another LEGO canister to your collection. With that canister added to your stash, fly to the area's center and destroy the turrets and satellite dishes on the surface.

Now follow the left wall to the north; you'll find the controls to the next force field ahead. Fly to the right side to collect the bombs you need. Destroy all four controls to shut down the force field so you can shoot the blue-and-gray wall blocking your way to the north.

Here's another canister to add to your collection.

FREEPLAY AREA

Fly a TIE fighter close to the red gate to open it and fly into the hidden room. A LEGO canister sits against the wall to the right behind a protective force field. Return to the gate you recently unlocked to the south and latch on to a rolling bomb using the snowspeeder. Bring it back to the force field and slam the bomb into the controls on one side of the force field. Get another bomb and do the same to the controls on the other side. When both sets of controls have been destroyed, the force field disappears. Destroy the gun turrets on the other side of the force field and grab the canister.

Fly into the next area and move to the wall on the left where you'll find a row of three turret guns. Break them to bits with your blasters, then continue to follow the wall on the right until another turnstile rises from the Death Star. Once again, shoot the green side to spin it around, causing a LEGO canister to appear in front of it. Collect your prize.

Continue to follow the wall to find some force field controls and many laser turrets. Ignore the controls for the moment and destroy all the turrets first. With the guns out of commission, follow the right wall to the bomb dispenser to grab some bombs to blast the force field controls until they are no more. Now fly to the center of the area and destroy the satellite dishes next to the TIE fighter chute. After the dishes are destroyed, head for the right wall and destroy more turrets. Now you can grab more bombs to use on the next set of force field controls.

Now that the last set of controls is garbage, the force field to the north disappears. Shoot out the wall behind the force field and head north. After you pass the force field you just destroyed, shoot the blue panels on the short left wall to uncover a hidden alcove. Fly into the alcove to get another LEGO canister.

Move the turnstile to find a hidden canister.

Shoot out the hard-to-see blue panels to find a secret canister.

Vader thinks it's time to send out the big guns...and that means him.

Vader and his crew stick in a tight formation as they fly in to stop Luke from destroying the Death Star.

This is it, the final straightaway! As soon as you enter the straightaway, you pick up a bomb. Fly quickly while shooting at the laser turrets mounted on the walls. Keep your speed up, and Vader, who is trailing behind you, won't be able to hit you. As soon as you get to the area where you need to drop your bomb, Han Solo comes out of nowhere in the *Millennium Falcon* to blast Vader off your tail. This gives you one less thing to worry about in the final area.

As soon as you enter the area at the end of the narrow passage you just flew through, drop your speed. In the center of the area is your target, but it is covered by a force field that you must

INTRODUCTION
GALAXY BASICS
STAR WARS CHARACTERS
TRANSPORTATION
MOS EISLEY CANTINA
WALKTHROUGH INTRODUCTION
iv EPISODE IV: A NEW HOPE
V EPISODE V: THE EMPIRE STRIKES BACK
vi EPISODE VI: RETURN OF THE JEDI
BONUS FEATURES

deactivate. To the north, west, and east of your target are holes containing turret guns. Once you fly over the holes, the turret guns will come out and start shooting. Starting at the left side, carefully loop over the corner hole to get the gun to come out. Blast it apart, then fly over another turret gun hole to get the next to come out so you can demolish it. Continue this method and take out all 12 turret guns that are surrounding your target one by one. After the last turret gun is destroyed, the force field is deactivated.

Eliminate the guard turrets one by one to drop the force field covering your target.

Before you go firing at your target, first fly to the back-left corner to cause a turnstile to rise from the surface. Again, shoot the green sides to spin the machine; a LEGO canister also rises from the surface. Next, fly to the back-right corner. There you'll find a hidden alcove with a red power brick to add to your collection. With the area clear, fire your bomb at the purple reticle at the center of the area to blow this joint.

It's just one more canister waiting to be yours.

Grab the red power brick hidden in an alcove in the back right wall.

> **NOTE**
>
> If you need another bomb, fly back down the straightaway you traversed and grab another one at the end.

With the bomb speeding toward the core of the Death Star, it's time to get out of here fast.

The Death Star explosion is huge. It sends debris and unfortunate stormtroopers hurtling into space.

Vader is out of commission for now, but he'll be back.

It's time for the heroes to celebrate.

What's that Imperial spy doing here? Get him out of here!

Chewbacca is still excited, even though he didn't get a medal. Poor Chewie.

EPISODE IV
A NEW HOPE

INTRODUCTION

GALAXY BASICS

STAR WARS CHARACTERS

TRANSPORTATION

MOS EISLEY CANTINA

WALKTHROUGH INTRODUCTION

iv EPISODE IV: A NEW HOPE

v EPISODE V: THE EMPIRE STRIKES BACK

vi EPISODE VI: RETURN OF THE JEDI

BONUS FEATURES

Chapter 7: Episode IV Bonus

The bonus section contains three parts. The first part requires you to play through all chapters of Episode IV in less than one hour while collecting 100,000 studs. The second part has you fighting your way through the mean streets of Mos Eisley spaceport in order to collect one million studs in under five minutes. And the third part has you flying along the surface of the Death Star gathering one million studs in under five minutes. After you successfully complete each part, you get a gold brick added to your collection. If you don't complete a mission in the allotted time, you just have to play again until you do, if you want to earn that brick.

SUPER STORY

The super story in this bonus chapter is nothing new. You are simply running through the previous six missions: "Secret Plans," "Through the Jundland Wastes," "Mos Eisley Spaceport," "Rescue the Princess," "Death Star Escape," and "Rebel Attack." The challenge this time is that you have to play thorough all six chapters consecutively while grabbing 100,000 studs in less than an hour. Since you've already played through these missions, you should have a good feel for them.

Don't waste time in areas where you aren't going to find many studs or that are way off the beaten path. As you move, be sure to hit the areas that have blue studs or many studs in a centralized location. The wall panels on "Secret Plans" hold a lot of easy-to-get studs. Fill up with more than 50,000 studs on this first chapter and you will be well on your way to ending up with more than 100,000 studs when you finish the sixth chapter. When you reach your stud goal, you can concentrate on getting through the levels quicker so you can finish in less than an hour.

The wall panels in the first chapter have a lot of quick-and-easy studs to collect.

Blast the orange and gray pillars during "Death Star Escape" to collect the valuable blue studs to add to your total.

CHARACTER BONUS (MOS EISLEY)

> While the Rebel Alliance struggles heroically with the oppressive Empire, and as Luke Skywalker moves closer to his epic destiny, daily life goes on across the galaxy.
>
> In the sprawling alleyways of Mos Eisley, intrepid adventurers compete to collect one million LEGO studs in the fastest time possible.
>
> It's the desperate, ruthless life of a world in turmoil....

You start this adventure on the mean streets of Mos Eisley, where you have five minutes to collect one million LEGO studs. This mission is played in a Freeplay mode style, so you can choose the main character you want to play and the game will pick the rest of your playable characters, all of whom will have different abilities. Play this mission after you have completed the game so you can use Anakin Skywalker (Ghost) as you play. Since Anakin is a ghost, he is impervious to blaster fire, which comes in very handy in this area. The second character that comes in handy is the bounty hunter with his thermal detonator.

After you start the mission, switch to your bounty hunter and toss a thermal detonator at the shiny equipment in the center of the area. All of the shiny equipment has lots of valuable studs hidden underneath it, so always make destroying the equipment a top priority. Pick up the studs that scatter on the ground and blast all the gray containers you see on the street. Switch to C-3PO and access the activation panel on the wall to unlock the only locked door around.

Use your thermal detonators to destroy the shiny equipment on the street because it gives off the best loot.

Use C-3PO to unlock the only locked door in the whole area.

Move through the open doorway and blast the stormtroopers on the other side. When the coast is clear, shoot more gray containers and be on the lookout for more shiny equipment that you can destroy. Also be on the lookout for the valuable purple studs lying on the ground, because these are worth the most. If you have to decide which ones to pick up first, always head for the purple studs immediately before they disappear off the ground.

Your bounty hunter can destroy a lot of equipment in a hurry, but he is always open to attack. After you take a few hits, quickly switch to Anakin Skywalker (Ghost) so you don't take any more hits. As Anakin, you can continue to destroy containers and enemies to refill your health and collect more studs. Switch back to the bounty hunter when you need to destroy more shiny equipment. Keep moving along the dirty streets, collecting studs until you reach the one million mark.

Switch from your bounty hunter to Anakin when you start taking too much damage.

Grab the valuable purple studs hidden along the streets.

Minikit Bonus (Death Star)

While the Rebel Alliance struggles heroically with the oppressive Empire, and as Luke Skywalker moves closer to his epic destiny, daily life goes on across the galaxy.

On the deadly surface of the Death Star, intrepid adventurers compete to collect one million LEGO studs in the fastest time possible.

It's the desperate, ruthless life of a world in turmoil....

You start this adventure buzzing along the surface of the Death Star. You have five minutes to collect one million LEGO studs. This mission is played in a Freeplay mode style, so you choose the main vehicle you want to fly and the game will pick the rest of your playable vehicles for the mission. It is a good idea to use the TIE interceptor on this level because of its speed and power. Many enemies are flying around with you; they will be constantly on your tail, so you need to be quick.

The Death Star is covered with lots of destructible objects that drop studs when destroyed. Just look for anything that has blue on it to know if you can break it. Breakable items that drop many studs are blue wall and floor panels, radar dishes, and blue turret guns. You can also blast the TIE fighters chasing you around the area, but they only drop hearts. Go after them when you get low on health.

Blast all the blue objects on the surface to reveal valuable studs to collect.

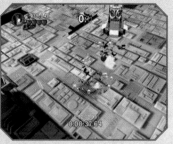

Enemy TIE fighters are always on your tail, but they can leave behind hearts after you destroy them. Do so if you need the health.

Shooting the blue objects in the area will get you studs, but there is a better source. After you start the mission, fly to the south until you get to the purple bomb dispenser. Loop around it three times to pick up three bombs that trail behind you. Fly south from the bomb dispenser to see four purple reticles on the ground around a pillar. Destroy all four targets, and you break the pillar at the center for a huge payday. Since the pillar never returns, you can concentrate on the other purple targets in the area. The first purple target is to the right of where the first pillar stood and the other two are up toward the northwest.

Continue to grab three bombs from the dispenser and fire at the purple targets so you can get the valuable studs they leave behind. Move from target to target until they respawn.

As you fly between the purple targets, don't forget to keep hitting the blue objects and continue to add more studs to your collection. When you reach one million studs you are declared the winner.

Destroy the four purple targets grouped together to get a big payday.

Grab three bombs at a time from the bomb dispenser so you can fire at the purple targets around the area.

CAUTION

If you lose all of your health, many of your studs will spill to the Death Star's surface. Be sure to fly around the spot where your ship broke up so you can pick up your spilled goods and minimize your losses.

EPISODE V
THE EMPIRE STRIKES BACK
Chapter 1: Hoth Battle

INTRODUCTION

GALAXY BASICS

STAR WARS CHARACTERS

TRANSPORTATION

MOS EISLEY CANTINA

WALKTHROUGH INTRODUCTION

EPISODE IV: A NEW HOPE

EPISODE V: THE EMPIRE STRIKES BACK

EPISODE VI: RETURN OF THE JEDI

BONUS FEATURES

STORY CHARACTERS

Snowspeeder

It is a dark time for the Rebellion. Although the Death Star has been destroyed, Imperial troops have driven the Rebel forces from their hidden base and pursued them across the galaxy.

Evading the dreaded Imperial Starfleet, a group of freedom fighters led by Luke Skywalker has established a new secret base on the remote ice world of Hoth.

The evil lord, Darth Vader, obsessed with finding young Skywalker, has dispatched thousands of remote probes into the far reaches of space....

The furry wampa almost eats Luke for breakfast. Never come between a Jedi and his lightsaber.

While Luke was out playing in the snow, Vader found the Rebels' hideout! And you know what that means...

...AT-AT walkers on the attack.

Why is Darth Vader so obsessed with finding Luke Skywalker? He even sent a probe droid all the way to the icy world of Hoth. Unfortunately for the Rebels, that is the exact location of their new hidden base. The Empire is not too thrilled with what happened to the Death Star and it has sent troops to the remote planet to take care of business. All kinds of ground troops arrive to crush the Rebels. Luke is going to have to be extra careful while driving the snowspeeder to repel this massive threat.

The area is crawling with a whole mass of troops and vehicles working for the Empire. While the AT-STs are the largest and easiest enemy to see in this area, the Imperial probe droids and speeder bikes are more nimble and can maneuver easily. All of your enemies have deadly blasters and orders from the man in black to send you to an icy grave.

The snow is covered with enemy troops.

Once you hit the snow, steer your craft down the left path. Along the way, you'll see a bomb deployment pad along the left canyon wall. When you get close enough, a red reticle surrounds the bomb, indicating that you can grab it with your tow cable. Since you

don't need the bomb yet, continue flying forward until you hit a locked red gate that only TIE fighters can open. Blast the enemies you see and the gun turrets on the ground and collect any goodies that spill out. Because this way is blocked for now, backtrack to your starting location and follow the icy canyon to the north.

At the beginning of your journey north, you will see a second bomb deployment pad on the left wall. Ignore it for now and blast any enemies that get in your path. Also shoot all the turret guns you find because they hide valuable hearts and studs for you to grab. As you move north, shoot the large gray rock formations along the path to uncover lots of hidden studs and hearts.

Blast those large gray rock formations because they hold plenty of secret stuff.

TIP

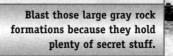

If you are low on hearts, just blast the bombs on the deployment centers to get more.

FREEPLAY AREA

Only a TIE fighter can open the gate to the left of the starting point, so fly in close and when the gate opens, head into the icy canyon beyond. Avoid going over the dark chasms because if you move too slowly, you can fall to your death. As you move, blast all enemies and turret guns in your path and collect anything they drop. At the end of the trail is a cave blocked by a large white wall that only bombs can destroy. Blast the dark-gray rocks to the right of the wall and collect a LEGO canister, then head back to the canyon's entrance to get a bomb.

Once you return to the locked gate you opened using the TIE fighter, use the snowspeeder to grab a bomb from the dispenser. Make your way slowly back to the large white wall, carefully keeping yourself and the bomb you're carrying on the snowy path so you don't slip into the chasms along the way. When you get to the end of the canyon, release the bomb you're towing into the white wall to open the cave entrance.

When you enter the cave, you can see that the enemy got there first. Race into the cavern and blow up those walkers and the speeder bikes. Destroy all the enemies in the cave, including the AT-STs, and you are rewarded with a LEGO canister. When your enemies are gone, fire your blasters at the small tanks along the walls of the cave. Hidden inside are valuable studs, and a tank on the right wall even has another LEGO canister. Clear out the cave before you return to the canyon outside.

Along your journey north through the canyon, you'll see large white walls on the sides. Fly back to the last bomb dispenser you passed and grab a bomb using your tow cable. With the bomb trailing behind your craft, steer toward one of the large walls. Quickly fly your craft toward the wall, then release the tow cable to send the bomb rolling toward your target. With a direct hit, the wall shatters, leaving behind hidden treasure for you to pick up.

Fly up the path and clear out all the AT-STs, probe droids, and speeder bikes before they can hurt you. Also blast all the gun turrets and gray rock formations so you can collect all the studs they were hiding. Use more bombs to destroy the white walls near the end of the canyon to the north, and you'll find your first LEGO canister on Hoth, not in a Freeplay area. At the end of the canyon is a closed gate, so backtrack and grab another bomb before returning. Release it at the closed gate when you get near. After the gate shatters, fly into the new opening.

Destroy the large white wall and grab the canister hidden behind it.

CAUTION

Imperial probe droids also have a grappling hook that they can use to grab onto bombs that you are dragging. This maneuver slows you down so the droids have an easier time shooting at you. Keep weaving back and forth to stay out of their crosshairs until you can detonate your bomb on its intended target. Or you can release the bomb, blow up the annoying droid, then grab another bomb and take it where you want it to go.

As soon as you fly into the next canyon, shoot the gray rocks on the ground for hidden stuff. Behind the rocks is a very large AT-AT walker. Before you start to tangle with that beast, fly around it and turn the little AT-STs into scrap metal. Also defeat any Imperial probe droids or speeder bikes that are flying around the area trying to shoot you.

With the little guys out of the way, you can now deal with the AT-AT walker. Fly in close to its legs and fire your tow cable. When the cable is deployed, it's time to fly loops around the walker's legs. Keep flying in circles until the legs are all wrapped up and the whole vehicle crumples to the ground. Another bomb dispenser is on the canyon wall nearby. Grab a bomb with your tow cable and drag it back to the downed AT-AT walker. Release the bomb to send it rolling into the AT-AT's helpless bulk.

You have to trip up the AT-AT walker with your tow cable before you can drag a bomb into it.

CAUTION

Downed AT-AT walkers won't stay disabled forever. After you tangle them up, you must quickly destroy them with a bomb before they can get up again.

FREEPLAY AREA

The passage in the left wall is blocked, so use a TIE fighter to get in. The area is crawling with AT-STs and Imperial probe droids. Circle around the small opening and blast all of your enemies. As you do this, take out the rock formations and turret guns so you can collect the studs and hearts that spill out onto the snow. Now the area is clear. For now, advance past the bomb dispenser and into the tunnel. Watch the tunnel's left wall as you travel along, and when you're about halfway through it, grab the LEGO canister that comes into view.

When you get to the end of the tunnel, blast the AT-STs coming toward you. Exit the cave to get back outside and blast the dark-gray rock formations just to the side of the exit. There, you'll find another LEGO canister to add to your collection. Head down the canyon outside and destroy all the enemies you see except the big AT-AT walker.

Move down the canyon past the walker. You'll find a large wall that only a bomb can destroy. Head back into the cave to the other side where you passed the bomb dispenser. Scrap any droids that get in your way, then use your tow cable to grab a bomb and drag it into the cave with you. When you get to the other side, fly past the AT-AT walker and release your bomb into the wall at the end of the canyon. Once the wall crumbles, you can grab the red power brick on the other side. Ignore the AT-AT walker and fly your craft back through the cave to the locked gate where you entered the area.

NOTE

If you really want to destroy the AT-AT walker, you have to grab a bomb from the dispenser and drag it back to the cave's exit. Drop off the bomb and use your tow cable to tie up the walker. Once the vehicle hits the snow, grab the bomb and swing it into the AT-AT to turn its hulking mass into garbage.

Destroy the dark-gray rock formations near the bomb dispenser and collect the valuables that spill out. Continue to follow the canyon until you see another large walker. Again, hog-tie it with your tow cable, then slam a bomb into its body to destroy the walker. The blast melts the ice and snow behind it, revealing a large gray wall. It's time to grab another bomb and destroy this wall.

After you destroy the wall, shoot the dark-gray rocks on the left canyon wall to find many studs and a hidden LEGO canister. Fly around the newly opened area and destroy all the swarming enemies. With the majority of enemies cleared out, head back and grab more bombs to destroy the white walls in the area. Continue to shoot all the turrets and gray rocks for even more loot.

At the end of the canyon are a narrow ice bridge and a large gray wall blocking the exit. When most of the white walls are gone, return to the bomb dispenser and grab one more bomb. When you get close to the end of the canyon, reduce your speed and steady the bomb so that it trails directly behind you. This way, you can keep it on the ice bridge. Once you get to the other side, send the bomb into the gray wall to open up a new passage. Before you move forward, fly to the right and shoot the container in the corner for another LEGO canister. When the canister is part of your collection, shoot the gray rocks that were on the other side of the wall that you demolished and continue forward.

Shoot the gray rocks to find another canister.

The ice bridge is narrow, so go slow to keep the bomb behind you.

Now you're in a large, circular battlefield. As soon as you enter the area, ten probe droids buzz in to get in your way. Circle the battlefield and drop all those droids unlucky enough to get caught in front of you. Other enemies are present too, but it is the droids you must focus on for now. As you fly around dropping droids, blast all the dark-gray rock formations to uncover two hidden LEGO canisters for your collection. Blast all the turret guns on the ground to pick up more studs and hearts as well.

Once all ten probe droids are nothing but debris, 14 AT-STs come marching in to greet you. Once again, the area is full of all kinds of enemies, but you must concentrate your fire on the AT-STs. After you destroy all 14, the big guys move in—AT-AT walkers. Two large walkers move slowly into the area to join the already-crowded battlefield. Choose one of the walkers and eliminate all the other enemies swarming around it. Next, use your tow cable to tie up the walker's legs. Once the beast goes down, grab a bomb from the dispenser in the area and slam it into the body of the AT-AT walker to destroy it. Repeat this process for the other walker as well. When the two walkers are history, more enemies enter the battle. Fly around the area and eliminate seven probe droids, ten AT-STs, and one more AT-AT walker to finish this mission.

The small battlefield gets crowed as you hunt down the AT-STs you need to destroy.

Although Luke is a good pilot, his snowspeeder goes down anyway.

That AT-AT walker almost steps on our hero! How rude!

Luke is able to grapple to the belly of the beast and bring it down to save the day.

Chapter 2: Escape from Echo Base

STORY CHARACTERS

Princess Leia (Hoth)

Han Solo (Hoth)

C-3PO

Chewbacca

Imperial forces have mounted a relentless assault on the Rebel base on Hoth. The Rebel fighters have held out bravely, but the enemy is overwhelming them.

In the Echo Base command center, carved deep into the ice of the frozen planet, Han Solo and Princess Leia monitor the evacuation of Rebel personnel.

But as snowtroopers breach the outer defenses, Han and Leia must quickly find an escape route for themselves....

Those AT-AT walkers are overwhelming the ground forces.

The Imperials have discovered the field generator that's keeping the Star Destroyers from breaching the planet.

Han and Leia? Could this be the beginning of something?

Han Solo and Princess Leia have just had a moment that will last a lifetime. Unfortunately that life won't be very long if they don't get out of Echo Base fast. Imperial troops have overrun the Rebel forces on the planet's surface and have destroyed the field generator. With the force field out of commission, the Imperial forces are storming the base. It's time to make a hasty retreat.

The room you start in is falling apart fast as chunks of the ceiling come crashing down. Scour the floor for studs to add to your stash, then head to the room's right side. When you get close, LEGOs fall from the ceiling and block the door. Assemble the loose pieces into a bomb, which blows up and destroys the door and gives you some studs. Smash the containers along the wall and collect the loot inside before you move through the doorway into the next room.

Get those LEGOs away from the door so you can escape.

FREEPLAY AREA

Use R2-D2 to access the activation panel in the wall near your starting location. Run into the room and grab all the studs on the ground, including a valuable blue one. Smash all the containers you see and collect the loot that litters the floor. Use the Force on the equipment in the room to open the compartment door, then quickly snatch all the blue studs that spill out.

FREEPLAY AREA

There are four broken screens around the room you start in. Use the Force to fix each one, and a LEGO canister appears in the center of the room for you to collect.

Follow the tunnel on the other side of the door and shoot the Imperial troops that rush toward you. The end of the tunnel is blocked, so assemble the loose LEGOs on the ground to make a heater. Once your device is complete, shoot at it until it turns completely orange and melts the ice in the doorway behind it. Smash the heater and collect the loot that spills out before you move on to the next room.

This room looks like a cafeteria with lots of tables for you to destroy. Pull the levers on the machine to the north for some hot brew before you collect all the studs on the ground. Get behind the heater along the right wall to collect a blue stud. Then push the heater along the checkerboard pattern on the floor. The heater stops in front of the door, and thaws the ice around it so you can move on.

Push the heater in front of the door to melt the ice.

FREEPLAY AREA

When you're in the cafeteria, use the Force on all the chairs in the room to make them dance. When the dance is done, valuable studs spill out. Add them to your stash.

Follow the tunnel beyond the door as it heads up, and shoot the snowtroopers who come charging in on you. The tunnel comes to an intersection where a snowtrooper sitting in a mounted gun is waiting for you. Let your natural dodging ability help you avoid getting blasted while you shoot the gun to destroy it and its gunner. When it's out of commission, move to the intersection and collect the studs on the ground. Assemble the loose LEGOs on the ground to put the mounted gun back together and blast the bars over the door behind you. Dismount from the weapon and drop any troops who heard the gun blast and rushed in to stop you.

The tunnel to the left is blocked with debris and the tunnel north has a door that only C-3PO can open, so move to the right. Blast the containers you find at the end of the tunnel and enter the room behind them. Inside you find more containers to blast and more loot to collect. Put together the loose LEGOs along the north wall to complete a cart. It starts to follow the track around the room. Jump on the cart as it moves, and from there, jump to a ledge on the north wall for some valuable studs. Drop back to the floor, where you can catch a ride on the moving cart again. This time, jump to a ledge on the right wall to get a LEGO canister for your collection.

After you put the cart together, you can get to those hard-to-reach high places.

Now that the room has been cleared of goodies, move to the turnstile at the room's center. Push on the green side to spin it and change the tracks on which the cart is moving. After you change the tracks, the cart travels out the door you came in, down the tunnel past the mounted gun, and crashes into the debris blocking the far end of the tunnel. Run out and collect the studs that were exposed by the explosion.

Move through the doorway that was once blocked with debris. Hey, there's C-3PO. He might come in handy. C-3PO joins your party. Shoot all the containers you find and grab the studs that spill to the floor. Four floor switches need to be stepped on at the same time, but you only have three members in your party right now. Return to the tunnel and move toward the locked door with the picture of C-3PO on the activation panel.

You need four characters in your party to press all the floor switches.

FREEPLAY AREA

In the room where you found C-3PO, you'll also find some shiny metal LEGO pieces. Switch to your bounty hunter and toss some thermal detonators at each one to destroy them. Both pieces of equipment leave behind some LEGOs for you to assemble. Each pile of LEGOs turns into a heater for you to shoot. You have to hit each one three times in order for it to turn on and melt the ice. Frozen in the ice are some more LEGO pieces for you to assemble. These pieces are bones, and after you put them together, you get two walking skeletons. Now step on one of the four green floor switches in the room's center and your buddy and those two dead dudes will step on the rest. When all four switches are pressed, a LEGO canister to add to your collection appears in the center of the room. Shoot each heater before you leave the room to reveal more studs for your account.

After C-3PO unlocks the door, move inside to find a large checkerboard pattern on the floor and lots of guards. Move across the room, shooting the snowtroopers as you go. The room's left side has two mounted guns pointed in your direction. Use the boxes in the area for cover as you blast the guns and the guards operating them to bits. Continue to shoot new guards as they enter the area to avoid taking damage.

Once the coast is clear, push the square boxes on the checkerboard pattern into the two square grates on both sides of the floor. This causes a fan in the ground between each set of grates to turn on and blast air upward. With the fans working again, assemble the LEGOs in the room's center to make a little cart and drive it next to one of the fans. As you wait there, C-3PO will walk over the fan and be blasted into the air so he can land in the back of your cart. Drive the cart to the ledge where you destroyed those mounted guns and turn your vehicle so the back of the cart is facing the ledge. As soon as you exit the cart, C-3PO will step onto the ledge.

Those mounted guns are still in pieces, since you destroyed them, so put them back together. Shoot the bars covering the door in the wall and blast any soldiers that enter the area to stop you. Destroy the gun again and collect more goodies. Use your droid to open the door, but before you leave, blast the debris above the open door and on the room's right side to find some hidden treasure. A door in the right wall can only be opened by R2-D2, so you'll have to come back later. After the room is bare, go through the open door.

C-3PO uses the wind from the fan to get on your cart.

FREEPLAY AREA

A pile of LEGOs blocks the checkered path leading into the left wall. Use the Force to move the loose pieces and turn them into a giant snowman and reveal a hidden door in the wall. Since no one will ever get to see your creation, smash it to bits and grab the studs. Get behind one of the moveable boxes in the main room and push it down the checkered pathway into the new room you discover. Push the box over the grate in the floor to the right to activate the fan in the floor. Jump on the fan and collect the blue studs floating above the ground. Add the rest of the studs in the room to your stash before you go.

FREEPLAY AREA

The boxes in the back of the room can only be moved by using the Force. Step on a box; your buddy will use the Force to lift you into the air. When the box reaches its highest level you can jump to a ledge nearby. Use the dark side of the Force to open the cage you find. Grab the valuables that spill out and grab the LEGO canister.

FREEPLAY AREA

Move to the door with the picture of R2 next to it and have him use the activation panel to get in. Move into the next room and blast all the snowtroopers trying to ice fish. Now that the enemies are gone, scour the icy floor for studs, and then assemble the loose LEGOs that are bouncing around in the center of the room. These turn into a sled on which you can use the Force to make it slide around the room. Use the Force again on the left hole in the ice to pull some LEGOs out and place them against the back wall. Assemble these to form a LEGO canister for your collection.

FREEPLAY AREA

A LEGO canister is floating in the air in the center of the room. Push one of the movable boxes next to the snow-covered area in the room's center and jump on top of it. From there, you can double jump into the center of the room and grab the canister for your very own.

As you run through the next hallway, don't step on the white grates on the ground. As soon as you step on one, they will all drop and take you with them. When you get to the end of the hall, some debris falls from the ceiling. Put the loose LEGOs together to form a bomb that detonates and opens the door for you.

In the next room, the path leads you to an intersection. The door to the north is locked. The path to the south is too steep to scale. So follow the path to the left as it loops around the room and stop when the trail turns north. Five red floor switches are located on the steep downward path to the north. You need to roll over them on your way down. Roll over as many as you can to turn them green. If you don't activate all of them, return to the top of the steep path and roll over the ones you missed. When all five switches are green, the door to the north opens for you to enter.

Roll over the red switches to turn them green.

In the next room, head to the south and collect all the studs you find, including a blue one. Just be careful that you don't step over the ledge or you'll fall to your doom. Next, shoot all the containers in sight to collect even more hidden goods and reveal some red floor switches. Push the boxes in the room over two of the buttons and step on the other ones to open the door in the back wall. Before you leave, use C-3PO to unlock the door in the left wall. Move inside and jump into the pink-lit alcoves on both sides of the room to collect some blue studs. Blast the containers you see and collect any additional studs on the ground. The rest of the room is blocked for now, so return to the previous room and go through the door you opened by pressing the floor switches.

FREEPLAY AREA

Some shiny debris is blocking the hallway in the left wall, so use a thermal detonator to blow it away. Collect the valuable studs on the ground as you move through the opening you created. In the next room, assemble the LEGOs in the center of the room to fix the equipment nearby. This lowers the water tank to your left and reveals a LEGO canister for you to collect. Move around the floor and collect all the studs you see. Use the Force on all the filing cabinets along the walls to uncover hidden goodies.

Move down the next hallway. You start to hear your old friend Chewbacca. A path leading off to the left is too steep to climb, so continue forward. The door at the end opens and you see your buddy fighting off some Imperial troopers. Give him a hand and blast them to little bits before they start shooting at you. Now that you have four members in your party, backtrack to the room where you saw the four switches on the floor. When you step on all four switches, a LEGO canister appears before you. Collect it.

FREEPLAY AREA

The tunnel in the left wall leading up has a slippery slope that you can't climb. Use the dark side of the Force to pull the black panels off the wall and create steps for you to jump to. Jump from step to step, being careful not to land on the snow, or you will slide back down the slope. Collect the studs that are on the hillside. Beyond the fourth step, it is safe to walk on the trail again.

Follow the trail north until the path splits left and right. Head left and move through the doorway. Use your ascension gun on the red circle swirl pad in the center of the room to grapple to the level above. There you find yourself in a giant glass dome looking out. Move to the other side of the dome. Switch to a Jawa so that you can move through the chute in the wall. Go through the tunnel on the other side until you get to another dome and can grab another LEGO canister for your collection. Use the Force on the walls of the second dome to break them apart, then backtrack to the intersection you passed.

Since you went down the left passage first, it's now time to travel down the right passage. Use R2 to access the activation panel on the door in the hallway. Run into the room and pull the lever on the right side of the room. Pulling the lever spins the wheels on the wall and turns them to a green and yellow pattern. Pull the lever on the left side of the room until you get a pattern with blue dots. A door with the green and yellow pattern over it opens in the hangar below. Next, pull the lever again on the left wall until you see a red and white pattern, then pull the lever on the right wall again to get the pattern of blue dots. This causes another door in the hangar to open. After you've opened the two doors in the hangar, return down the slippery slope you came up in the first place.

Go back to the hallway where you found the slippery slope heading up and follow the hallway to the hangar at the end where you found Chewy. Inside are the *Millennium Falcon*, a whole lot of guards, and two mounted guns. Quickly blast your enemies to pieces before they can hurt you. Once they are out of the way, pull the levers on the wall next to the door you came through. Some blue see-through doors along the wall nearby open up for you.

Move into the alcoves behind each door to find two boxes that you can push across the room. Push each one into the black metal grates on the floor. Another see-through blockade in front of you raises up. In the alcove beyond are two tauntauns. Jump on one and ride it to the *Millennium Falcon*. Jump to the roof and assemble the loose pieces to fix the gun at the center of your ship, then fall off the left side. There, you can assemble more LEGOs to fix another part of the *Millennium Falcon*. As soon as the repairs are complete, run up the ramp on the left side to get out of there.

Push the boxes into the metal floor grates so you can get those tauntauns out from behind the glass.

CAUTION

Getting too close to the *Millennium Falcon* only brings more Imperial troops down on you, so keep your distance.

FREEPLAY AREA

The levers you pulled in the room above opened two doors in the hangar near the *Millennium Falcon*. Hidden inside one is a LEGO canister and in the other, a red power brick. Grab them.

When the lights are off, Han sneaks a little kiss.

Just as Vader arrives, the *Falcon* is gone.

Now that the party is over, it's time for Luke to hit the road as well.

Chapter 3: *Falcon* Flight

STORY CHARACTERS

Millennium Falcon

Led by the evil Darth Vader, Imperial forces have overrun the Rebel base on the ice planet Hoth.

Having bravely stalled the enemy advance, Luke Skywalker has made his escape by X-wing fighter.

And as the last Rebel transports lift off from the planet, Han Solo, in the Millennium Falcon, engages the Imperial ships above....

Just when you thought you were going to escape, the Imperial fleet shows up.

Foolhardy or brave, Han Solo is ready for any fight.

EPISODE V
THE EMPIRE STRIKES BACK

INTRODUCTION

GALAXY BASICS

STAR WARS CHARACTERS

TRANSPORTATION

MOS EISLEY CANTINA

WALKTHROUGH INTRODUCTION

iv EPISODE IV: A NEW HOPE

V EPISODE V: THE EMPIRE STRIKES BACK

vi EPISODE VI: RETURN OF THE JEDI

BONUS FEATURES

Just when Han Solo and his crew thought they were out of trouble, the Empire reared its ugly head. While the ground forces were invading Echo Base on the surface of Hoth, the Imperial fleet was waiting out in space for anyone trying to escape. These aren't just TIE fighters, but Star Destroyers as well. It's going to be a difficult fight, and if you want to live, you'll have to bring out your best.

Four Imperial Star Destroyers have the escaping Rebels surrounded while the Empire sends in the TIE fighters to cut them down. Your first mission is to take out the four turret guns on each of those big ships. Head to the first Star Destroyer on the right and fly behind the upper control tower on the ship. Hidden up there is a LEGO canister for your collection, so blast away. After you have the canister, it's time to take out those guns. The turret guns are lined up on each vessel, so fly in a loop toward the end of the row and fire at the first gun. Keep flying in circles in front of the first gun to avoid taking fire as you blast it. After a few hits, the gun explodes and you can get to work on the next one in the row. Be sure to fly in and collect the studs that each gun leaves behind.

After you destroy the four guns on the first ship, speed to the next Star Destroyer in view. Fly behind the upper control deck like you did on the first ship and collect the red power brick that is hidden up there. Fly along the deck of that ship and destroy the four guns you find. Destroy the remaining eight turret guns on the last two Star Destroyers to teach the Empire a lesson it will never forget.

The only way to shake these bad guys is to head for the asteroid field.

Your friends aren't worried, are they?

The asteroid belt is a very dangerous place to be flying around, but desperate times call for desperate measures. Unfortunately the Empire wants you really bad: They follow you in. As you fly into the belt, blast all the asteroids with blue and black metal chunks sticking out of them. As the asteroids explode, they leave behind pink bombs for you to pick up, as well as gray LEGO chunks. Shoot these chunks to find valuable studs and hearts. A red gate in the left asteroid can only be opened using a TIE fighter, so skip it for now. Shoot the asteroids just beyond the locked gate; you'll find the wreckage of a ship hidden in one of them.

Continue to follow the asteroid field until you find a really big chunk blocking your path. It has four pink targets in an alcove at its center. When you get close to the large asteroid, fly your craft to the left and follow the wall of large asteroids. When you see the little gray satellite, blast it to get a LEGO canister added to your collection. Now shoot more small asteroids in the area to collect some bombs, then head for the targets in the alcove. When the pink reticle lights up, fire your bomb.

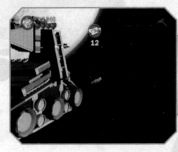

Maneuver your ship behind the control towers of the first and second ships to collect a canister and a red power brick.

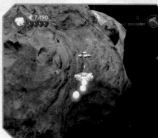

Shoot at the satellite along the wall of large asteroids on the left to find a hidden canister.

Each Star Destroyer has four turret guns for you to take out.

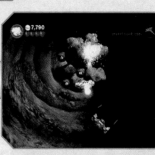

Fire those bombs at the center of the large asteroid.

TIP

When you get low on health, retreat and take out a few of the TIE fighters buzzing the area to get more hearts.

CAUTION

TIE interceptors hound you during this entire mission, so keep on your toes and avoid flying straight toward the enemy because you will take a lot of damage. Instead, fly your craft in loops to come up behind the enemy ships and take them out with ease.

FREEPLAY AREA

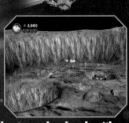

The first large asteroid to the left of the asteroid belt has a locked red and black gate. Use a TIE fighter to open the gate and fly inside. The large crater you're in has red floor switches on the left and right sides. On the back wall as you fly in is a bomb dispenser. Use a snowspeeder to grab a bomb with the tow cable and drag it over each floor switch. Be sure to take your time; avoid rolling the bombs into deep craters or you'll lose them and have to get others. When you successfully hit your target with a bomb, a LEGO canister rises to the surface where the switch used to be. Shoot the canister to collect it. After you collect both LEGO canisters, return to the asteroid field.

After you destroy all four targets in the alcove of the large asteroid, a tunnel opens up through its center. Fly through to the other side, where you are again greeted with more small asteroids and TIE interceptors. Continue to blast the asteroids for hidden loot as you fly along the right side of the asteroid field. A large asteroid on the right side juts out into the field, partially obscuring your view ahead. Right in front of it is a satellite for you to blast. Do so; you'll collect another hidden LEGO canister.

Continue to fly along the asteroid field until your path is once again blocked by a very large chunk of rock. At the center of the asteroid is an alcove with four targets in it. Before you do anything else, shoot the asteroids around the entrance to the alcove to uncover another LEGO canister. With the canister in hand, get some bombs from the small asteroids in the area and go into the alcove. Fire when you see the reticle to blow up your targets. After all four targets are gone, a tunnel opens up in the large asteroid for you to travel through.

Check behind all the large asteroids for hidden canisters.

The tunnel leads you to a large crater in this giant asteroid. Collect the studs on the ground, then fly into the giant hole on the surface. That was no cave you just flew into—it was a space worm! And it just closed its mouth behind you, so keep flying forward. When you get to the bottom of the path and can't go any farther, shoot all the junk on the ground to uncover hidden studs and bombs to collect. Shoot the container on the right side to add a LEGO container to your stash.

After you clean out the bottom area, the worm unclenches its teeth, so you can race back out of this worm to the crater. Along the large crater floor you'll find some targets to hit. Fire your bombs when a reticle appears over them. After they explode, collect the valuable studs that appear. One of the side walls of the crater has

a tunnel blocked with rubble. Luckily, the rubble has some targets on it at which you can fire your bombs. When you run out of bombs, fly back into the worm and shoot the debris inside to pick up three more bombs. Return to the surface and shoot the remaining targets to unblock the tunnel and fly inside.

This worm's previous meals provide you with lots of good stuff.

Use the bomb to blast the target on the side of the crater to get out of there.

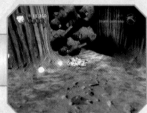

FREEPLAY AREA

The large crater has a locked red and black gate on one of the walls. Use a TIE fighter to open the gate and fly inside where you'll find a pink target on the ground. Fire a pink bomb at the target to get a LEGO canister.

The tunnel out of the crater leads your craft back into space toward more asteroids and enemy ships. Fly the *Falcon* to the large asteroid on the right and fire into the alcove on its side to find another LEGO canister. Follow the line of large asteroids on the right and shoot at all the smaller ones going by. One of those smaller asteroids has a LEGO canister inside that will be added to your stash after you hit it.

At the end of the asteroid field is a larger asteroid with pink targets on it. Shoot the smaller asteroids in the area to collect some pink bombs, then fire them at the pink targets when you get close. Destroy all the targets on the large asteroid and the rock explodes. With your path clear, head out into open space toward the Star Destroyer waiting for you.

The alcove in the large asteroid holds a canister for you.

EPISODE V
THE EMPIRE STRIKES BACK

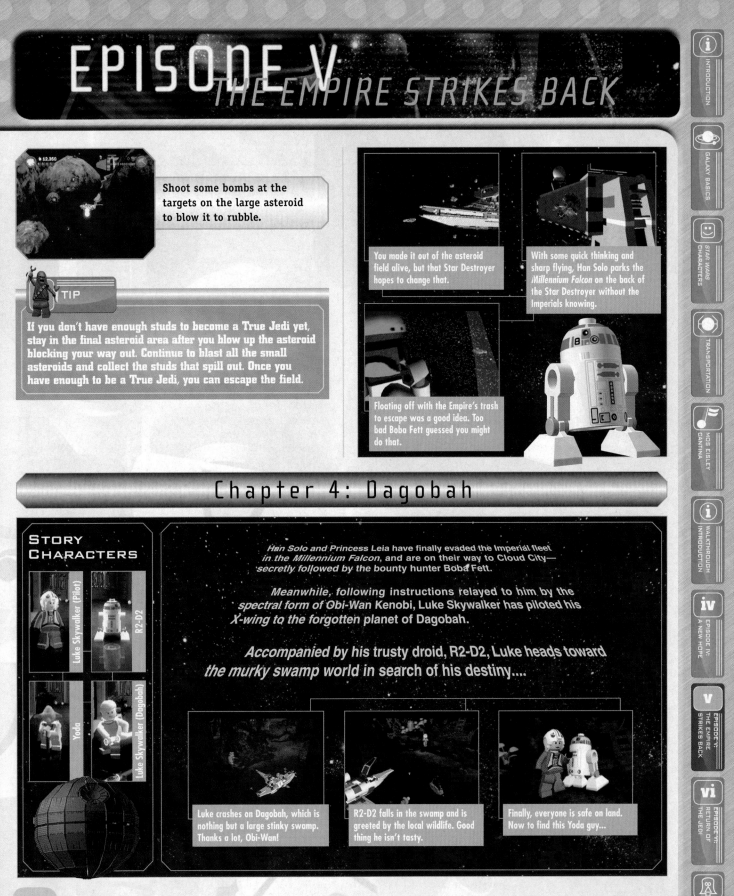

Shoot some bombs at the targets on the large asteroid to blow it to rubble.

TIP

If you don't have enough studs to become a True Jedi yet, stay in the final asteroid area after you blow up the asteroid blocking your way out. Continue to blast all the small asteroids and collect the studs that spill out. Once you have enough to be a True Jedi, you can escape the field.

You made it out of the asteroid field alive, but that Star Destroyer hopes to change that.

With some quick thinking and sharp flying, Han Solo parks the *Millennium Falcon* on the back of the Star Destroyer without the Imperials knowing.

Floating off with the Empire's trash to escape was a good idea. Too bad Boba Fett guessed you might do that.

Chapter 4: Dagobah

STORY CHARACTERS

Luke Skywalker (Pilot)

R2-D2

Yoda

Luke Skywalker (Dagobah)

Han Solo and Princess Leia have finally evaded the Imperial fleet in the *Millennium Falcon*, and are on their way to Cloud City—secretly followed by the bounty hunter Boba Fett.

Meanwhile, following instructions relayed to him by the spectral form of Obi-Wan Kenobi, Luke Skywalker has piloted his X-wing to the forgotten planet of Dagobah.

Accompanied by his trusty droid, R2-D2, Luke heads toward the murky swamp world in search of his destiny....

Luke crashes on Dagobah, which is nothing but a large stinky swamp. Thanks a lot, Obi-Wan!

R2-D2 falls in the swamp and is greeted by the local wildlife. Good thing he isn't tasty.

Finally, everyone is safe on land. Now to find this Yoda guy...

One minute you're hanging around with your friends and the next minute the form of Obi-Wan Kenobi tells you to go to Dagobah to find Yoda. Ben forgot to mention that Dagobah was nothing but swamp with no place to land safely. At least no one got hurt, and since you're not going anywhere anytime soon, you had better go find Yoda the Jedi Master.

Since Dagobah is just a swamp, plenty of plants grow here. Shoot the tall spiky ones and collect the studs that spill out. Since only R2 can take a dip in the swamp behind you, fly over the swamp to the right. There you find an island covered in valuable studs. After you're done collecting them all, head back to your starting location. Go north and assemble the loose LEGOs to form some ramps leading up and over the boulders.

INTRODUCTION
GALAXY BASICS
STAR WARS CHARACTERS
TRANSPORTATION
MOS EISLEY CANTINA
WALKTHROUGH INTRODUCTION
iv EPISODE IV: A NEW HOPE
V EPISODE V: THE EMPIRE STRIKES BACK
vi EPISODE VI: RETURN OF THE JEDI
BONUS FEATURES

Many goodies are hidden in the vegetation.

FREEPLAY AREA

When you are still in the starting area, use the Force to pull up the plants growing in the mud. Use the Force to uproot any similar plants that you see along your Dagobah adventure. Next, use the Force to stack the three boxes you see lying around the swamp. Jump to the top box, then on to the tree branches above them. Switch to R2-D2 and fly to the right to land on some more branches. Add a LEGO canister to your collection.

Follow the path over the rocks until you get to the next trail. Ahead, black bats are flying in the air above the trail, so blast them before they swoop down on you and take away your health. Follow the trail while smashing the spiky plants as you go. Be sure to grab all the studs on the ground before moving on. The path curves around to the right where you can see another watery part of the swamp. Shoot the plants and the bats in the area and collect any loot on the ground. As you do so, a giant snake slithers out of the water. Start shooting it as soon as you see it; the snake requires many shots to take it down.

A spiky plant along the water's edge has a red circle swirl hidden under it. After the plant is gone, use your ascension gun to swing over the water to the trail on the other side. There, you'll find more plants to shoot and more studs to pick up. Continue to follow the path as it leads to the left until a break in the trail stops you. Send R2-D2 to hover across the water to the left and access the activation panel. This raises a bridge out of the swamp so Luke can get across. Blast the tall spiky plants nearby and follow the trail as it bends to the left under the stone archway.

Because of the dangerous water in the way, Luke must use his ascension gun to swing across.

FREEPLAY AREA

After you break the fence along the right wall, you can see some black spiky plants sticking up. Use the dark side of the Force to pull them out of the ground and turn them into compost. As soon as the plants are destroyed, quickly grab the studs that fall on the ground. Switch to R2-D2 and fly across the chasm to the north. Use the Force to pull some plants out of the ground for some studs, then follow the trail north. At the end of the trail is a racetrack. Grab the red power brick that's close by.

Destroy the spiky plants around the track and use the Force to pull out the others to find some hidden loot. Now run around the racetrack until you find a blue container to the left. Break it open, then assemble the LEGO pieces that spill out. Congratulations, you made a tractor! Grab the blue stud that comes from your creation, then hop on and take that tractor for a spin around the track.

FREEPLAY AREA

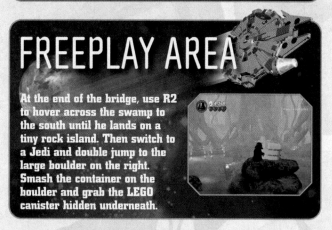

At the end of the bridge, use R2 to hover across the swamp to the south until he lands on a tiny rock island. Then switch to a Jedi and double jump to the large boulder on the right. Smash the container on the boulder and grab the LEGO canister hidden underneath.

On the other side of the archway are some loose LEGOs and, surprise, dirty water. Put the LEGOs together to form a red switch on the ground. Step on the switch to make a pillar rise out of the swamp. The pillar has another red switch. Use R2-D2 to hover out to the pillar and land on the switch. A shorter pillar rises out of the swamp in between the two previous switches.

As you wait, Luke jumps on this new switch, raising yet another pillar and bridge farther out in the swamp. Cross the bridge and step on that red switch. A low pillar rises to the left of the bridge with another red switch. Roll R2 back onto the bridge and watch as Luke jumps on the new switch. This raises one more pillar out of the swamp to the north. Now Luke and R2 can safely make it across the swamp to Yoda's hut.

EPISODE V
THE EMPIRE STRIKES BACK

Raise the pillars out of the water so Luke can get to the other side.

That's the powerful Jedi Master Yoda?

Yoda gives Luke a little demonstration of his powers—much to Luke's chagrin.

Even a small dude like Yoda can move great things through the power of the Force.

Before now, all Luke had to defend himself with was his blaster. Learning the ways of the Force will make him even more powerful. And with a powerful Jedi like Yoda training him, Luke should be able to learn to master the Force in no time. Hopefully he won't let all that power go to his head. As a Jedi, Luke will no longer be using his blaster since Jedi Knights only use the lightsaber.

Because you are a Jedi in training, your powers are still weak. To fully use the Force you need Yoda's help, and for him to give it, he needs to ride along on your back.

With Yoda firmly settled on your back, hack at the large cap on the ground until it opens. You have opened one of three caps around the area that lead to a surprise. Unfortunately, you also let out a lot of bloodthirsty bats, so chop them to bits with your new lightsaber.

Why must Yoda ride on your back for the training? Don't ask questions: He's the Jedi Master.

A few bunches of plants in the area need to be trimmed up. With Yoda's help, use the Force to pull up some of the plants from the ground. Plants that can't be manipulated using the Force must be hacked apart with your lightsaber. Under each bunch of plants are some boards. Use the Force to move all three groups of boards into the swamp to form a bridge that you can cross.

The bridge leads to a small island with some spiky plants for you to chop up. Collect the loot on the ground, then hack at the giant cap on the ground until you open the area's second cap. Back up, and when the bats swarm out, hack them to pieces with your lightsaber. Jump on the small platform in the swamp to the north and step on the red switch on top. This causes another platform to rise out of the water in front of you. Continue to move from platform to platform (as you raise them out of the swamp using the Force) until you get to the water's other side.

Use the Force to lift the platforms out of the water so that you can cross the swamp.

When you get to solid ground again, chop at the giant cap on the ground to the left. This is the third and final one you need to open. After you do so, a LEGO canister appears in the air to the right. Collect the canister and chop up the bats that fly out of the open cap. Wipe out the plants in the area and collect the studs on the ground as you move to the right.

Run to the right side of the clearing where you can see two large mushrooms. Use the Force to lower the smaller mushroom and then the taller one. Switch to R2-D2, then roll onto the cap of the smaller 'shroom. After a while, it rises back into the air. From there, fly to the left and land on the top of the taller mushroom. Wait for it to rise into the air, then fly to the platform on the left, where R2 can access an activation panel. After he activates the controls, the gate in the wall opens up and you can pass through.

Help R2-D2 get to the controls so that he can open the gate for you.

Yoda is quite the teacher. Luke is fast on his way to becoming a True Jedi and can already use the Force on his own without always having Yoda on his back. When you get to the new area through the gate, follow the dirt trail south. You'll come back to this area in a little while. On your way south, smash all the spiky plants that you see and collect the studs on the ground. Collect the blue stud at the end of the trial. Then jump down to the ground below to find yourself back at the area near Yoda's hut.

Use the Force on the plants in the area to pull them out of the ground. Collect the studs hidden underneath them. Hack apart with your weapon any plants that aren't affected by the Force. Now, use the Force to stack three stones in the center of the area. Jump to the top, then double jump in the air to grab a valuable blue stud. Use the Force again on Yoda's dwelling to pull some LEGOs off the sides and turn them into a step in front of the ledge from which you came. Go into Yoda's place because he has some valuable studs lying around his pad. Grab them and return to the swamp.

INTRODUCTION

GALAXY BASICS

STAR WARS CHARACTERS

TRANSPORTATION

MOS EISLEY CANTINA

WALKTHROUGH INTRODUCTION

iv EPISODE IV: A NEW HOPE

V EPISODE V: THE EMPIRE STRIKES BACK

vi EPISODE VI: RETURN OF THE JEDI

BONUS FEATURES

Follow the trail south to get to Yoda's hut.

takes you to the shore in the distance. When you get back to solid ground, chop all the spiky plants you find and collect the studs that fall to the ground. Use a thermal detonator to destroy some large LEGO bricks in the back of the area and uncover a hidden LEGO canister for your collection.

FREEPLAY AREA

While you're in Yoda's hut, use the Force on his high-definition plasma television to turn it into junk. The good news is it leaves behind a nice LEGO canister for your collection.

FREEPLAY AREA

Right before you enter the cave, find a red circle swirl on some of the tree roots. Use your ascension gun to grapple into the branches, where you can add a LEGO canister to your stash.

Outside the hut, run to the right and use the Force to pull up more plants. Congratulations! You found the parts to an old bike. Follow the muddy trail to the right until you find more swamp water. You can't do anything else here for now, so backtrack the way you came and use the step you made from pieces of Yoda's house to return to the high ledge from which you came. Follow the narrow path that leads back to the north. This takes you back to the area beyond the gate that R2 unlocked earlier. Head north and use the Force to pull a tractor and a cart out of the swamp. Use the Force again to turn that cart into a ramp to the north.

Steer R2-D2 up the ramp you just made. From there, have him hover around the tree through the air to the left until he lands on an old wooden dock. Access the activation panel to make a platform rise from the swamp behind you, allowing Luke and Yoda to follow you. Jump along the roots of the trees to the left until you get to a cave in the hillside. Go inside.

The cave might be dark and scary, but you're a Jedi now so you should have nothing to fear. Follow the narrow path along the left side of the cave. When the trail ends at the deep, dark chasm, you find a platform floating in front of you. Double jump to the platform to lower it, and from there, double jump again to the next one floating nearby. From the second platform, jump to a ledge along the left wall. Chop up the plants to uncover a hidden red circle swirl.

Since you can't use the circle swirl, jump to the next platform ahead and then onto the next part of the rocky trail. Follow the trail until you get to another dangerous chasm. Use R2 to hover to the wooden platform to the north. Hover from platform to platform to get across and Luke and Yoda will join you. Follow the trail up as it heads north until you reach the top.

Use R2-D2 to hover around the tree where Luke and Yoda can't go.

Carefully jump from platform to platform to get to the other side.

FREEPLAY AREA

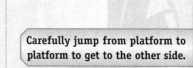

When you get to the edge of the swamp that's to the right of Yoda's hut, use the dark side of the Force to break the crate at the water's edge. Assemble the remaining loose pieces to create a raft on the water. Switch to R2 and fly to the raft until it

TIP

You can tell when it is safe for R2-D2 to land on something because you can see his shadow below him.

CAUTION

Be careful not to fall off the sides of the trail and into the dark chasm or you'll be dead in an instant.

FREEPLAY AREA

After you enter the cave, use the dark side of the Force to pull some black LEGO pieces from the chasm nearby to form half of a bridge. Run to the edge of the partially completed project and use the dark side of the Force to pull some black LEGO pieces from the ledge across the gap to complete the bridge. Cross the bridge to the ledge along the cave's right side. Toss a thermal detonator at the pile of shiny metal equipment to reveal some loose LEGOs. Put the LEGOs together to create a red circle swirl pad. Stand on the pad and grapple to a smaller ledge in the cliff wall above. There, add a LEGO canister to you stash.

FREEPLAY AREA

Run up a series of narrow ledges along the left cliff wall until you get to the top. Switch to R2-D2 and access the activation panel to open the gate nearby. Head through the open gate and blast the small cage hanging to the south. The chain holding the cage breaks, and the cage falls to the ground and breaks apart. Drop down to the floor and pick up the LEGO canister that was inside. Head back up the narrow ledges, but stop when you get back to the ledge that is farthest north. Now double jump to a ledge on the right and grab the loot on the ground. Double jump from ledge to ledge as you head north through the cave, grabbing all the studs that you find along the way.

FREEPLAY AREA

As you venture through the cave, you find a red circle swirl hidden under some plants along the right wall. Stand on the swirl and use your ascension gun to grapple to the ledge above. Throw a thermal detonator at the shiny LEGOs covering the cave entrance up there to break them apart. Once the cave is open, go inside and grab some blue LEGO studs for your collection.

FREEPLAY AREA

A cave along the right wall is blocked by shiny metal LEGOs. Use a thermal detonator to break them apart and go into the cave. The middle of the large cave floor is covered with pillars that collapse shortly after you touch them. You'll be safe as long as you move quickly and don't stop. Double jump your way across the left side of the room, moving from pillar to pillar until you get to solid ground on the cave's north side. There, collect a LEGO canister and more studs. Now double jump your way back along the room's right side until you get to the cave entrance and solid ground.

FREEPLAY AREA

Along the cave's right wall you'll find a travel chute. Use a small character and go inside. This takes you to a ledge above where you can collect more studs.

That trail leads you to...Vader! What is he doing here? When Vader rushes in to get you, jump at him and slash him with your lightsaber. Quickly get some distance between the two of you, then jump attack him again to send him retreating to a ledge on the left. Now that you have some breathing room, assemble the LEGO pieces on the ground into a box. Use the Force to move the three boxes on the room's right side to a spot against the wall to the right. Next use the Force to move the boxes on the left side over to the left wall.

Jump on one of the boxes you moved to the left. Yoda jumps on the other. As soon as both of you are on boxes, use the Force to raise each other's boxes into the air. The boxes lift you to the ledge above where you can once again fight Vader. Remember to block his attacks before you take one swing with your lightsaber. Only swing once before blocking again to avoid getting hit. After

he takes a couple of hits, Vader flies across the room to a ledge above the right wall. Climb the boxes you stacked over there and attack Vader. When he loses all of his health, he disappears and the large gate in the back wall opens up. Collect the studs on the ledge and run through the open gate.

> With teamwork, Luke and Yoda get to the ledge high above the ground.

> Move the boxes in the area so you can get to Vader as he moves about the room.

> One creature's trash is another creature's treasure. Turn this trash into something more useful.

The gate brings you back outside to the swamp and to another bat for you to take out. Smash all the spiky plants. A blue stud is hidden behind one growing on the area's right side. Next, use the Force on the plants in the center of the area to uncover some hidden loot and loose LEGOs. Put the pieces together to create a turnstile. Push on the green side of the turnstile to raise a bridge out of the swamp ahead.

When you get to the other side, use the Force to assemble the loose LEGOs to create a ramp at the end of the bridge so that R2 can cross. Dangerous bats are flying around the sky in this area, so chop them up whenever they get close. Move to the left after you get off the bridge until you see a large cap on the ground. You can't open this now, so run to the rock to the left of the cap. From there, use R2 to hover across the water to the left and grab some valuable studs on the roots of a nearby tree.

Assemble these pieces into a box with an activation panel showing R2's picture on it. Once R2 accesses the panel, back away from the box because it will blow up, destroying the gate behind it. Now, smash all the spiky plants left in the area and collect all the studs on the ground before you run through the open gate. In the swamp beyond the gate is your X-wing. Use the Force to lift it out of the water.

> Hover to the tree roots to get some valuables for your stash.

When you get back to dry land, run along the left side of the area until you find two boxes on the ground. Jump onto one and Yoda jumps onto the other. Use the Force to lift his box. He will do the same to yours until both of you can reach the platform high above you. Jump to the platform above the ground and push the box you find there along the platform until the box falls to the ground and shatters into tiny pieces. Return to the ground and turn those LEGO pieces in to a motorcycle and some loot to collect.

Hidden in the swamp to the north of the motorcycle are some more LEGOs. Use the Force to pull them out of the water to make a washing machine. Now use the Force to break apart the motorcycle and put its pieces in the washer. Now use the Force to activate the machine, making it shake this way and that until it breaks into a whole lot of LEGOs.

FREEPLAY AREA

Along the right side of the clearing you'll find a travel chute in the large tree trunk. Switch to a small character and jump inside. The chute takes you to a branch high above you. Switch to R2 and fly along the tree branches to the left until you find a lever. Pull the lever to make a container on the ground below you break open. Drop to the ground and assemble the loose pieces to create a red circle swirl pad. Use your ascension gun while standing on the pad to grapple to a tree branch above. After you get there, double jump to the branch on the right to add a LEGO canister to your stash.

EPISODE V
THE EMPIRE STRIKES BACK

INTRODUCTION
GALAXY BASICS
STAR WARS CHARACTERS
TRANSPORTATION
MOS EISLEY CANTINA
WALKTHROUGH INTRODUCTION
iv EPISODE IV: A NEW HOPE
v EPISODE V: THE EMPIRE STRIKES BACK
vi EPISODE VI: RETURN OF THE JEDI
BONUS FEATURES

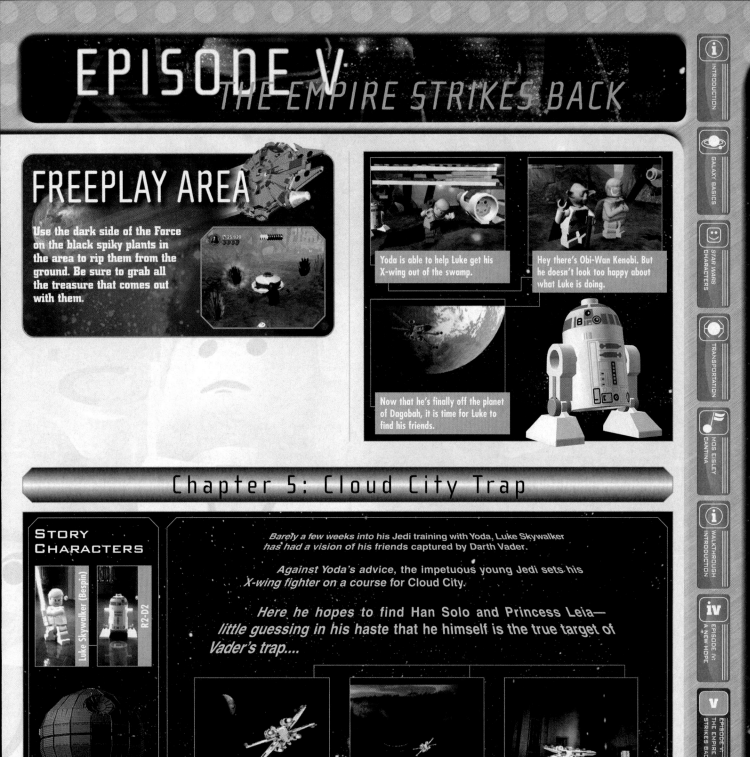

FREEPLAY AREA

Use the dark side of the Force on the black spiky plants in the area to rip them from the ground. Be sure to grab all the treasure that comes out with them.

Yoda is able to help Luke get his X-wing out of the swamp.

Hey there's Obi-Wan Kenobi. But he doesn't look too happy about what Luke is doing.

Now that he's finally off the planet of Dagobah, it is time for Luke to find his friends.

Chapter 5: Cloud City Trap

STORY CHARACTERS

Luke Skywalker (Bespin)

R2-D2

Barely a few weeks into his Jedi training with Yoda, Luke Skywalker has had a vision of his friends captured by Darth Vader.

Against Yoda's advice, the impetuous young Jedi sets his X-wing fighter on a course for Cloud City.

Here he hopes to find Han Solo and Princess Leia— little guessing in his haste that he himself is the true target of Vader's trap....

Luke makes the long journey through space to find his friends.

There's the Cloud City of Bespin.

The landing on Bespin seems a little too easy.

Training with Yoda on Dagobah was going so well, it was a shame Luke had to leave. But having had a vision of his friends in trouble, there was no way he could stay. Yoda and Obi-Wan Kenobi are fearful of what might happen to Luke without the proper training. But if Luke survives his attempt to save his friends, he should be back to complete what he started.

A quick X-wing ride takes him to the landing pad of Cloud City. Jump to the top of your fighter and grab the blue stud, then collect the rest scattered about the landing pad. Some stormtroopers on a ledge in the distance try to blast you, so use your lightsaber to deflect their shots back at them and knock them out. When the guards are gone, have R2-D2 hover over to the ledge to collect the valuables on the ground and use the activation panel on the wall. This brings out part of a walkway to the right.

Fly R2 back to the landing pad and have Luke use the Force to turn part of his X-wing into another piece of the walkway. Jump across the walkways until you get to another ledge against the wall. Assemble the LEGOs on the ground to make an activation panel for R2-D2 to use. This opens the door on the left for you to enter.

Use your lightsaber to deflect enemy shots back at the shooter.

R2-D2's ability to hover in the air sure does come in handy.

FREEPLAY AREA

After R2-D2 flies over to the platform against the wall and accesses the panel, switch to your bounty hunter. Throw a thermal detonator against the far side of the shiny gate in the wall and keep your distance until it explodes. Run inside and grab the LEGO canister for your collection.

When you arrive in the next room, use your weapon to chop apart all the stormtroopers that drop from the ceiling. After the last one falls to pieces, collect all the studs on the ground, including a blue one in the back corner. Have R2-D2 use the activation panel on the back wall to open the nearby door and reveal a box inside. Jump behind the box and push it along the checkerboard pattern on the floor.

When the box reaches the end of the pattern, it sinks into the floor to form a stand. Next, slash at the LEGOs on the back wall to the left of the door. Assemble the loose LEGOs that remain on the floor into a gun. Now use the Force to move the gun over to the base you made. Jump into the gun's controls and blast away the bars on the right wall. Leave the gun and run down the hall that was behind those bars. Take out the stormtroopers that get in your way and grab the studs lying on the ground.

CAUTION

Take care of business in this room quickly because more stormtroopers drop from the ceiling after a while.

FREEPLAY AREA

Use a bounty hunter to access the activation panel on the left wall. Go inside the small room and grab a LEGO canister.

At the end of the hall, have R2 use the activation panel to open the door. Go inside. You are on a narrow walkway in a dark room. Follow the walkway to the right; you'll see a helmet dispenser on the wall to the north. Pass this up for now and continue to follow the trail to the right and down a flight of stairs to a circular platform. There you see Vader waiting for you.

Get your weapon ready and block Vader as he swings his lightsaber at you three times. After his attack, swing your lightsaber once to score a direct hit, but immediately go back to blocking. After Vader tries to hit you again, you can swing your weapon to score another hit. After he suffers a couple of hits, Darth Vader leaps to one of the black steam vents on the ground. When he does this, use R2 to access the activation panel at the bottom of the stairs to cause steam to come up through the vents. The steam disorients Vader for a moment, so have Luke rush in and take another swing at him.

The steam coming out of the vent will not only clear Vader's pores but also disorient him long enough for Luke to take a swipe at him.

After that hit, Darth Vader is back to his usual self, so block his attacks and then take one swing at him before you go back to blocking. After two successful hits, Vader jumps back to a steam vent where you can use R2 to blast the steam so you can attack again. Repeat this process until Darth Vader has had enough, flies across the room, and retreats out the door.

On his way out, Vader causes some LEGOs to fall around the circular platform. Put these pieces together to complete the crane on the south side of the platform. Jump into the crane's controls and pick up R2. Carry your friend over the abyss to the walkway against the far right wall and drop him. When he hits the ground, he moves to an activation panel on the wall and extends a walkway over the abyss for you to cross.

Before you cross over to the other side, go back up the stairs to the helmet dispenser. Pull the lever to have a stormtrooper helmet placed on your head. Return to the circular platform and double jump to the bridge that R2 extended for you. Run up on the walkway along the wall and grab all the valuable studs you find. While wearing your stormtrooper mask, use the activation panel on the wall to open the door and run inside.

Vader is a sore loser and he makes a mess on his way out.

Pretending to be a stormtrooper can be fun and can get you into forbidden areas.

FREEPLAY AREA

Use the dark side of the Force to pull the lever that's located at the back of the platform where you fought Vader. When you do, the center of the platform drops out, so watch your step or you'll fall to your death.

In the next area, you and Vader are on a narrow ledge high above the inner workings of Cloud City. On the wall nearby are some LEGOs. Use the Force on them to change them into a fan on the path ahead. As you move forward, Darth Vader takes off to get out of your way. Use R2-D2 to continue down the path to the right where he can use the activation panel on the wall. This activates a moving platform along the wall above you. Now have Luke jump on the fan on the ground and ride the currents into the air so you can reach the ledge above.

From this ledge you can jump on the moving platform that R2 activated. Ride it along the wall until you can jump to a ledge below you. Step on the gray LEGO platform at the left side of the ledge to lower it so R2 can fly across and join you. Use the Force to move the fan in the center of the ledge so that the wind currents are pointing up. Before you ride the currents, move R2-D2 to the right of the fan. From there fly him south to pick up a LEGO canister hovering in the air before quickly returning to the ledge.

Fly R2-D2 into the air to grab the hovering canister.

FREEPLAY AREA

After you ride the air from the fan to the ledge above you, throw a thermal detonator at the wall to the right. The explosion causes some LEGOs to fall and a small step to form on the wall. Jump to the step and then double jump in the air to get the LEGO canister floating nearby.

Now jump on the fan in the ledge and ride the currents to the ledge in the wall above. To the right is another gray platform and an activation panel that R2 can access. Activating the panel moves the gray platform up and down. When the platform reaches its highest point, fly R2-D2 through the air to the left until he can get the LEGO canister floating in the air. Return to the moving platform and ride it up to arrive at an even higher ledge. Grab the studs on the ground, then enter the open doorway.

Vader is waiting for you in the next room. Use the same fighting technique as you did before to get a few hits on him and send him retreating to a ledge high above the room. After he flees, stormtroopers drop from the ceiling, so cut them down with your lightsaber before they blast you. After the stormtroopers are dead, use the Force to move the two blocks along the back wall and turn them into a ramp. Roll R2-D2 up the ramp to the ledge with the activation panel. Access the panel. Steam shoots out of the vents that Vader is standing over on the ledge above you. This causes him to jump down to your ledge, so fight him off using Luke's lightsaber. After two hits, Vader retreats back to the ledge from which he just came.

Make a ramp on the back wall so R2 can get to the activation panel.

CAUTION

After you defeat a wave of enemy troops, you get a few seconds of peace. But work quickly because more troops are on the way.

INTRODUCTION

GALAXY BASICS

STAR WARS CHARACTERS

TRANSPORTATION

MOS EISLEY CANTINA

WALKTHROUGH INTRODUCTION

EPISODE IV: A NEW HOPE

EPISODE V: THE EMPIRE STRIKES BACK

EPISODE VI: RETURN OF THE JEDI

BONUS FEATURES

77

FREEPLAY AREA

Switch to a small character and jump into the chute in the back wall. This takes you to a locked cell to the left where you can grab a LEGO canister for your stash.

Return to the main floor of the room and quickly assemble the LEGOs in the room's center to create a turnstile. Move to the blue platform next to the right wall and assemble some more loose LEGOs to fix the machinery nearby. After everything is put together, R2-D2 moves over to the blue platform. As soon as he does, push the green side of the turnstile around and around to raise the platform to the ledge above. When R2 gets high enough, he uses the activation panel on the wall to release the steam under Vader. Once again, Vader comes down to fight you, so use your lightsaber skills to send him packing back up to the ledge above.

Vader should have less than half of his health at this point. Move R2 back up the ramp to activate the panel on the wall to fire off the steam again. Vader will come down again, so once again give him a beating to make him retreat. Push on the red side of the turnstile to lower the blue platform you raised earlier. When it gets back to floor level, R2 jumps back on. Push the green side now to raise the platform to the ledge above, where R2 can use the activation panel again. Once the steam is released, Vader drops back down for you to attack. After his health is gone, Vader makes a run for it through the door to the right, so follow him.

Push the green side of the turnstile to raise the blue platform or push the red side to lower it.

Follow the narrow walkway to a small platform in the middle of the room. On a ledge to the north you can see Vader and two Stormtoopers. As soon as they see you, the troops open fire. Use your lightsaber to deflect their shots back at them and knock them out. While you defend yourself from blaster fire, use your double jump attack on the square LEGO pieces in the right side of the platform. The LEGOs break apart, causing you to fall through the platform. You land on a rising pillar. Grab the LEGO canister you find there as you return to the platform.

While the stormtroopers are still shooting at you, send R2-D2 flying through the air to the north toward the ledge with Darth Vader. Collect the studs on the ground, then use the activation panels on the walls. This causes the platforms that the stormtroopers are standing on to close, defeating them instantly, as well as causing some debris to fall on the ground around you.

Send R2 across the room to shut out those stormtroopers.

Taking out his stormtroopers doesn't make Vader very happy. He uses his powers of the Force to hurl the debris through the air at Luke. Fly back to the platform you came from and take control of Luke when nothing is being hurled at him. As Vader sends in debris to hit you, use your own powers of the Force to send it right back. As soon as Vader takes a hit, he comes leaping over to your platform to fight you. After you hit him, block his next attack. When he is done, use your double jump attack to send him retreating back to the ledge he came from.

The platforms those stormtroopers were standing on open back up and more enemies rise up through the floor to blast you. Send R2 back to the ledge to the north to access those activation panels on the walls again. Once the platforms are closed and the storm-troopers are gone, Vader tries to send more junk at Luke, so fly back with R2 and take control of Luke. As the debris comes flying in, use the Force to send it right back at Vader. This makes Vader angry. He jumps over to fight you again. After he takes two hits, he retreats back to the ledge he was on before.

This causes those platforms near Vader to open again with more stormtroopers. Send R2 back over and use the activation panels to shut them down again. When the platforms are closed, fly R2 back to the platform he came from. Take control of Luke and use the Force to send any incoming garbage back at Vader. This time Vader goes crashing through the window behind him, leaving shards of glass in his wake. Use the Force to turn the broken window into the platform nearby so you can cross to the window Vader just fell out and jump on through.

Don't take any garbage from Vader! Send it right back in his face.

Unfortunately, Vader is waiting for you on the other side of the broken window, so have your weapon ready. Block his shots, then attack. After two hits, Vader retreats down the right side of the narrow walkway. Collect the LEGO canister to the left, then use the Force on the LEGOs to the right to make a ramp. Run up the ramp and jump to the next ledge, where you get to fight Vader again. Hit him twice to send him packing. While you're on this ledge, send R2 flying to a small platform to the south where you find another LEGO canister.

After you get the canister, hover back to the ledge and fly to a platform to the right. Access the activation panel on the wall and jump on the brown platform to the left. Ride it to the ledge above, where you can fight Vader again. Hit him twice, and he runs farther down the walkway. As you run after him, collect the studs and the

EPISODE V
THE EMPIRE STRIKES BACK

INTRODUCTION

GALAXY BASICS

STAR WARS CHARACTERS

TRANSPORTATION

MOS EISLEY CANTINA

WALKTHROUGH INTRODUCTION

iv EPISODE IV: A NEW HOPE

v EPISODE V: THE EMPIRE STRIKES BACK

vi EPISODE VI: RETURN OF THE JEDI

BONUS FEATURES

LEGO canister on the path. Run along the walkway to the right until you find Vader again. As you fight the Sith Lord, hit him four times to take away all of his health.

Collect the LEGO canister floating to the south of the ledge before you move on.

FREEPLAY AREA

There's a door in the wall that is locked. Switch to a stormtrooper, then use the activation panel to get inside and buy a mini-kit canister.

Give a hand to Luke. He fought Vader bravely until, well, he lost his hand.

Vader explains that he is Luke's father, and he has the picture to prove it.

Since Luke doesn't want to join with dear old dad, it's down the hatch.

First Luke got his hand chopped off, then he found out Vader was his father, and finally, he fell down the waste chute only to be left hanging for dear life above nothing. Can anything go right?

Chapter 6: Betrayal over Bespin

STORY CHARACTERS

Lando Calrissian

Princess Leia (Bespin)

Chewbacca

R2-D2

C-3PO

Escaping from the Rebel defeat on Hoth, Han Solo has sought sanctuary on Cloud City, high above the planet Bespin.

His old friend Lando Calrissian is now baron-administrator of this self-governing colony, and Han hopes for a warm welcome.

But in this time of galactic upheaval, nothing is as it seems....

The *Millennium Falcon* lands at Cloud City and Han Solo is greeted by his old friend Lando Calrissian.

Unfortunately the Empire got to Lando first and Vader was just waiting for the Rebels.

The bounty hunter, Boba Fett, finally gets his man as Chewbacca and Princess Leia watch helplessly.

All is not lost because Lando Calrissian has a plan up his sleeve.

Friends are hard to come by around the galaxy as Han Solo and his Rebel friends found out the hard way. Darth Vader and Boba Fett set the perfect trap to catch the Rebels and they used Lando to do it. Even though Lando had to go along with the Empire's plan to catch Han Solo, it doesn't mean he is in league with them. As soon as the opportunity arises he sets Chewbacca and Princess Leia free in the hopes of rescuing Han from Boba Fett before he is able to leave Cloud City.

As soon as you start this mission, Boba Fett is firing at you from down the hall while upset citizens of Cloud City run around in a panic. Let your natural ability to dodge blaster fire help you as you fire at Boba. He takes few hits and runs off down the hall. As soon as he runs away, stormtroopers charge at you, so blast them to pieces. The door in the wall to the left can only be opened by a protocol droid so head down the hall after Boba Fett.

Put the loose LEGOs together to make one of the hidden towers in the area.

Before you can hurt him, you first have to shoot Boba Fett out of the air.

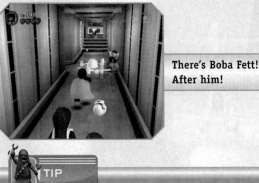

There's Boba Fett! After him!

TIP

It might not seem very baron-administratorlike, but you can shoot the people of your fair city if you need some hearts.

When you get to the loose LEGOs in the path, you see Boba at the end of the hall. Blast him again until he runs away. When the coast is clear, put the LEGO pieces together to build one of three towers around the area. Collect all the studs on the ground, including a blue one to the right of the tower you built, then advance to the end of the hall. Blast the metal grating on the left wall to uncover a lever. Pull the lever to make the ramp in front of you turn into some stairs; climb them to get to the next room.

Grab the studs in the room at the top of the stairs and head to the right. Immediately you see Boba Fett, and immediately he starts shooting at you. Give him a taste of his own medicine and fire back until the coward runs off down a side hallway. Follow him down the hall and into the next room where he's waiting for you.

Shoot Boba Fett as he hovers above the ground to knock him back to earth. Only when his feet are touching the floor can your blasters hurt him. As soon as he starts to hover again, shoot him back down again where you can actually hurt him. Keep shooting him until he takes enough damage and decides to run back out of the room you just entered. When you get back to the main room, you see him enter a door at the end right before stormtroopers charge in to stop you. Shoot them down, then follow Boba Fett through the open door. The door next to it can only be opened by R2-D2.

FREEPLAY AREA

The stark white room has some interesting designs. Use the Force on the tower in the center to start it spinning. Keep it going until it breaks apart leaving a hole in the floor. Jump in the hole and grab the LEGO canister to add to your collection.

FREEPLAY AREA

Use R2-D2 to open the door that has his picture on the activation panel next to it. After you move through the door, you're on a small ledge outside. Pull the lever on the wall to lower a platform in the distance. Now use the Force to lower a platform from the wall that is closer to you. Quickly jump to the closest platform as it rises back up. But as it rises, double jump to the left and grab a LEGO canister to add to your inventory.

That doorway leads to more citizens running around in a panic and one bounty hunter with an itchy trigger finger. Blast Boba to make him run off down the hallway to the left. The hallways to the right and straight ahead have doors that can only be opened by droids, so you better follow Boba Fett. As you move toward the next door, take out the stormtroopers charging at you. After you go through the door, you see the bounty hunter again, so blast

him before he hits you. Follow him as he runs down the hall and shoot him again when he stops at the end to make him run through a door to the right.

When you get to the end of the hall where Boba Fett just fired at you, some stormtroopers enter the area to blast you. First shoot the stormtroopers in front of you, then get the ones that followed you down the hallway. When the coast is clear, assemble the LEGO pieces in the room's center to make the second of three towers located around this part of Cloud City. Grab the studs that scatter on the floor and head through the open door to the landing platform outside.

Boba Fett is trying to get away with Han's frozen body.

Unfortunately, your blasters have no effect on Boba Fett's ship and he gets away.

R2? What is he doing here?

FREEPLAY AREA

In Freeplay mode, Boba's ship *Slave 1* is still on the landing pad. Run to the front of the ship and grab the red power brick to add it to your collection.

Boba Fett might have gotten away with Han Solo, but it's good to see R2-D2. There's nowhere to go outside so collect the studs at your feet and go back inside. As soon as you walk through the door, some stormtroopers try to rush you. Blast them quickly to get rid of them. Backtrack down the hall you came through until you see gas blocking your way. Use R2-D2 to access the activation panel on the right wall to shut off the gas. Some more guards rush you from the hallway ahead so shoot them until they are all dead. With the hallway free of gas and guards, you can continue.

Follow the hallway until you get to the room with the locked doors that only the droids can open. Skip the one with the picture of C-3PO on the activation panel and find the one with the picture of R2-D2. Use R2 to open the door, then go inside. Blast the purple

boxes around the room, as well as the pile of spare parts at the room's center. Also, be sure to drop the Ugnaughts in the back of the room as well before they shoot R2.

Now that the room is clear, push the machinery located in between the red and grey track along the floor. Push it all the way to the wall where the posts on the machinery fit with the holes in the wall. This fixes the lever on the wall to the right and makes it usable. Pull the lever to start the conveyer belt next to you; many golden pieces come tumbling down into the room. Put all those loose pieces together and you make...C-3PO! What happened to him?

Have R2-D2 use the activation panel on the wall to turn off the deadly gas.

It's not your concern why C-3PO is in pieces, just figure out how to put him back together again.

Now that you've fixed C-3PO, get moving again. Outside the door that R2 just opened is a door that only a protocol droid can open. Before you open the door, return to the area where you started this mission and use C-3PO to access the activation panel on the left wall to open the door. Grab the LEGO canister inside and pull the lever on the right wall if you want to change your look with a new hat or hairdo.

After the canister has been added to your collection, return to the locked door you just skipped. Use C-3PO to open the door and go inside where you will immediately have to shoot the guards that try to shoot you. When the area is secure, shoot the equipment hanging from the ceiling to the right. After all the equipment comes crashing to the ground, it leaves behind a pile of loose LEGO pieces. Put the pieces together to form a mini car.

Shoot the equipment on the ceiling to cause it to crash on the ground.

After you put the car together, put on a stormtrooper helmet from the helmet machine against the wall. Next, follow the hallway to the left and pick up the studs on the ground as you go. Shoot all the stormtroopers that try to stop you. The room at the end of the hall has two elevators: One for bounty hunters and one for stormtroopers. Before you take a ride, shoot the stormtroopers in front of the elevators, as well as those lounging in the room to the right. Once the area is clear, and while still wearing your helmet, use the activation panel to ride the elevator up.

FREEPLAY AREA

While you're in the lounging area, use the Force to stack the chairs on the tables. To thank you for being so considerate, a LEGO canister appears over- head after the last set of chairs is stacked.

FREEPLAY AREA

Next to the elevator that only stormtroopers can use is an elevator that only bounty hunters can use. Access the activation panel using your bounty hunter and ride the elevator to the roof. There you find lots of beautiful plants...for you to destroy. Blast the planter boxes, then the trunks of the palm tress. Be sure to collect all the valuables that spill to the floor in the process. When all the vegetation is gone, use the Force to put two of the nearby blue pots together. After a few seconds, they break apart, leaving a LEGO canister for you to collect.

NOTE

If you get shot and lose your helmet, go back and get another one.

The ride in the elevator takes you to a walkway outside. Grab the LEGO canister to the right of the elevator when you get out, then follow the walkway to the round landing pad ahead, which is heavily guarded. As you shoot the guards stationed there, more drop down to blast you. Keep firing and use the boxes around the area as cover until every last enemy is history. Some LEGO pieces fall to the landing pad. Shoot any boxes still intact around you, then put those loose pieces together to make a red circle swirl pad.

Collect any studs on the ground, then use your ascension gun to swing to the walkway along the wall in the back of the area. Grab more studs on the ground. Then jump into the crane. Move the head of the crane over the droids back on the landing pad. Use the crane to lift up the droids one by one to bring them over to the ledge with you.

Blast all the stormtroopers until the LEGO pieces fall from the sky.

When everyone is across, use the red circle swirl on the other side of the walkway to grapple to the ledge above you. Assemble the LEGO pieces on the ground to make a lever on the wall. Pull the lever to lower the elevator nearby so the droids can use it to get up to you. With the elevator lowered, follow the walkway to the right until you get to a conveyer belt. Jump over the red beam crossing the conveyer belt and step on the button on the ground. This stops the conveyer belt from moving and allows the rest of your party to catch up.

Follow the narrow ledge as it wraps around the building until you get to some equipment that blocks the path of the droids. Use R2-D2 to fly around the blockage to the other side of the ledge. On the other side, he can follow the side of the build and fly to another ledge across the way. Once he activates the panel on the wall over there, a blue and grey bridge comes out so everyone but C-3PO can cross.

Fly R2 around the equipment blocking the path so he can get to the other side.

Now that most of the characters can cross the bridge, use Princess Leia to use her ascension gun on the red circle swirl near the activation panel to get to a ledge above. Run to the left of that short ledge and shoot the equipment on the wall. The debris rains down on the path below and destroys the blockage that is stopping C-3PO. Now he can rejoin your group.

The rest of the walkway is blocked with two movable orange boxes and a stationary blue one. Blast the blue box, then push the two orange boxes into the right. By moving the orange boxes, the rest of your team should be able to get by to the door. C-3PO can use the activation panel on the wall to open the door.

The boxes should be pushed to the south so the others can get by.

Inside the hallway beyond the door are more stormtroopers. Drop them quickly when they start shooting at you. Move down the hall shooting any more troops that charge into the area. When you get to the center of the hall, assemble the loose LEGOs you find to form the third of three towers in the area. A LEGO canister appears next to you; add it to your collection.

Continue down the hall and shoot more stormtroopers that rush in to greet you. Follow the hall as it bends to the right and run past the red circle swirl on the ground—you don't need to use it yet. The main hallway ahead is blocked by deadly gas and a small hall to the left has a door that only R2 can open. Skip the side hall for now and use R2 to roll through the gas and use the activation panel on the left wall. This shuts off the gas and makes it safe for everyone to join you.

Use R2 to shut off the deadly gas.

FREEPLAY AREA

Use your ascension gun when you're standing on the red circle swirl to grapple to a ledge above. Grab the studs you find, then use R2-D2 to fly to the other three ledges nearby for even more goodies.

FREEPLAY AREA

On the right wall, before you get to the poisonous gas, is a black wall lock. Use the dark side of the Force to bust the lock open and open the door next to it. Inside is a large grey table at which somebody probably had a pretty good meal. Collect the studs on the ground, then shoot the chandelier over the table. This causes a LEGO canister to appear on the table. Grab it.

Follow the rest of the main hall as it bends to the left until you get to a small room looking out at the *Millennium Falcon* out on the landing pad. Step on the red floor switches on both sides of the room to turn them green and fix the levers at the center of the room. Pull the levers to make a bridge extend out to the landing pad outside.

Now backtrack to the locked door you recently skipped and have R2-D2 access the activation panel on the wall to open it. Run outside and across the bridge to get to the *Falcon*. As soon as you step on the landing pad, stormtroopers drop from the sky to stop you. Blast each and every one until the coast is clear. Run up the ramp on the left of the *Falcon* to blow this joint.

Fight off the swarm of stormtroopers so you can get the heck out of here.

FREEPLAY AREA

It's hard to reach the roof of the *Millennium Falcon*. Switch to a Jedi and double jump to the top where you can grab a LEGO canister for your collection.

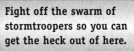

INTRODUCTION

GALAXY BASICS

STAR WARS CHARACTERS

TRANSPORTATION

MOS EISLEY CANTINA

WALKTHROUGH INTRODUCTION

EPISODE IV: A NEW HOPE

EPISODE V: THE EMPIRE STRIKES BACK

EPISODE VI: RETURN OF THE JEDI

BONUS FEATURES

Lando might not be the best fighter, but he leaves his enemies in pieces.

Just when the going gets good, Leia wants to go back to Cloud City.

There's Luke hanging from the city. It's time to pick him up and get out of town.

The Rebel fleet is on the move again with the escaped heroes.

C-3PO doesn't think Luke's losing his hand was that big a deal. He can take his hand off anytime he wants.

Luke's hand gets a little out of hand as Lando and Chewy set off to find Han.

Chapter 7: Episode V Bonus

The bonus section for Episode V contains three parts. The first part requires you to play through all the chapters of Episode V in less than one hour while collecting 100,000 studs. The second part has you fighting your way through the dangerous landing pads and walkways of Cloud City to collect one million studs in under five minutes. And the third part has you flying along the white snowfields of Hoth in search of one million studs in under five minutes. After you successfully complete each part of this bonus section, you get a gold brick for your collection. If you don't complete a mission in the allotted time, you just have to play again until you are successful.

SUPER STORY

The super story in this bonus chapter is just like the super story for Episode IV. Here you have to run through the previous six missions: "Hoth Battle," "Escape from Echo Base," "*Falcon* Flight," "Dagobah," "Cloud City Trap," and "Betrayal over Bespin." You must play thorough all six chapters consecutively while grabbing 100,000 studs in less than an hour. As was the case for the first bonus chapter, you have already played through these missions, so you should know them pretty well and know what areas have studs. Don't waste time in areas where you aren't going to find many studs or that are way off the beaten path and might cause you to waste precious time. As you move, be sure to hit the areas that have the blue studs or many studs in a centralized location. "*Falcon* Flight" is a great chapter because you can fly through it in a hurry while collecting a substantial number of studs—without going out of your way. Blast the small asteroids as you fly along to get some studs for your collection. When you get to the large crater with the wormhole, be sure to hit the small purple reticles on the ground for lots of blue studs. The two chapters that take place on Cloud City are great places to load up on the studs that you need. Many studs can be found on the floor, as well as behind destructible wall panels.

The pink targets around the worm hole on *Falcon* Flight give off lots of blue studs.

Cloud City has many wall panels hiding studs.

CHARACTER BONUS (CLOUD CITY)

While the Rebel Alliance struggles heroically with the oppressive Empire, and as Luke Skywalker moves closer to his epic destiny, daily life goes on across the galaxy.

In the dangerous corridors of Cloud City, intrepid adventurers compete to collect one million LEGO studs in the fastest time possible.

It's the desperate, ruthless life of a world in turmoil....

EPISODE V
THE EMPIRE STRIKES BACK

You start this adventure on the dangerous landing pads of Bespin, where you have only five minutes to collect one million LEGO studs. This mission is played in a Freeplay mode style so you can choose the main character you want to play, and the game will pick the rest of your playable characters, all of whom have different abilities. Make sure you choose Boba Fett and Obi-Wan Kenobi (Ghost) for this mission. Boba Fett is needed for his dangerous blaster rifle that mows down your enemies and for his thermal detonator that you can use to destroy any shiny equipment you find. The ghost of Obi-Wan will be useful to get you out of danger.

The landing pads around Bespin are connected by a system of walkways. Sometimes these walkways are not extended. If this is the case, find a red switch on the ground near the side of the landing pad. Step on the switch and the walkway in front of you will extend and connect to the next pad. But by using Boba Fett, you don't always need the walkways to get from landing pad to pad; you can just fly across the gaps. Not extending all the walkways prevents your enemies from chasing you.

Collect the studs scattered around Bespin.

When you want to extend a walkway to the next landing pad, just step on the red floor switch.

After you start the mission, begin blasting all the gray fence pieces around you because they are loaded with studs. But other things give more studs than the fences. Look for large blue boxes around the landing pads and blast them open to spill a large quantity of studs on the ground. The very best items to destroy, though, are the pieces of shiny metal equipment. Use your thermal detonator to blast that equipment to bits to find valuable purple and blue studs.

Follow the system of walkways to the south as far as you can go. There you'll find three landing pads in a row and each one has some great things to destroy. Two have shiny metal objects and the third has a large number of destructible blue boxes. Stay in this area, moving back and forth, destroying everything in sight and collecting everything that litters the ground. When enemy troops drop in to stop you, switch to Obi-Wan (Ghost) and take them out so you don't take any damage. When the coast is clear, you can switch back to Boba Fett and continue destroying items looking for more studs. Keep moving along these landing pads, collecting studs until you reach the one million mark.

Use Boba Fett's thermal detonator to destroy the shiny metal equipment.

Switch to Obi-Wan's ghost when you need to take out some enemies without getting hurt.

MINIKIT BONUS (HOTH)

> While the Rebel Alliance struggles heroically with the oppressive Empire, and as Luke Skywalker moves closer to his epic destiny, daily life goes on across the galaxy.
>
> On the frozen planet Hoth, intrepid adventurers compete to collect one million LEGO studs in the fastest time possible.
>
> It's the desperate, ruthless life of a world in turmoil....

You start this last part of the bonus chapter by flying over the icy lands of Hoth. You have five minutes to collect one million LEGO studs. This mission is played in a Freeplay mode style so you can choose the main vehicle you want to fly, and the game will pick the rest of your playable vehicles, which you can use at any time during the mission. The vehicle you will use most on this mission is the snowspeeder because of its useful tow cable. As you skim across the planet's snowy surface, many TIE fighters, AT-AT walkers, and AT-ST walkers are out to get you. Luckily, the snowspeeder has just the right amount of quickness and maneuverability to get you through this mission alive.

The mission takes place on a large circular ice field on Hoth, with a large mountain in the field's center. Hoth might be a frozen planet, but the land is covered in green trees. As you buzz around the area, fire your guns at the greenery and studs will litter the ground for you to pick up. Hidden among the green trees are some shiny metal ones that can't be destroyed with your blasters, so fly on past them. If you start to get low on health, be sure to destroy any enemy vehicles in the area. There is a good chance they will leave hearts behind for you to grab to replenish you health.

INTRODUCTION
GALAXY BASICS
STAR WARS CHARACTERS
TRANSPORTATION
MOS EISLEY CANTINA
WALKTHROUGH INTRODUCTION
iv EPISODE IV: A NEW HOPE
V EPISODE V: THE EMPIRE STRIKES BACK
vi EPISODE VI: RETURN OF THE JEDI
BONUS FEATURES

Blast the green trees to find some hidden loot.

Destroy the AT-AT and AT-ST walkers on the ground if you need to refill your health.

As you fly around the snow, you'll also see large white barricades scattered about. These barricades hold many valuable purple and blue studs, but blasters have no effect on them. Luckily, a rolling bomb dispenser is on the side of the center mountain. Fly your snowspeeder in close to the dispenser and grab the round bomb with your tow cable. As you drag the bomb behind you, shoot all the trees that might be in your way. When you get to a barricade, release the tow cable to send your bomb rolling toward your target. After the barricade is destroyed, fly amongst the debris and grab all the good loot. Continue to destroy the barricades and the purple targets until you reach one million studs and are declared the winner.

Fire your purple bombs at the purple reticle on some nearby equipment.

While the trees are a good source of studs, they are not the best source. On one side of the ice field is a purple bomb dispenser. Fly past the bomb dispenser a few times to pick up three bombs, then fly around the circular field to the opposite side of the area until you find the piece of equipment with the pinkish reticle on it. Fire your bomb at the reticle, and the equipment shatters, spilling valuable purple and blue studs to the snow below. Fly in quickly to pick up the loot before it disappears. It doesn't take long for the equipment to respawn, so you can fire more bombs at it and collect more studs.

Those white barricades hold lots of purple and bluestuds to collect.

EPISODE VI
RETURN OF THE JEDI
Chapter 1: Jabba's Palace

INTRODUCTION
GALAXY BASICS
STAR WARS CHARACTERS
TRANSPORTATION
MOS EISLEY CANTINA
WALKTHROUGH INTRODUCTION
EPISODE IV: A NEW HOPE
EPISODE V: THE EMPIRE STRIKES BACK
EPISODE VI: RETURN OF THE JEDI
BONUS FEATURES

STORY CHARACTERS

Princess Leia (Boushh)

Chewbacca

Luke Skywalker (Jedi)

C-3PO

R2-D2

Luke Skywalker has returned to his home planet of Tatooine in an attempt to rescue his friend Han Solo from the clutches of the vile gangster Jabba the Hutt.

Little does Luke know that the Galactic Empire has secretly begun construction on a new armored space station even more powerful that the first dreaded Death Star.

When completed, this ultimate weapon will spell certain doom for the small band of rebels struggling to restore freedom to the galaxy....

Vader boards the Empire's new and improved superweapon. Unfortunately it requires a bumpy shuttle ride to get there.

On Tatooine, the droids pay a visit to Jabba.

As part of the plan, Leia and Chewbacca follow right behind them, whether Chewy likes it or not.

Luke had better know what he is doing back here on Tatooine at Jabba's palace. He sends the droids in first, and then Leia and Chewbacca, to get Han Solo back! That is some friend. Hopefully everything will go according to plan because Jabba and his friends are a dangerous bunch and somebody is likely to get killed.

For now, stick to the plan for getting inside Jabba's palace. From your starting location, follow the narrow path to the left and collect the blue stud at the end. Search the rest of the ground around the area for more studs to add to your collection. Be sure to shoot the brown LEGO piles for more hidden goods. The shiny metal piles of LEGOs can only be destroyed with thermal detonators, so you'll have to come back later.

Run at the huge door in the distance and grab the gold stud inside the left-hand alcove in the door. Grabbing the stud opens a small window behind it and a turret gun comes out to shoot at you. Retreat back to where you started and fire at the turret from a distance while avoiding its fire. After the gun is destroyed, repeat the process with the gold stud on the right. Now return to the door and assemble the loose LEGOs you find there. Collect any studs and hearts that appear and jump on top of the platform you made. From there, grab the last gold stud in the door. Another turret appears; destroy it like the others. After it blows, the door opens for you.

Only grab one stud from the door at a time because you have to take out a turret gun behind each one.

FREEPLAY AREA

To the left of your starting location is a pile of black LEGO bricks. Use the dark side of the Force to break them apart and collect the studs that spill out. Switch to a character with an ascension gun and use the red circle swirl that is now visible to grapple to the ledge above. Run to the left until you find another red circle swirl, then grapple to yet another ledge.

Run to the left and jump down when you get to the end. Collect the blue studs on the ground. Use the Force to assemble the loose LEGOs on the ground. This creates a hook on the side of the cliff and a red circle swirl on the ground. Use your ascension gun on the circle swirl to swing back to where you started.

On your way into Jabba's palace, shoot the platform you put together for a few extra studs. As you enter into the palace hallway, some Gamorrean guards drop through chutes into the palace to greet you. These guys are tough and take three shots before they die! Each one deflects your first blaster hit with his axe, but two more direct hits drops each guard to the ground. Clear out all the guards from the area near the entrance.

With the immediate threat gone, you have to act fast. Near the entrance to the palace, quickly assemble the LEGO pieces on the ledge to the left of the hallway. The loose pieces form a jukebox that starts to play music. When more guards slide down chutes into the hallway, they immediately start to rock out, playing air guitar on their axes. While they rock out, pull the lever on the wall under each chute to close them so no more guards can slide down. With the chutes closed, you can finish off these rockers.

The jukebox you made from the loose LEGO pieces cause the guards to rock out and ignore you for a while.

TIP

Smash all the light fixtures along Jabba's walls to find lots of hidden studs.

FREEPLAY AREA

After you enter the palace, go down the first hallway to the right. Some water cuts through your path and it's too wide to jump over it. Switch to R2 and fly across to the other side. Pull the levers on the wall to make the door between them open. Go into the room and use the Force on the equipment in the center to make it deposit studs on the ground. After you collect the loot, go back across the water to the main hallway.

Move down the hall and be sure to shoot the lights on the walls for some hidden loot. The gate at the end of the hall is closed and only a bounty hunter can open it. Run into the room to the right and find two more guards who need to be taught a lesson. Assemble the loose LEGO pieces on the ground near the cage door to form an access panel that only a protocol droid can use.

FREEPLAY AREA

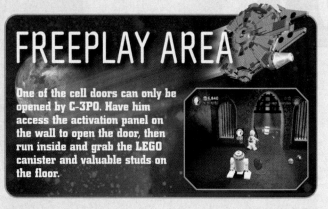

One of the cell doors can only be opened by C-3PO. Have him access the activation panel on the wall to open the door, then run inside and grab the LEGO canister and valuable studs on the floor.

Only a bounty hunter can open the large door at the end of the hall. Head into a room to the left and eliminate the guard that slides down the chute in the ceiling. Then pull the switch under the chute to close it. Dispatch any additional guards that might have dropped down to stop you. When the coast is clear, pull the other lever in the room to get a new helmet. Now you look just like a bounty hunter.

Return to the locked door outside the room and access the control panel to the left of the door. Because you look like a bounty hunter, the door opens for you. Open the door to find Luke waiting for you. Once he joins your party, run back outside and use your thermal detonator on all the shiny pieces of metal outside. After you destroy the pile to the left of the main entrance, you see a red circle swirl on the ground. You can't do anything with it now, so just collect the studs on the ground.

After you blow up all the metal pieces outside, run back to the room where you found Luke. Some Gamorrean guards are waiting for you, so take them out quickly. Pull the levers on the wall in the back of the room to close the two guard chutes in the ceiling. Be sure to blast any more guards that get too close.

Hey, Princess Leia looks just like a bounty hunter. And she can throw thermal detonators like one, too.

FREEPLAY AREA

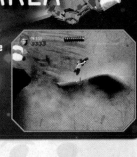

After you uncover the red circle swirl to the left of Jabba's palace entrance, use an ascension gun to get to the ledge above. From there, double jump to another ledge on the left where you can grab a LEGO canister for your collection.

NOTE

It takes a lot of blaster fire to bring down a Gamorrean guard, but Luke can easily use the Force to break them into pieces in a much easier and safer way.

Now that the guards are gone, you can safely explore the room and shoot any light fixtures for hidden loot. Move to the right of the door you came through and put the LEGO pieces together to form a moveable box. Slide the box until you cover up the red flashing button on the ground. As soon as the button is pressed, a red circle swirl appears on the ground next to you, so use your ascension gun to grapple to the walkway above. Follow the path above to collect studs and a red power brick.

Near the red circle swirl on the ground is a cover in the wall that only the Force can move. Use Luke to move it to the ground nearby. Collect the studs that were behind the cover in the wall, then use the Force again to open the newly moved cover in the ground. Once the cover is open, jump inside and grab some blue studs. With all the studs in hand, move to the big door in the back of the room and put the loose pieces together to form an activation panel. With your bounty hunter disguise on, access the panel, open the door, and run inside.

Use your ascension gun to get to the walkway above and grab a nice red power brick for your collection.

NOTE

If you are shot and lose your bounty hunter disguise, you can always go back to the machine and get a new disguise as many times as you need to.

FREEPLAY AREA

Use R2-D2 to access the activation panel at the door on the left side of the room. When the door opens, go inside and snatch all the goodies on the ground, including a LEGO canister.

FREEPLAY AREA

A black grate covers the center of the room. Use the dark side of the Force to break it into tiny pieces. Don't fall into the opening you created or you'll die a painful death.

At the entrance to the new room is a bounty hunter helmet dispenser that you'll use later. The back wall of the room has a large brown gate, and the room corners each have a locked cell. The room also has alcoves on the left and right walls. The first thing you need to do is run to the alcove in the left wall to find a chute coming out of the ceiling. Dispatch Gamorrean guards that tumble out, then quickly pull the lever on the wall nearby to close the chute.

Run across the room and use the Force to break the pieces of an old droid on the ground to uncover hidden studs. Next, run into the small alcove to the left of the droid. Shoot the equipment on the ground, then assemble the loose pieces into a platform. Jump on the platform, and Luke uses the Force to lift you high above the ground. When you stop moving, jump to the ledge that runs along the wall next to you. Follow the ledge to the left and drop into the small room below you. Take out the guard who's waiting for you. Run to the locked gate; when you get close, it opens up, allowing your friends to move inside. Now run back inside the cage and pull the levers on the wall. This opens the large gate in back of the main room.

After you assemble the platform, Luke uses the Force to give you a boost up.

INTRODUCTION
GALAXY BASICS
STAR WARS CHARACTERS
TRANSPORTATION
MOS EISLEY CANTINA
WALKTHROUGH INTRODUCTION
EPISODE IV: A NEW HOPE
EPISODE V: THE EMPIRE STRIKES BACK
EPISODE VI: RETURN OF THE JEDI
BONUS FEATURES

FREEPLAY AREA

Use C-3PO to access the activation panel on the wall near the cell on the right. The cell door on the right opens up, allowing you to enter. Run inside and grab the LEGO canister, then smash the blue bed frame to find some hidden loot.

FREEPLAY AREA

The back-left cell has a small chute next to it. Switch to a small character and head through the chute to get inside the cell. Smash the bed frame, then move through another chute that you find in the cell. This one takes you to the front-left cell where you can smash another bed frame and collect more studs. Exit the room, but throw a thermal detonator in behind you to destroy the grate on the ground. Run back into the cell and jump into the hole where the grate used to be. Follow the tunnel under the ground and clean out all the studs you find. Follow the tunnel to the right until you get to some debris that blocks your path. Use a thermal detonator to clear the way, then continue moving to the right until you step on the elevator at the end of the tunnel. This raises you back up to floor level and into a cell in the front-right of the large room. Grab the LEGO canister in there if C-3PO didn't already grab it earlier.

Behind the large gate you opened is a lot of silvery debris blocking your path. If you don't already have a bounty hunter mask on, return to the room's entrance and put one on. Now that you look like a bounty hunter, toss a thermal detonator at the blockage, and when it explodes, the whole thing crumbles to pieces. Now you can run into the next room.

Immediately run to the lever in the back of the room and pull it to close the guard chute coming out of the ceiling. Put down any guards that made it into the room before you continue. Next, assemble the LEGOs along the left wall to create an explosive bomb. Shoot it a few times; it turns orange until it explodes and takes a chunk of the wall with it. Grab the blue stud it leaves behind, then move inside to get the LEGO canister.

Destroy the wall so you can get the canister inside.

Run to the right wall to find a closed gate. Shoot the orange LEGOs on both sides of the gate until they are completely destroyed. After the last one is gone, the gate rises up. Follow the hallway beyond the gate until you get to a spot where you see white grates on the floor. Continue forward while avoiding the grates—they drop out of the floor when you touch them. When you get to the end of the grates, shoot the two guards waiting for you. After they fall, run past the gate and follow the hallway to the next room.

Take out the set of guards in the back. When they rush you, shoot them before you get hurt. After eliminating them, use your lightsaber to smash the brown grates on the floor near the entrance. Jump under the grates and follow the tunnel as it leads to the left and to a hidden LEGO canister. After you grab the canister, a platform below you raises you back up to floor level. Then, use the Force to move the LEGOs on the wall over to the floor nearby. Assemble the LEGOs into a step platform. Use the Force on the droid parts scattered about the room to find even more studs.

Smash the blue grate to get the hidden canister underneath.

Now pull the two levers located on the equipment to the right to deposit more LEGOs on the ground. Assemble all the pieces to create four red buttons on the floor. These floor buttons are the controls to the step platform you made earlier. Step on the button pointing up to move the platform to the north until it sits next to the tank holding C-3PO in the back. Jump on the platform, then double jump into the enclosure with your golden pal. With your added weight, the floor drops, allowing both of you to escape.

Return to the buttons on the floor and step on the one on the right. Move the step platform all the way over to the enclosure holding R2-D2. Jump on top of the platform, then into the tank with your other droid. Once again, the floor of the enclosure drops, setting you both free. Now use C-3PO to access the activation panel to the left of the door, and use R2-D2 to access the panel on the right. After you activate the panels, the door opens so you can continue.

Step on the red floor buttons to move the step platform where you want it to go.

EPISODE VI
RETURN OF THE JEDI

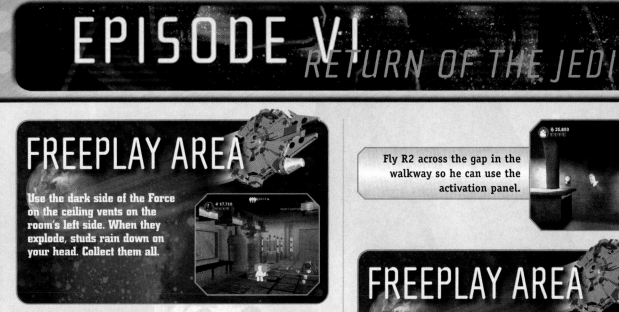

FREEPLAY AREA

Use the dark side of the Force on the ceiling vents on the room's left side. When they explode, studs rain down on your head. Collect them all.

Follow the hallway behind the door as it snakes upward. Pick up the studs on the ground as you go and assemble the loose LEGOs that you find to turn them into another jukebox. Go up the hallway to find some Gamorrean guards playing air guitar to the music you created. Give them a beat-down to secure the area, then use R2 to access the panel on the wall to open the door. Move into the next room.

You enter the room from a doorway in the left wall. Immediately run across the room to the right corner and pull the lever on the wall to close the guard chute in the ceiling. Use the Force to break apart any guard foolish enough to try to stop you. To the left of the lever, on the wall, are some movable boxes of various heights. Push the tallest box along the floor and over the holes in the ground next to the upper walkway on the left. Then push the medium-size box next to the first. And finally, push the smallest of the three boxes next to the medium one. After all three boxes are lined up, use the Force to unfold the top of the boxes to create a ramp leading to the walkway above you.

Push the boxes against the wall in descending order.

Run up the ramp and follow it to the upper walkway; assemble the LEGOs you find into a platform. Use the Force to move the platform you created against the wall nearby to form half a bridge. Stand on the bridge and use the Force again to pull some LEGOs off the wall in the distance, and turn them into the other half of your bridge. Eliminate the guards on the other side, then pull the lever on the wall to ensure no more enter the area.

Follow the walkway around the room to the left until you get to a drop-off point. Use R2 to fly along the wall to the left until he gets to another walkway. Access the panel on the wall; a bridge extends and connects the walkway you're on to the one you came from, allowing your friends to cross. Follow the new walkway until you find some LEGOs on the ground. Assemble them to create an activation panel on the wall. Have C-3PO access the panel to open the nearby door, then go through it.

Fly R2 across the gap in the walkway so he can use the activation panel.

FREEPLAY AREA

When you get to the room with the movable ramps, use the dark side of the Force on all the black and red pieces of equipment on the floor. Move along the upper walkway around the room until you get to the back wall. Use the dark side of the Force to shatter the black grate on the wall. Collect the studs that drop out, then double jump into the alcove behind the grate to add a LEGO canister to your stash.

Follow the stairs opposite the door down to a darkly lit room. When you get there, use the Force to crush the guards, then run to the left wall and pull the lever to close the guard chute in the ceiling. Quickly run to the back wall and pull a second lever to close another guard chute. After you close the second chute, a door in the left wall opens and more guards charge out for you to dispatch. Before you go running into the next room, search along the walls of the room you're in for some valuable studs, including a blue one in the back-right corner. Next, assemble the LEGOs in the back-left corner to create another jukebox. After you get the music going, head into the next room.

As you enter it, use the Force on any guards rocking out to the music. Follow the left wall, breaking lights and collecting studs as you go. When you get to the back-left corner, pull the lever on the wall to close the guard chute in the ceiling. Quickly run across the area and pull another lever on the right corner wall to close yet another chute.

The back wall displays Han Solo frozen in carbonite; only a bounty hunter can get him out. Move to the gate to the right of Han. It opens up for you and lets you to proceed. Run up the steps to a small platform and collect the studs on the ground, then pull the lever on the wall to get a bounty hunter helmet. Go back to Han and access the activation panel to the right of your frozen buddy.

Pull the levers in the back of the room to stop the guards from entering.

INTRODUCTION

GALAXY BASICS

STAR WARS CHARACTERS

TRANSPORTATION

MOS EISLEY CANTINA

WALKTHROUGH INTRODUCTION

iV EPISODE IV: A NEW HOPE

V EPISODE V: THE EMPIRE STRIKES BACK

vi EPISODE VI: RETURN OF THE JEDI

BONUS FEATURES

There's Han Solo frozen in carbonite! Only a bounty hunter can get him out.

A door in the left wall can only be opened by a stormtrooper. Run to the gate to the right of where Han is frozen in carbonite. After it opens up, run inside and pull the lever on the wall to get a stormtrooper helmet. Now you can access the activation panel on the wall on the left side of the room and open the gate that is to the right of the panel. Eliminate the guard inside, then add the studs and LEGO canister to your collection.

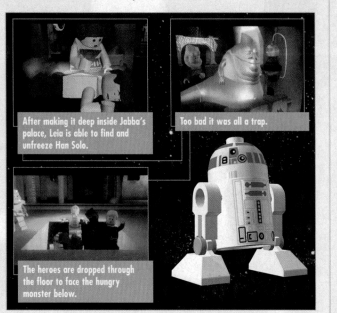

After making it deep inside Jabba's palace, Leia is able to find and unfreeze Han Solo.

Too bad it was all a trap.

The heroes are dropped through the floor to face the hungry monster below.

You're dropped into the monster's small lair and it's hungry! As soon as you hit the dirt floor, the monster charges in to make you its snack, so run for it to stay safe. To the south is an alcove; it has many sharp spikes on the ground that can kill you instantly. To the north is a giant, locked gate that prevents you from escaping. The left wall is an activation panel with a picture of a protocol droid; the right wall has a panel with a picture of an astromech droid.

Run to the left wall and switch to C-3PO, who stands nearby. Have him use the activation panel to make a Gamorrean guard fall from the guard chute in the ceiling. The monster can't resist the fresh meat and chases down the guard. With food in hand, the monster retreats to the back-left corner to enjoy its meal. As soon as it gets there, use Chewy or Princess Leia to blast the explosive container at its feet and hurt it.

The monster drops its snack and comes after you again. Use R2-D2 to access the panel on the right wall to make another guard slide down the chute into the area. The beast grabs the guard and moves into the front-right corner to munch on its new treat. When it gets there, blast the explosive container at its feet to cause some massive damage. Switch back to C-3PO so that he can use his activation

panel one more time to release another guard. The beast once again grabs the helpless guard, but after suffering two hits already, it heads this time for the large locked gate. As soon as it gets there, pull one of the levers on either side of the gate.

Blast the container below the beast to cause a big explosion.

When the beast finally retreats toward the large gate, pull one of the levers on the sides of the gate to crush it.

FREEPLAY AREA

Assemble the LEGOs in the back-right corner of the monster pit to create a red circle swirl pad. Grapple to the ledge above, and from there, double jump up to the ledge on the right. Grab the LEGO canister there.

Pulling the lever on the wall brings down a gate, crushing the monster and saving your butts.

Unfortunately, you're still a prisoner at Jabba's palace and there's no escaping that many Gamorrean guards.

Jabba thinks Princess Leia needs a makeover.

The gold bikini is certainly a new look for the princess.

Chapter 2: The Great Pit of Carkoon

STORY CHARACTERS

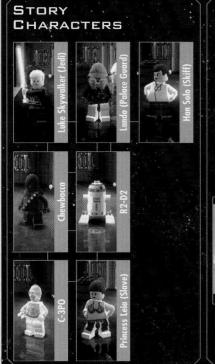

Luke Skywalker (Jedi)

Lando (Palace Guard)

Han Solo (Skiff)

Chewbacca

R2-D2

C-3PO

Princess Leia (Slave)

Work continues on the new Death Star, and the future of the galaxy appears increasingly bleak. On Tatooine, Luke Skywalker is in the grip of Jabba the Hutt, along with Han Solo, Chewbacca, and Princess Leia.

Jabba takes his prisoners across the Tatooine dunes to the Great Pit of Carkoon, where he plans to feed them to the fearsome Sarlacc beast.

But, even with backup from Boba Fett, Jabba has severely underestimated the powers of a Jedi....

Jabba's skiffs are taking Luke and his friends to the Sarlacc pit out in the desert.

Could this really be the end of our hero Luke? He looks a little nervous.

Luckily it was all part of the plan, and Luke is able to get free and escape from the evil clutches of Jabba the Hutt with his friends.

Jabba's plan to feed Luke and his pals to the great Sarlacc beast in the Pit of Carkoon didn't go exactly as planned. Instead of walking the plank and falling into the mouth of the giant beast, Luke (with the help of R2-D2) is able to get his lightsaber back and take control of his skiff. With the others free, it's time to teach Jabba and his thugs that it doesn't pay to make a Jedi mad.

You start this level out on a small skiff high above the desert floor. In the distance is the large barge that Jabba is on and that's where you want to go. As soon as the mission begins, you see an explosion on the barge behind you and an endless supply of skiff guards rush out on the deck. Once they spot you they relentlessly try to shoot you off the skiff.

There's Jabba's barge in the background—that's where you want to go.

FREEPLAY AREA

Use the dark side of the Force to break the floor grate on the first skiff. Use the Force again to pull the LEGO pieces out of the floor and turn them into a tall mast on the ship.

NOTE

Smash all the guard rails along the skiffs and barge to find hidden studs.

Break the railing around the skiff and collect all the studs on deck. Break the two boxes on the side of the boat that's facing north to find some loose LEGOs. Assemble both piles of LEGOs to make two turret guns on the side of the craft that you can use to shoot the skiff guards across the way. The guards' onslaught is nonstop, so when you get tired of blasting them, move to some loose pieces on the ground to the right. Assemble these LEGO pieces to form levers. Pull the levers to make a ramp extend from

INTRODUCTION

GALAXY BASICS

STAR WARS CHARACTERS

TRANSPORTATION

MOS EISLEY CANTINA

WALKTHROUGH INTRODUCTION

iv EPISODE IV: A NEW HOPE

v EPISODE V: THE EMPIRE STRIKES BACK

vi EPISODE VI: RETURN OF THE JEDI

BONUS FEATURES

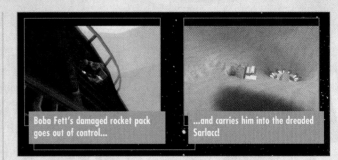

Boba Fett's damaged rocket pack goes out of control...

...and carries him into the dreaded Sarlacc!

the right side of the skiff you're on to the right side of the nearby skiff. Grab more studs on the ground and run across the ramp to the back of the next skiff.

When you get there, you find that Han and Chewy are safe, but they have company. Drop the guards who were watching them, then stand at the back of the craft. Use the Force to lift the LEGOs from the floor and turn them into a tall pole.

Use the Force to create a pole extending into the sky.

FREEPLAY AREA

Walk the plank on the side of the second skiff; you'll see a LEGO canister floating out in the air. Use R2-D2 to fly out there and get it, then return to the plank before he falls to his doom.

Run to the back of the skiff and pull the lever to raise a box out of the floor on the left. Push this box all the way to the front until it explodes into little LEGO pieces. Assemble these pieces into a turret gun to shoot the guards on the large barge in the distance. Return to the lever and pull it again to bring up another box. Push it along the path all the way to the right and then to the north until it explodes, leaving some LEGOs behind. Use the Force to put these pieces together to form another turret gun that you can use to take out more guards. After you have assembled all four turret guns, a LEGO canister appears at the top of the pole for you to collect.

Move to the right and use the Force on the pieces on the ground to turn them into a lever. Pull the levers to make a bridge extend from the front of this craft out to the next. Follow the bridge to the next boat, where you are greeted with more guards and Boba Fett! Use your lightsaber to hack apart the skiff guard and then the Gamorrean guard. Boba Fett is a little bit harder to fight. Chase him down and hack him with your weapon when he lands. This causes him to fly around some more, so follow him. When he drops down to the floor of the skiff, hit him again. Keep hitting him until his jet pack ruptures.

Hit Boba Fett with your weapon every time he lands.

Now that the bounty hunter is out of the way, run to the right of the skiff. Jump from the front of your ship to the front of the fourth skiff. Use your double jump to take out the two skiff guards, then use the Force to dispose of the Gamorrean guard who gets too close. Run to the back of the craft to get a closer look at Jabba's barge nearby. Use the Force to pull some LEGOs from the barge and create a floating platform. Jump onto this new platform, and from there, to Jabba's barge.

On the deck of the barge, kill any guards you see and collect all the studs on the floor. Use the Force to lift up the panels along the barge wall to reveal a walkway and more studs. Most of these panels eventually fall back into place, but a few explode when you lift them. Continue to use the Force to lift up the panels until you find a lever hidden behind one of them. Pull the lever to make a platform extend out from the barge farther to the left. Continue lifting panels until you find a second lever to pull. This one extends another platform out from the barge to the left.

Use the Force to lift the panels on the barge until you find the hidden levers.

FREEPLAY AREA

When you get to the back of the fourth skiff, use the dark side of the Force to pull some wooden planks off the main barge and create a floating platform to the right. Double jump to the new platform, and from there, to the large barge. Collect the studs along the walkway, then use your ascension gun when you get to the red circle swirl. This takes you to an upper deck where you can assemble some loose LEGOs lying on the ground to form a lever. Pull the lever and a LEGO canister appears, so nab it. Drop down to the previous walkway and continue to

INTRODUCTION

GALAXY BASICS

STAR WARS CHARACTERS

TRANSPORTATION

MOS EISLEY CANTINA

WALKTHROUGH INTRODUCTION

iv EPISODE IV: A NEW HOPE

v EPISODE V: THE EMPIRE STRIKES BACK

vi EPISODE VI: RETURN OF THE JEDI

BONUS FEATURES

move around the barge. Step on the next circle swirl and grapple to a deck above you. Pull the lever on the left wall to extend a platform farther down the barge. The hall down the right is blocked for now, so drop back down to the deck on which you were traveling.

The next part of the barge is lined with panels that can be lifted by using the Force. Some just lift up and fall back down, but some explode. Lift the panels until you find an activation panel with a picture of R2. Use him to access the panel and raise a gate in a walkway above you. Continue to lift panels until you find another activation panel that only C-3PO can use. This opens another gate above. A few panels down, one reveals a lever that you can pull to raise a platform farther down the barge.

Keep lifting panels. Near the end, you'll find an activation panel that R2 can access. This raises a third gate in the walkway above you. Backtrack down the barge and grapple to the walkway above from the last circle swirl you saw. Follow the walkway to the right, collecting studs as you go. Throw a thermal detonator at the shiny metal debris blocking your path. Once the way is clear, grab the blue stud and the LEGO canister for your collection.

Return to the barge's main walkway and follow it to the right. When there is a break in the walkway, jump on the platforms you raised by pulling those levers. Jump from platform to platform until you get to the other side of the barge. The rest of the walkway takes you to the back of the barge where you would normally go.

Use the Force to lift the panel next to the last lever you pulled. While the panel is still raised up, use Luke to double jump on top of it. From there, double jump to the ledge nearby. Move into the small alcove of the barge and get behind the box you find. Push the box along the path and over the ledge, causing it to smash on the deck near your friends. Assemble the LEGOs that the box leaves behind into a red circle swirl platform.

Use a character with an ascension gun and grapple from the circle swirl to a walkway high above the deck. Grab any studs on the ground, then follow the walkway to the right behind the walls of the barge. At the end of the walkway is a lever for you to pull. This extends a third platform from the barge, near the other platforms you extended. There's nothing else to do up here, so return to Luke down on the deck.

Use your ascension gun to get to a walkway high up on the barge so that you can pull another lever.

Jump across all three platforms that you extended from the barge's hull to the left. You're now on a deck at the back of the barge and skiff guards start to drop from the sky to fight you. As you fight them off, you'll see two sets of lights on the back of the ship. After you defeat a wave of enemies, quickly use the Force on each set of lights to fix them.

After you fix the second set of lights, a turnstile rises from the deck in between the two. Your goal is to make the right set of lights look like the left set of lights. Push on the green side of the turnstile to move it. You'll see the bottom color of the right set of lights start to change. Keep pushing the turnstile until the bottom light turns blue. Return to the right set of lights and use the Force to turn the middle light yellow. When the right set of lights matches the left set, a door opens into the barge in between the two sets. Enter it.

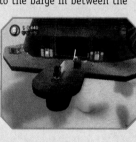

Fix the lights so that they are identical.

TIP

Skiff guards drop down on you in waves. Fight them until the area is clear, then use the Force on the lights because it takes a long time to fix them. If a guard does happen to drop in on you as you're using the Force, stop what you are doing and drop him because you don't want to take unnecessary damage.

FREEPLAY AREA

When the back of the barge is enemy free, use the dark side of the Force to shatter the box on the left. Put together the pieces on the deck to create a red circle swirl pad that you can use to grapple to a deck above. Blast the enemies you find before they can hurt you, then look at the levers on the back wall. Pull the center lever and then the right lever, then use the dark side of the Force to pull the lever to the left. This makes a LEGO canister appear. Grab it for your collection.

You finally made it into Jabba's barge! The first thing to do is celebrate by smashing the equipment lining the right and left walls. Collect all the studs on the ground, then assemble the loose LEGOs on both sides of the room that were left behind from the equipment. Both piles of LEGOs turn into a turret gun. Jump into the controls of the gun and blast the gate in the north wall. Once you destroy the wall, guards try to rush in from the next room. Stay in the gun and mow them down with your laser fire until the coast is clear.

In the next room you find your old friends C-3PO and R2-D2. You also find more of Jabba's stuff to mess up. Break the container to the left of the door to leave it in pieces, then use the Force on some equipment on the right to move it to the left wall. Now use the Force again to combine all the pieces along the left wall into more equipment. Follow the left wall until you find more LEGOs on the ground. Assemble these pieces into an activation panel and collect the studs that spill out. Have C-3PO access the panel to make a lift in the center of the room rise and fall. Jump on the lift and ride it up to the next room.

Blast the gate blocking your path and all the guards behind it.

FREEPLAY AREA

In the back left corner of the room, you'll find a travel chute. Switch to a small character and go through to get to the other side of the fence. Take out the guards you find, then move to the right until you find two levers on the wall. Pull the levers and a LEGO canister appears on the wall nearby. Collect it.

FREEPLAY AREA

When you get to the next level of the barge, there is a room to your right. The lift you rode up is on the left. Ignore the room for now and run around the opening to the lift on the left until you find a metal cage blocking your path to the next room. Throw a thermal detonator at it to blow it apart. Run inside and blast the guards you encounter. After you get rid of the guards, follow the walls of the room to collect all the studs on the ground, including two valuable blue ones. The right and left walls are lined with stacks of more equipment. Use a blaster rifle and destroy every last one of the stacks and collect anything that spills on the ground.

Move to the room that's on the right of the lift you rode earlier. As soon as you enter, use the Force to pull some LEGOs from the left and turn them into some equipment near the back of the room. To the right of that equipment are some loose LEGOs for you to put together to make a jukebox. After you make your sound

machine, shoot all the brown pipes along the walls and collect the studs that were hidden from view.

Destroying some brown pipes on the right wall enables you to use the Force to pull some white half-circle LEGOs from the wall and place them on the floor. This creates a red circle swirl nearby that Han Solo can use to grapple to the walkway overhead. Assemble the loose LEGOs to form a bracket on the ceiling. Follow the walkway behind the wall until you find a box. Push this box to the left until it falls over the ledge and breaks into tiny pieces on the ground.

The shattered box leaves behind tiny LEGO pieces for you to assemble into another jukebox in the corner of the room. Now return to the white half circle LEGOs you pulled from the wall and switch to Luke. Use the Force to move the disco ball up to the bracket on the ceiling. This opens a panel on the floor, revealing blue and pink lights. Step on one of the two pink lights on the ground and one of your friends steps on the other. The pair of pink lights turns green and another pair of blue lights turns pink for you to step on them. Continue to step on all the pink lights until the whole floor is nothing but green lights. Once that happens, the door in the north wall opens up.

Use the ascension gun to get to the upper walkway.

You and a buddy must step on all the pink lights on the floor to turn them green and get the dance party started.

NOTE

You only have a certain amount of time to step on all the lights or they start to change back to their original pink color and you have to repeat this process—so move quickly.

As soon as the door goes up, some Gamorrean guards come rushing in to check out the scene. When they hit the dance floor and hear that music, they just have to rock out; all thoughts of killing you go away. While they are distracted, run into the room from which they came. As soon as those guards realize you're gone, they come after you, so use the Force to crush them. Then crush the wooden paneling on both sides of the room. Pick up any studs that drop to the ground, then assemble the LEGOs that are lying along the left wall. These turn into a LEGO canister that floats in the air nearby. Use Luke to double jump in the air and make it part of your collection. After you get the canister, go through the door in the back.

EPISODE VI
RETURN OF THE JEDI

INTRODUCTION

GALAXY BASICS

STAR WARS CHARACTERS

TRANSPORTATION

MOS EISLEY CANTINA

WALKTHROUGH INTRODUCTION

iv EPISODE IV: A NEW HOPE

v EPISODE V: THE EMPIRE STRIKES BACK

vi EPISODE VI: RETURN OF THE JEDI

BONUS FEATURES

Princess Leia chokes Jabba with her chain.

R2-D2 is always there when you need him...like for breaking the chain keeping you attached to a bloated, dead Hutt.

You've finally reached the top of Jabba's barge. Even though Jabba is dead, he still has guards running about, so drop them whenever they get close. Smash the brown circular grate on the deck nearby. Then use the Force to move the pieces underneath and attach them to the large pole on the left. Run past the pole to the rear-left side of the barge and smash the gray panel on the ground. This brings up a movable box for you to push along the path on the deck. Push it along the path all the way to where you see a large spinning target trapped in a see-through casing. A similar target is directly across from it on the left side of the ship.

Move around to the back side of the target on the right. As you do, some Gamorrean guards drop in to say hello. Use the Force to break them apart as you go. On the other side of the target, push another box along the path on the deck until it rests next to the target. Once both boxes are next to the target, a huge explosion happens. The casing around the spinning target is now gone and you can collect any studs on the ground. Switch to C-3PO and move to the other target on the barge's other side. Access the activation panel on the side to make the casing over that target explode as well.

Push the boxes to the sides of the right moving target to destroy the protective casing.

FREEPLAY AREA

After you get to the top of Jabba's barge, use the dark side of the Force to break the box on deck. Piece together the LEGOs that spill out and turn them into a red circle swirl pad. Grapple from the pad to the ledge above and collect some studs. Switch to R2 and fly to another ledge to the right. Stand on the red circle swirl on the ground and use your ascension gun to get to the small deck above you, where you can add more studs and a LEGO canister to your stash.

Return to the area where you originally found the second movable box. Nearby is a large brown box on the deck. Keep your distance and blast this explosive box to make a hole in the deck. Jump in the hole and follow the attached tunnel as it winds under the deck to the right. Follow the passageway until you get to the end, where a tiny elevator lifts you up to a locked cabin. Pull the lever on the wall and the blue door of the cabin leading back to the deck opens up.

Skip the exit for now and move to the gray wall in the cabin. Chop it with your lightsaber to destroy it and find a movable box hidden behind it. Get behind the box and push it along the path on the floor and out the door to the cabin. Continue to push until it stops against the side of the vessel. Construct the LEGOs nearby to form part of a ramp. Now use the Force on the box you pushed out of the cabin to finish the ramp leading to the next deck.

Follow the passageway under the deck to get to hard-to-reach areas.

Climb the ramp and collect the valuable studs on the ground of the next deck. Run to the south, find the box there, and smash it to reveal some loose LEGO pieces. Assemble the pieces to form a red circle swirl pad then use an ascension gun to grapple to a platform high above the area for some hard-to-reach studs.

At the center of that deck you'll see some targets on the floor. Blast them into little bits. Use the Force to pull out the boards that were underneath and turn them into part of a ramp. More targets are on the wall to the next deck on the right. Blast each target, then use the Force on the LEGOs between the two destroyed targets. This completes the ramp leading to the next deck.

More guards run down to greet you. Use the Force to dispose of the Gamorrean guards, then slash at the skiff guards. When the coast is clear, run to the very top deck and pick up all the studs you find. There, you'll also find a very large turret gun. The green lights under the gun indicate how many shots you have left: each one turns red after each shot. Have R2 access the activation panel on the gun if you need to reload. Jump into the controls and use the big turret gun to fire at the right spinning target first. Now run to the lower deck where the gun used to be, and stand on the platform it was on. The floor drops you down into a secret tunnel under the deck. Follow the tunnel to the south where you can add a LEGO canister to your collection. Return to the hole in the floor where you came from, then go back to the upper deck. Run back to the big gun and destroy the second target. Destroying these targets takes down Jabba's floating barge.

Smash the targets on the sides of the barge to get more pieces for your ramp leading to the next deck.

FREEPLAY AREA

Right before you get to the upper deck with the large turret gun, you find two travel chutes in the wall. Switch to a small character and go on through. The chute takes you to a small room where you add a LEGO canister to your inventory.

FREEPLAY AREA

After you use your ascension gun to get to a platform over Jabba's barge, switch to R2-D2. Fly over to a platform on the left and then to another platform even farther to the left. Grab the red power brick for your stash.

Jabba's barge is going down fast!

It's a good thing that smaller skiff was floating nearby.

Oh, C-3PO! Can Luke take him anywhere?

Chapter 3: Speeder Showdown

STORY CHARACTERS

Luke Skywalker (Endor)

Princess Leia (Endor)

The Rebel Alliance has learned of the new Death Star, and launches a daring plan to destroy this evil weapon before its construction can be completed.

The Rebel fleet is readied for an assault, and a small strike unit lands on the nearby forest moon of Endor.

Led by Luke Skywalker and Han Solo, the unit's mission is to destroy the shield generator that protects the deadly Imperial space station....

There's the forest moon of Endor and the new Death Star.

Luke tries to sneak up on the Imperial guard, until he falls on his face.

That Imperial guard doesn't like the look of you and races off on his speeder bike.

vi

For a Jedi, Luke isn't very graceful. Just when the Rebels thought they had the element of surprise, he makes a big racket by tripping on the dirt. That Imperial guard who saw him isn't going to keep this news to himself. He races away on his speeder bike through the thick forest. If he gets away and tells his buddies, then your plans really are in trouble. Don't let that happen. You have to stop him at all costs!

From the start, destroy all the LEGO vegetation around the area and collect the studs that spill out. When you destroy the plants to the north near the fallen tree you'll find some wooden planks. Use the Force to put these together into a wooden platform. Jump on the platform with Leia. Luke uses the Force to lift the platform up so you can jump to the other side of the fallen log.

Shoot the plants in the back right corner for some more studs and to reveal a red circle swirl on the ground. Use your ascension gun and grapple to the ledge on the right and shoot more plants. Follow the ledge to the south and jump on the wooden platform at the end to lower it. This raises up some platforms back near Luke and he is able to join you on top of the fallen tree. Return to the circle swirl on the ground to find a pile of LEGOs to the left. Use the Force to turn those LEGOs into a ramp leading over the next fallen tree. Climb the ramp to get to the other side.

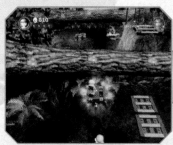

Get on the wooden platform and Luke lifts you up.

The LEGO vegetation around the area can hold lots of hidden treasure.

Jump down the cliff wall to the right and assemble the LEGOs on the ground to create a red circle swirl pad. Collect the loot on the ground. Then shoot the nearby plant for even more studs. Run along the dirt to the right to find yourself on a large dirt trail. To the right is a large force field with four blue posts. As you stand there, a pair of Imperial speeder bikes races in from the north and a force field blocks the rest of the path. When a bike stops in front of you, the guard gets off, giving you the perfect chance to put your lightsaber right through him. After both of the drivers have been dealt with, you can jump on your new ride. After you get on your Imperial speeder bike, the force field that was blocking the path disappears.

Since those stormtroopers won't be using their bikes anymore, they're all yours.

> **NOTE**
>
> The speeder bike trail around the forest follows a circular loop, so you will see the same terrain over and over again. If you happen to miss something on the first pass, you'll get another chance to shoot or collect it the next time around. Your bike goes pretty fast and there are plenty of plants and trees that you might miss destroying on your first few passes.

As soon as you get on your new ride, two more enemy speeder bikes zip past you to the north. Before you go racing after them, you have some business to take care of in the forest. First, blast the large white turret gun up ahead that's trying to gun you down. Collect the studs it leaves behind. Now follow the trail those bikes are on and shoot the LEGO plants as you go and grab the goodies they leave. On the left side of the trail on the ground, you'll find a wooden lever with red lights on either side of it. Drive over the lever to turn the lights green and raise a wooden ramp behind it. Drive up the ramp and collect the LEGO canister at the top.

Continue to follow the trail ahead and shoot all the white turret guns and plants you see. Be sure to circle back and collect all the studs they leave behind. Keep moving along the path until you see three rectangular levers lined up along the ground on the trail's right side. Ride your speeder bike over a lever to turn the lights on it from red to green. Run over all three, and a LEGO canister appears at the end of the row for you to grab.

Fly up the ramp to get the canister at the top.

Ride over all three levers to get another canister.

Keep moving along the trail and you come to an area where there are two more ground levers on the right side of the trail. Ride over both to turn the red lights on them to green. A ramp rises up at the end. Follow this ramp up to a ledge on the side of the trail and grab the LEGO canister you find. Not too much farther up the trail you'll find four more ground levers on the trail's left side. Ride over all four, and a LEGO canister lowers from the trees down to the end of the row of levers. Ride through it to add it to your stash.

Keep moving forward until you see another lever on the right side of the trail. Run over the lever; a ramp rises up ahead. Follow the ramp up to the ledge on the right and run over the levers lined up ahead of you. Run over all three levers on the ledge. Another ramp rises up ahead. Speed up the ramp and grab the LEGO canister at the top. When you get to the end of the ledge keep to the right side of the trail. As soon as you drop down, you find another LEGO canister to add to your stash.

Run over the two levers on the ground to raise a ramp leading to the ledge ahead.

Run over the lever on the right of the trail to raise the ramp ahead.

Now that you have all those canisters, you can go after those Imperial speeder bikes! Ride as fast as you can and you'll catch up to them in no time. Ignore the stuff in the terrain for now and focus your attention on stopping those stormtroopers. The bottom of the screen shows that you must take out two speeder bikes. When those bikes get in range, start blasting away with your guns. After a few hits, each bike breaks into tiny pieces. After the last one falls apart, your speeder bike automatically stops at a force field blocking the path. When your bike stops, you automatically get off and discover not only stormtroopers waiting for you, but also an AT-ST.

Quickly get in close to the large vehicle and use the Force to pull the driver out of the AT-ST's cockpit. Now jump in and take over the controls. Walk toward the blue force field generator to the right of the force field. Fire your guns at the generator until it completely falls apart. Destroying this generator not only allows you to continue down the trail in front of you, but it also destroys one of the posts of the larger force field that is farther down the road. Blast any stormtroopers still on the ground and walk the AT-ST over to the upper ledge on the trail's right side. Hop out of the vehicle to land on this ledge, where you can shoot the vegetation to find more studs.

Use the AT-ST to destroy the nearby force field generator.

CAUTION

Don't get too close to an enemy AT-ST or it will step on you and disable you for a few seconds.

FREEPLAY AREA

When you get to the upper ledge on the path's right side, switch to a Sith character and use the dark side of the Force to pull out the black spiky plants from the ground. Be sure to collect all the studs that are uprooted with each plant. After you destroy every plant, you can see a chute in the trunk of the large tree nearby. Switch to a Jawa and enter the chute to reach a platform high above you. Now switch to R2-D2 and fly to another ledge to the left. Pull the lever on the trunk. A cage holding a LEGO canister will drop to the trail nearby. Get back to your speeder bike and run over the cage to add the canister to your collection.

With the generator gone, you can jump back on your speeder bike. The force field blocking the path disappears. Ride down the trail. Two more enemy speeder bikes race past you. Race up behind them and blast them with your guns to break them apart. After the first two bikes are eliminated, a third bike races in, so take it out as well. After all three bikes are destroyed, you automatically stop in front of another force field that is blocking the trail and hop off your bike.

Run to the trail's right side and assemble the brown LEGOs on the ground to create a large step. From here, jump to the ledge above and smash the vegetation in the area for some hidden loot. When you're done, run to the trail's left side and smash the large collection of plants on the ground. Hidden underneath are two AT-ST feet, which you will use in a minute. Stormtroopers start dropping from the sky. Break them into little pieces as you follow the trail's edge to the south. When you see the brown box lying on the ground, use the Force to move it to the ledge on the left. Now you can jump on the box to get to the ledge above.

Hey, where's the rest of the AT-ST?

When you're on the upper ledge, use the Force to move another box and stack it on the last. Now Leia can run up the boxes and join you. Assemble the loose LEGOs on the ground to form a red circle swirl pad. Then use your ascension gun to grapple to the platform in the trees, where you can pull the lever that's up there. This releases some LEGO parts that were hanging from the tree you're on. They drop to the ground.

EPISODE VI
RETURN OF THE JEDI

Drop down to the ground yourself and blast any more stormtroopers that come to stop you. Have Luke use the Force on the new LEGO pieces to put the rest of the AT-ST on top of the feet you found a moment ago. Jump into the walker's controls and blast the force field generator in the upper-left corner. Destroying it eliminates the second post of the larger force field in another section of the jungle. Jump on your speeder bike; the smaller force field blocking your way disappears.

> Pull the lever on the tree to get some more LEGOs so that you can build an AT-ST walker.

FREEPLAY AREA

When you are on the ledge on the right side of the trail, switch to a bounty hunter. Throw a thermal detonator at the two pieces of shiny metal equipment to uncover a hidden brown box inside. Another brown box is leaning on a tree trunk nearby. Use the Force to stack all three boxes, then jump to the top of the stack. From there, jump to the platform on the large tree and pull the lever that you find. This lowers a cage with a LEGO canister down to the trail. Return to your speeder bike and blast the cage to add the canister to your collection.

Move down the trail again. You have to destroy four more enemy speeder bikes. After the fourth one breaks apart, your speeder bike stops in front of another force field and you dismount from your bike. Quickly run to the large AT-ST walker nearby and use the Force to send the driver crashing to the ground. Jump inside the empty cockpit and drop any stormtroopers that are roaming around. When the coast is clear, fire at the blue generator in the upper-left corner. When it blows up, a third piece of the large force field down the path is destroyed.

Run to the trail's right side and follow the upper ledge to the south until you see a pile of brown LEGOs. Use the Force to turn these into a large brown box. Jump on top of your creation, then jump to the ledge above. Destroy all the vegetation you find and collect the goods that are hidden underneath. Now return to your speeder bike. The force field that was blocking your path is gone.

> Blast the field generator in the upper-left corner with the big guns.

FREEPLAY AREA

When you are on the ledge in the upper-right side of the screen, use the Force to move the platform on the right tree over to the center tree. Now switch to a bounty hunter and use a thermal detonator to destroy the shiny metal equipment nearby. This leaves behind some loose LEGOs. Assemble them to create a red circle swirl pad. Stand on this new pad and grapple up to the platform you moved. Move to the left and pull the lever on the tree trunk to lower a cage holding a LEGO canister. Return to your speeder bike below and blast the cage to add the canister to your collection.

CAUTION

After you drop the five enemy speeder bikes in the next paragraph, you can no longer explore the jungle. Make sure you have thoroughly explored everything before you take out the fifth stormtrooper.

Zoom down the path again. This time you have to destroy five enemy speeder bikes. As they drive past you, speed up behind them and fire away. Keep shooting until all five are nothing more than spare parts. After the fifth one goes down, you stop in front of yet another force field that blocks your path. Drop the stormtroopers on the ground, then run to the south. A deep chasm cuts through the trail, but there is a narrow bridge for you to cross.

On the other side, smash all the vegetation you see. Some AT-ST feet are hidden under some plants, as well as some loose LEGO parts. Assemble the pieces to create a turnstile. Push the green side and the wooden cage holding some loose AT-ST pieces goes down. Keep pushing the green side until the cage completely disappears. Use the Force on the pieces inside the cage to construct the AT-ST walker.

Blast any stormtroopers that might be around, then head to the edge of the nearby chasm. Shoot the LEGO crates hanging from the trees on the other side. Some loose pieces go crashing to the ground. Exit the vehicle and use the Force to turn those loose pieces into a large bridge that spans the chasm. Get back into the large walker and cross the bridge. Head for the blue shield generator in the far-left corner and blast it to pieces. This destroys the last post of the large force field in the jungle on the right.

> Shoot the basket of hanging LEGOs on the other side of the chasm.

INTRODUCTION
GALAXY BASICS
STAR WARS CHARACTERS
TRANSPORTATION
MOS EISLEY CANTINA
WALKTHROUGH INTRODUCTION
EPISODE IV: A NEW HOPE
EPISODE V: THE EMPIRE STRIKES BACK
EPISODE VI: RETURN OF THE JEDI
BONUS FEATURES

There's the large force field that is blocking you from the rest of the jungle.

Now that the large force field is gone, you can head down the path it was blocking. When you get to the other side, start blasting all the vegetation you see, including plants and trees. Be sure to collect all the valuable studs that drop to the ground as you go. In the distance is a metal structure with two support beams sticking into the ground.

There's no reason to go to the left beam for now, so go toward the one on the right. Assemble the loose LEGOs on the ground to create a red circle swirl pad. Grapple from the pad to the structure above to get some valuable studs. Now drop back to the ground and pull the levers on the beam nearby to open the door. Head inside and ride the elevator up to a walkway above. Follow the walkway to the left and jump in another elevator to continue your journey up to the top of the structure.

Smash all the vegetation, then head for the right side of the structure in the distance.

FREEPLAY AREA

Go to the left support beam of the large structure in the forest. Push the movable box along the ground until it is right up against the beam. Switch to a small character, like a Jawa, and enter the chute. This takes you to a walkway above, where you can grab a red power brick for your collection.

FREEPLAY AREA

While you're walking along the structure's walkway, you see an activation panel with a picture of a stormtrooper. Switch to a stormtrooper and use the panel. A cage with a LEGO canister lowers to the ground below you. Get in the elevator to the right and ride it back down to the forest floor. Throw a thermal detonator at the cage and add the canister to your inventory.

From the top of the structure, you can see a large AT-AT walker in the distance. Before you can even think about that beast of a machine, some stormtroopers grapple to the roof to take you out. Walk along the roof's edge and use your lightsaber to smash all the grappling hooks to stop the stormtroopers from coming up. After all the hooks are gone, move along the roof, smashing all the gray fence pieces to find hidden studs.

Also on the roof are four blue levers that control small force fields over the four radar dishes surrounding the AT-AT in the distance. After you pull a lever, the corresponding force field disappears from a radar dish. Move around the rooftop and pull all four levers to disable all four radar dish force fields. Now run to the back of the roof and step on the white pad in between the green lights. The white pad flings you through the air until you land at the controls of the AT-AT walker.

Pull the blue levers around the rooftop to disable the force fields protecting the radar dishes in the distance.

Now that you control the giant walker, spin it around and fire at the four radar dishes surrounding you. Each time you destroy one, the corresponding lever on the rooftop also explodes. The explosions on the rooftop leave behind studs and some loose LEGO pieces. When all four dishes are gone, exit the AT-AT and you'll fly back to the rooftop.

Move toward the center of the rooftop. You'll see two sets of loose LEGO pieces. Assemble each pile of LEGOs to fix the levers nearby. When everything is back together again, pull one of the levers and your partner will pull the other. That begins the destruction of this Empire-controlled structure.

Put the broken levers back together again.

The structure doesn't seem so stable anymore. It's time to get moving.

Run for it! The place is going to blow!

Time to celebrate.

Chapter 4: The Battle of Endor

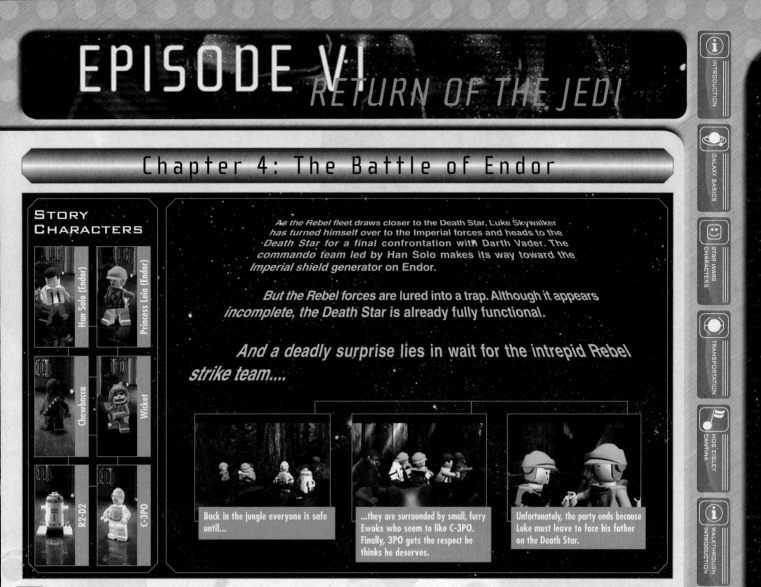

STORY CHARACTERS

Han Solo (Endor)

Princess Leia (Endor)

Chewbacca

Wicket

R2-D2

C-3PO

As the Rebel fleet draws closer to the Death Star, Luke Skywalker has turned himself over to the Imperial forces and heads to the Death Star for a final confrontation with Darth Vader. The commando team led by Han Solo makes its way toward the Imperial shield generator on Endor.

But the Rebel forces are lured into a trap. Although it appears incomplete, the Death Star is already fully functional.

And a deadly surprise lies in wait for the intrepid Rebel strike team....

Back in the jungle everyone is safe until...

...they are surrounded by small, furry Ewoks who seem to like C-3PO. Finally, 3PO gets the respect he thinks he deserves.

Unfortunately, the party ends because Luke must leave to face his father on the Death Star.

INTRODUCTION

GALAXY BASICS

STAR WARS CHARACTERS

TRANSPORTATION

MOS EISLEY CANTINA

WALKTHROUGH INTRODUCTION

EPISODE IV: A NEW HOPE

EPISODE V: THE EMPIRE STRIKES BACK

EPISODE VI: RETURN OF THE JEDI

BONUS FEATURES

It's a good thing that the Rebel friends had C-3PO with them. Those furry Ewoks think he is some kind of god, and they actually *like* to hear him talk. At least somebody does. Otherwise, our heroes would have ended up as the main dish at an Ewok barbeque. As the Rebels prepare their final plans, Luke must leave to find Vader on the Death Star. So much for the happy reunion.

Luke might be gone, but you still have to carry on with the mission. You start high above the forest in the Ewok village in the trees. Show your thanks and blast the pots against the wall behind you. Collect the studs and shoot the boards that cover the doorway so you can shoot the blue pot inside. Shoot the container in the other doorway and grab the valuable goods that spill out. Now follow the path and run around behind the doorway where you just shot the pot. While you're out of view, grab some valuable studs. Follow the path until you loop back around to where you started.

Move to the left of the village and smash more pots for more goodies. Break the purple box to find some loose LEGO pieces to assemble. Assembled, they form a turnstile; as before, push the green side to spin it. Keep pushing to make an elevator platform along the giant tree to the northwest raise to a horizontal position. Send R2-D2 over to the new elevator; it raises him up to a platform above. He can collect the LEGO canister and some studs there. There's nothing more to do here, so fly back to the main part of the village.

Move to the right and you'll find another pile of loose LEGOs. Put the pile together to create a barbeque and collect the studs that are released. Continue moving to the right, shooting more pots and collecting more studs. Blast the brown boards blocking the doorway, then blast the blue pot behind them to get another blue stud.

Shoot all the blue pots you find because they can contain valuable blue studs.

Push the turnstile to raise the elevator on the tree nearby.

FREEPLAY AREA

After you fly R2-D2 over to the platform against the tree, pull the lever on the trunk. This drops a crate of supplies over to the right, spilling its contents on the ground. Assemble the LEGO pieces that spilled out to create a red circle swirl pad. Now use your ascension gun to grapple to a ledge over to the right. Shoot the blue pots you find and collect the blue studs that are inside them.

FREEPLAY AREA

Jump into the large wooden chair near the turnstile. Your partner uses the Force to move the chair to a platform in the trees above you. From there, jump on the platform and add some more studs to your collection.

FREEPLAY AREA

Use the dark side of the Force on the barbeque to get the burners going. Once it is fired up, use the dark side of the Force on the nearby pot to move it onto the grill. The pot's contents start bubbling out and so do some studs. Snatch them up. Now you have food but no place to eat. Use the Force on the LEGOs near the grill to form a table and some chairs. After everything is put together, use the Force on the cups and plates on the table to get a few more studs.

The path to the right eventually leads to a small chute in the wall. Switch to Wicket and hop inside the chute. It takes you to a walkway on another tree to the right. Assemble the loose LEGOs you find to the left of the chute exit. This fixes the controls for a bridge that rises up and connects to the walkway from which you just came. Your friends can now run across and join you.

Now follow the village walkway to the right. As you move, continue shooting all the pots and boxes along the path to find hidden treasures. An elevator to the north takes you to a ledge above. Switch to R2 and fly to a ledge on the left, and from there, fly to another ledge on the left to get some valuable studs. Go

back to the village and continue moving to the right. When you see some boards covering a doorway, blast them apart. Use C-3PO to access the activation panel in the doorway. This causes a crate to drop to the walkway and shatter into tiny pieces.

Use Wicket to assemble the loose LEGOs and fix the bridge so that your friends can cross it.

FREEPLAY AREA

When you get to the second platform above the village, use the Force on the ball hanging over your head. This pulls the ball down and lowers an elevator on the right. Quickly double jump to the elevator. It takes you to a lever overhead. Pull the lever; a cage door opens below you, so grab the LEGO canister that was behind it.

Assemble the loose pieces from the crate that broke on the walkway to create a red circle swirl pad. Use your ascension gun and grapple to the ledge overhead. Pull the lever on the tree trunk. A bridge rises up below you. Drop back down to the village and run to the right to cross the bridge. On the other side, be sure to break all the pots to add more studs to your collection.

Continue following the walkway through the village. It eventually starts to wind down to a lower level. When you get to the lower level, smash more pots and follow the walkway to the right. As soon as you run down a small ramp, some stormtroopers grapple up the sides of the village to greet you. Fight them off and then run along the fence of the village, blasting all the grappling hooks you see. After you destroy the last one, no more troops can come up to shoot you in this area.

Shoot those grappling hooks to stop enemy troops from coming into the village.

104

FREEPLAY AREA

When you get to the platform with the lever on the tree trunk, use the Force to lower a platform in the tree to your right. Now you can jump on the platform you moved. From there, jump to another platform to the right and collect some studs. Remember that platform you just lowered? Well, use the Force again to raise it back up to its original location. From the ledge you're standing on, you can jump to the top of the ledge you just moved. From there, jump to a new ledge to the left and add a LEGO canister to your stash.

When the coast is clear, destroy all the equipment on the checkerboard pattern in the center of the walkway. Some of the equipment leaves behind some loose LEGOs that you can assemble. Put them together to form a piece of equipment that you can push all the way to the left until it fits into the slot in the floor. This raises a large platform to the south.

Now use Wicket to jump into the travel chute in the large tree nearby. This chute takes you to a platform above where you pull a lever attached to the tree. This causes a crane to lower and grab that piece of equipment you just pushed along the floor below. The crane deposits it on a checkerboard pattern on a small platform to the right. Push this piece of equipment into the slot in the tree to the right of the larger tree. Doing so raises up a platform with some red floor switches in the south.

Push the equipment you put together across the checkerboard pattern on the floor.

Drop back to the village walkway and run to the south. Stand on one of the red floor switches to turn it green. The rest of your party does the same. After all the switches turn green, the platform you're standing on lowers to the forest floor. Shoot the guards standing around in the south, then blast the ones on a walkway to the right.

When the coast is clear, run to the left of the clearing. Shoot all the vegetation and collect the stud on the ground. Destroy a purple box nearby and then assemble the LEGOs it leaves behind to create a circle swirl pad. Use your ascension gun while standing on the pad to grapple to a platform overhead. Destroy all the pots you see and collect the goodies that spill out. Shoot the boards covering the doorway and collect the LEGO canister that is hidden behind them.

Blast the boards covering the doorway to get a hidden canister.

Drop back to the forest floor and move to the right. The rest of the trail is too high to get to for now, so destroy all the vegetation on the ground and snatch the studs that litter the ground. Put together some loose LEGO pieces from under the plants to form a red and green turnstile. Push the green side to raise a platform against the cliff wall to the right. After the platform rises as high as it can go, use Wicket to get in the travel chute in the wall.

The chute takes you to a ledge directly overhead. Once you get there, step on the red floor switch. This causes a hook hanging nearby to move to the right, and a red circle swirl to appear on the ground below. Continue to stand on the switch while another character uses the circle swirl to swing to the next part of the trail on the right. Once that character gets there, pull a lever to raise a ramp so that everybody can get up to the next part of the trail.

Keep standing on the red floor switch so someone from your party can use the ascension gun to swing to the next part of the trail.

Now blast the stormtroopers who are in your way. Move to the left and destroy all the plants you see. You'll find a red circle swirl pad on the ground. Stand on the swirl and grapple to a platform overhead. Destroy all the pots you see and blast the boards covering the doorway. Hidden behind them is a blue pot that you can turn into junk, then collect the blue stud inside. Now drop back down to the trail and follow it as it crosses a small stream. The current is strong, preventing you from going too far upstream for now, but you'll be back later.

When you get to the stream's other side, blast any guards that you see, then get to work destroying the plants on the right side of the area. While you're on the right side, destroy the wooden fence as well as the purple boxes that were penned up. Then get the loose LEGOs on the ground. Put them together to make a tractor. Lots of valuables spill out for you to grab.

Put the loose LEGOs together to make a tractor and be a real-life farmer!

INTRODUCTION

GALAXY BASICS

STAR WARS CHARACTERS

TRANSPORTATION

MOS EISLEY CANTINA

WALKTHROUGH INTRODUCTION

EPISODE IV: A NEW HOPE

EPISODE V: THE EMPIRE STRIKES BACK

EPISODE VI: RETURN OF THE JEDI

BONUS FEATURES

FREEPLAY AREA

Some black spiky plants down by the river are impervious to blaster fire. Switch to a Sith character and use the dark side of the Force to pull up each black plant and grab the studs that come out with them.

FREEPLAY AREA

Switch to a bounty hunter character and throw a thermal detonator on the right side of the farm. The large explosion leaves some brown LEGOs on the ground for you to put together. These form an elevator on the tree behind you. Jump on the elevator and use the Force on the hanging ball to the right. This raises the elevator up to a travel chute located in the trunk of the tree. Switch to your small character, like an Ewok, and go inside the chute. The chute takes you to a platform overhead. Grab the studs on the ground, then jump on the elevator to the left and ride it up to another platform. When you get there, add more studs to your stash.

Drive the tractor you just created to the left side of this farm. Drive the tractor over the tops of the carrots that are planted in the ground to make them grow. After everything sprouts, some studs pop up too. Keep moving over the carrots until every last one has sprouted from the ground. When all the vegetables are above ground, chop them down for even more goodies.

Now drive the tractor into the water and head upstream. When you get to the waterfall at the end, jump off and grab the LEGO canister you find.

After you get the canister, go to the back of the farm. In the center of the area is a tan box. Blast it apart. It leaves behind some LEGOs that you can assemble into an activation panel. Move C-3PO over to this panel and have him access it. This causes some red floor switches to be revealed to the left and right of the gates nearby.

Use C-3PO to access the activation panel to open some red switches on the ground nearby.

Move to the right of the activation panel and step on the red floor switches; the rest of your party does the same. After all the switches turn green, the gates in front of you rise up, opening the path ahead. Run forward and assemble the loose LEGOs on the ground to create a small wooden ramp. This ramp is perfect for the droids to use to get up to the walkway's next level.

Run around the activation panel that C-3PO used and head for the open gate on the left. In the wall beyond the gate is a travel chute that Wicket can use to get to a platform in the trees above. Pull the lever on the trunk to make a crate drop to the floor below. Drop down and assemble the pieces into a red circle swirl pad. Use your ascension gun to swing to the next part of the trail that is too high to reach otherwise. Step on one of the red switches on the ground. The rest of your party follows suit. When everyone is standing on a floor switch, the gate in front of you lowers into the ground, opening the trail ahead.

Step on the red floor switches to get those gates out of the way.

Move forward down the next part of the trail and blast the stormtroopers charging you. When they're dead, destroy all the vegetation on the area's left side. Doing so uncovers a travel chute hidden on the large tree trunk nearby. Have Wicket jump into the chute to arrive at a platform above. From there, jump to another platform to the left and shoot the pots for some hidden loot.

Drop back down to the ground and head to the right side of the area. Blast all the plants you find and collect the goodies that litter the ground. Some purple boxes can also be found here, so break those apart to be rewarded with even more hidden treasure. Once the area is loot free, follow the trail farther to the north.

Clear the plants away from the tree trunk to find a hidden travel chute.

FREEPLAY AREA

After you travel to the ledge in the trees using the travel chute, switch to R2-D2. Fly to the platform in the trees to the right and pick up another LEGO canister for your inventory.

FREEPLAY AREA

On the trail's right side, you'll find some shiny metal equipment, so switch to your bounty hunter and toss a thermal detonator at it. When the smoke clears, use the Force to stack the loose LEGOs in the area to form a tall pole. Double jump to the top of the pole, then jump to the platform in the tree nearby. Smash the boards covering a hole in the tree, then smash the pot inside for a blue stud. Smash the rest of the pots on the platform for even more goodies.

In the next area, start shooting the vegetation on the ground to find some hidden studs. As you do so, be sure to take out the stormtroopers that come rushing in to stop you. When the area is enemy- and plant-free, head down the path until you find a catapult. Jump into the controls and starting firing at the debris that blocks the path in front of you. After a number of hits, the debris shatters into tiny pieces, spilling studs all over the ground. Don't leave the controls of the catapult just yet because an AT-ST comes charging at you. Fire a direct shot at the body of the AT-ST to knock its driver out of the controls.

When the walker is lacking a driver, quickly exit the catapult and jump into the AT-ST. Now that you have control of it, blast all the nearby stormtroopers who were trying to shoot you. Continue along the path ahead and shoot all the plants along the trail to find some more valuables. The trail is eventually blocked by a flimsy fence. One shot from your AT-ST turns it into garbage.

Use the catapult to take out the AT-ST's driver before it hurts you too much.

Continue advancing past the broken fence. You're in a large clearing. Use your AT-ST to blast all the stormtroopers running around the area trying to kill you. Move into the clearing and follow the left cliff wall. Be sure to destroy all the vegetation as you collect more studs. You eventually get to some destructible purple boxes on the ground. These boxes leave behind some LEGOs for you to put together. Once assembled, they form a turnstile. Get out of your vehicle and push the green side. As the turnstile spins, a platform comes down on the tree nearby. Blast the vegetation to the left of the boxes and you uncover a red circle swirl pad. You can't do anything there yet so get back in your AT-ST.

Now walk to the north of the clearing. When you get to the end, jump out of your walker and blast all the vegetation to find some more studs. Get back in the AT-ST and blast the large pile of debris to the right. After a few hits, the pile explodes, leaving behind many valuable studs. Be sure to jump out and grab them.

Press the green side of the turnstile you created out of the loose LEGO pieces.

FREEPLAY AREA

While you're in the AT-ST, move to the ledge on the left side of the area. Exit the vehicle so that you land on the ledge. Give the stormtroopers that greet you a beating. Break all the equipment on the ground. Then assemble the loose LEGOs that you find. Next, throw a thermal detonator at the two shiny metal boxes nearby to destroy them and create more LEGO pieces. Now use the Force to put all these pieces together to make a trailer. Use the Force again on the top of the trailer. The lid on top opens up so some Ewoks can jump in for a ride.

FREEPLAY AREA

Use your ascension gun 'while standing on the red circle swirl pad to grapple to the elevator above. Use the Force to pull on the ball to the right and the elevator you're standing on ascends the tree. When it reaches its top height, quickly double jump to a ledge on the left before the elevator drops back down again. Stand on the elevator you find there and again use the Force on the ball hanging to the left. When this second elevator reaches its top height, quickly switch to R2 and fly to a platform to the left. Move across those platforms until you can grab the LEGO canister that was up there.

Jump back into the walker, and from there, jump to a platform in the trees nearby. Step on the red floor switch you find to make a red circle swirl pad appear on the ground below. Someone in your party uses the ascension gun to grapple to another platform to the right. That character pulls the lever on the tree trunk. A crate drops to the ground and shatters into pieces.

INTRODUCTION

GALAXY BASICS

STAR WARS CHARACTERS

TRANSPORTATION

MOS EISLEY CANTINA

WALKTHROUGH INTRODUCTION

iv EPISODE IV: A NEW HOPE

v EPISODE V: THE EMPIRE STRIKES BACK

vi EPISODE VI: RETURN OF THE JEDI

BONUS FEATURES

Jump to the area where the crate fell and assemble the loose pieces on the ground to create a red circle swirl pad. Use your ascension gun to grapple to a platform in the tree to the right. Then step on the red circle swirl pad and swing to the roof of a building to the right. Blast all the vents you see and collect the loot that falls to the ground. Two of the broken vents leave some LEGO pieces behind. Assemble the leftover pieces to finish the checkerboard pattern on the roof. Now push the box you find up there along the pattern and over the edge of the building to shatter on the forest floor below you.

Use the red circle swirl pads on the platforms in the trees to swing over to the roof of the Imperial building nearby.

Jump off the edge of the building and blast the plants to the left. Collect anything that drops to the ground. Then assemble the loose LEGOs on the right side of the building. These pieces turn into an access panel that only R2-D2 can use. Head to the south of the panel and put together a few more LEGO pieces to form a ramp. Now the rest of your party can join you in front of the building.

Before you do anything else, run down the path to the right, blast any plants that are still alive, and collect any studs scattered about the area. When the area is clean, use R2 to access the panel on the building's side to open the door and head inside.

Assemble the LEGOs in front of the building to create a ramp that your friends can use.

FREEPLAY AREA

When you get to the clearing's right side, use a thermal detonator to break up the shiny metal boxes. Assemble the LEGO pieces that are left behind after the explosion to create an elevator platform on the tree behind you. Stand on the platform and use the Force on the ball to the right to raise the elevator. When it gets to its top height, switch to your small character and jump into the travel chute in the tree.

The travel chute takes you to a ledge higher up in the tree. Use the Force to break apart a ledge to the left and reassemble it in a lower location. Jump to the ledge you moved and then to another ledge to the left. When you are safely across, use the Force to put the first ledge you moved back where you found it. Now jump to the ledge you moved, and from there jump to a higher ledge to the right. There you can add another LEGO canister to your stash.

NOTE

If the enemy AT-STs in the area are giving you trouble, move to the center of the clearing and jump into the controls of one of the catapults. Fire a direct hit at the walkers to send the pilots flying out of the cockpits. Now mow them down.

Upon entering the building, shoot the wall panels and the white containers on the ground. Be sure to collect any studs that spill onto the floor as you go. Follow the walkway inside and go down the ramp until you get to a locked door. Fire your blaster pistol at the red lights in the center. After a few hits, the doors open and Imperial troops rush out to greet you. Keep your weapon ready and shoot them down as they get close.

When the coast is clear, go through the open doors into the next room. Blast all the white equipment lying around and any guards that might still be alive. There are doors to blast open both on the left and the right, and the pathway ahead is blocked by a force field. For now, go to the back-left corner of the room and pull the lever on the wall. This undoes one of the four locks holding the force field in place.

Blast the red lights on the door to open it up.

FREEPLAY AREA

Inside the Imperial building, you find some brown pipes on the walls. Use the Force to break each pipe and collect the studs that spill out.

EPISODE VI
RETURN OF THE JEDI

INTRODUCTION
GALAXY BASICS
STAR WARS CHARACTERS
TRANSPORTATION
MOS EISLEY CANTINA
WALKTHROUGH INTRODUCTION
EPISODE IV: A NEW HOPE
EPISODE V: THE EMPIRE STRIKES BACK
EPISODE VI: RETURN OF THE JEDI
BONUS FEATURES

FREEPLAY AREA

Some unbreakable equipment stands in the back-right corner of the first room in the building after you run down the hall. Use the Force on the equipment to open a secret compartment and collect the studs that spill out.

Since the walkway ahead is still blocked, move to the door in the left wall. Shoot the red lights at the center of the door until they are gone, then head into the room beyond. As soon as you enter, you are fired on by a swarm of enemy troops. Blast all the guards at floor level, then hit the guys that are on the walkways above the room. When the coast is clear, assemble the loose LEGOs at the center of the room to create a model of a TIE interceptor.

Now move around the room, blasting all the white containers and grabbing anything that drops to the floor. Hidden beneath two of these containers are red floor switches. Step on both switches to make two platforms drop into place along the left wall. Shoot the wall panels in the back-left corner of the room and you'll discover a third floor switch. Step on this last switch to make a third platform move into place between the last two you created.

Jump up the platforms until you reach the narrow walkway at the top. Shoot the panels on the wall, and you'll find a piece of moveable equipment behind them. Jump behind the equipment and push it south and then to the left into a slot in the wall. This causes those platforms you just climbed to tilt and become a ramp. Now the rest of your friends can come up and join you. Switch to C-3PO and access the activation panel on the wall. This causes a force field on the right to disappear and a lever on the wall to become accessible. Pull the lever to destroy another lock on the large force field in the other room.

Step on the red floor switches to create a platform you can climb on the left side of the room.

Push the equipment on the walkway at the top of the room into the wall slot to create a ramp.

FREEPLAY AREA

Use the dark side of the Force to lift a piece of equipment out of the ground. Next, push it along the path on the floor to the right, then push it into the slot in the wall. After that, the equipment slides through the wall. You can see it through the large window in the wall as you enter the next room. Next, access the activation panel on the wall nearby using a stormtrooper. The stormtrooper in the other room runs back toward the large window and stands at the nearby controls.

Return to the walkway above the room near the lever you had C-3PO pull, and use R2-D2 to fly across the room to the right. Switch to C-3PO and use the activation panel on the wall. This causes some equipment in the next room to fall on the head of that stormtrooper at the controls, and opens a travel chute in the wall below you. Before you drop down, use a thermal detonator on the shiny metal pipes along the wall to destroy each one and collect the goodies that spill out.

Now drop to the floor and get in the travel chute to go to the room on the other side of the window. Get behind that box you pushed through the wall earlier. Push it along the path on the floor all the way to the end of the hall. When it slides into the slot in the wall at the end of the hall, a force field in the wall disappears. Grab the red power brick that was hidden behind it.

Go back to the main room and run to the locked door on the room's right side. Shoot the red lights at the center of the door, then head into the room beyond. Inside, blast all the Imperial troops trying to mow you down. After your enemies have been eliminated, shoot all the white containers on the room's right side. One of them has a red floor switch for you to step on. As soon as you do that, a trapdoor drops you down to a hidden tunnel under the floor. Collect all the studs you find under the floor, and when you're ready to go back up, follow the tunnel to the north. When you reach the end of the tunnel, a small elevator lifts you back to floor level.

On the floor level, shoot all the wall panels in the back of the room and collect the studs that drop to the ground. Next, use R2 to access the activation panel against the back wall. This activates a small elevator to the right of the panel. Ride the elevator to the ledge above the room and exit to the right. Assemble the loose LEGOs on the ledge to fill in the gaps in the path so the droids can get across. Switch to C-3PO and follow the walkway to the right. Use him to access the activation panel with his picture on it.

This opens up a lever in the wall to the right. Pull the lever to make a third lock on the large force field in the other room bust apart.

Use R2 to access the panel on the wall to start the small elevator moving up and down.

FREEPLAY AREA

Hidden behind some of the wall panels in the back of the room are some compartments. Use the Force to open all the compartments, causing LEGO studs and pieces to fall out. Collect the studs, then assemble the loose pieces on the floor to make a LEGO canister to add to your collection.

FREEPLAY AREA

When you get to the top of the room, throw a thermal detonator at the shiny pipes along the upper wall. After they break apart, collect the blue studs hidden behind them.

Switch to R2-D2 and follow the upper walkway to the room's left side. When you get to the end, follow the wall and fly across the room to the left. You eventually reach a small ledge on the other side of the room. Use the activation panel on the wall. A plug in the wall opens, spilling loose LEGOs onto the ground. Assemble the loose pieces to create a travel chute in the wall. Use Wicket to move through the chute to get into a room to the left. Once you get to the new room, drop the stormtroopers guarding the area, then pull the lever to the right. This destroys the last lock on the force field in the main room.

Luckily, Wicket is small enough and can travel through the chute in the wall to get to the other room nearby.

FREEPLAY AREA

After you pull the lever using Wicket, switch over to R2. Fly across the gap in the walkway to the back of the room. There you can add another LEGO canister to your stash.

Go back to the main room and move to the center of the area. Now that the four locks have been destroyed, the controls at the room's center are functional again. Pull the lever on the center control; the force field blocking the path ahead disappears. Head down the path and kill any stormtroopers that enter the room to stop you. When you get to the new area, you see four piles of LEGO pieces on the ground. Assemble each pile to create an explosive device on the wall. After you build the last bomb, your plan is set in motion.

Pull the levers on the controls at the center of the room to make that force field disappear.

Run for it. This baby's going to blow!

The Empire's shield generator is history.

Han feels pretty good about himself ...until the large dish falls on him.

Chapter 5: Jedi Destiny

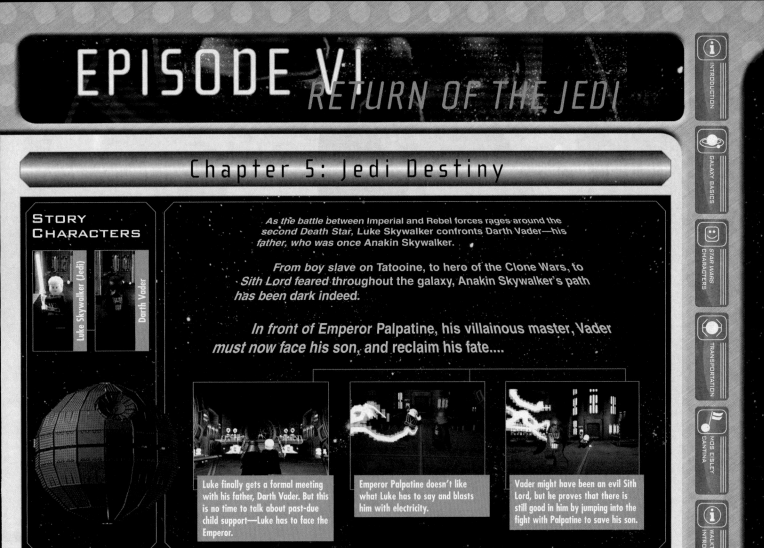

STORY CHARACTERS

Luke Skywalker (Jedi)

Darth Vader

As the battle between Imperial and Rebel forces rages around the second Death Star, Luke Skywalker confronts Darth Vader—his father, who was once Anakin Skywalker.

From boy slave on Tatooine, to hero of the Clone Wars, to Sith Lord feared throughout the galaxy, Anakin Skywalker's path has been dark indeed.

In front of Emperor Palpatine, his villainous master, Vader must now face his son, and reclaim his fate....

Luke finally gets a formal meeting with his father, Darth Vader. But this is no time to talk about past-due child support—Luke has to face the Emperor.

Emperor Palpatine doesn't like what Luke has to say and blasts him with electricity.

Vader might have been an evil Sith Lord, but he proves that there is still good in him by jumping into the fight with Palpatine to save his son.

Luke Skywalker bravely turns himself over to the Empire to get a meeting with Darth Vader. Luke believes there is still good in his father, and is willing to try and convince him to change his ways. Vader is adamant about what side of the Force he is on and he escorts Luke to his master, Emperor Palpatine. If Luke thought Vader was bad, he gets a rude awakening with Palpatine, who shocks him with evil electrical Force. Unfortunately for the Emperor, that was just the trigger Vader needed to find his true self, Anakin Skywalker, within. Vader valiantly jumps into the path of the electrical attack waves hitting his son to try to save Luke.

After the mission starts, the Emperor charges in to take both father and son. Jump at your attacker and hit him with your lightsaber to cause him to lose one of his hearts of health. He flies back across the room, but comes charging right back in again. Fly at him again and slice him with your weapon. Repeat this until you take away four of his hearts. That's when the Emperor tries a new trick and sends the electrical currents at you. When the currents surround your body, quickly switch over to Darth Vader, who is standing close by. While the Emperor is still distracted by dealing with Luke, you can jump at Palpatine and hit him with your lightsaber. After the fifth hit, Palpatine goes flying across the room and runs to another area.

When the Emperor blasts you with electrical energy, switch over to your other playable character so you can keep up your attack.

TIP

The Emperor's electrical blasts don't have a lot of range. If your other character isn't around for you to switch to, run to the end of the upper platform and fall to the lower area. Palpatine can't touch you there and you'll avoid taking damage. Just run back up the stairs when you are ready to fight again.

Before you go chasing after Palpatine, run to the back of the throne room. Using the dark side of the Force, turn on the red lights on the wall, on both sides of the throne. After you switch on the eighth light, a red Power Brick appears on the Emperor's actual throne. Jump on the seat and add that red Power Brick to your collection. Run to the room's left side and use the Force to turn some floor panels into a large step. Jump to the top of the step you created, and from there, into the small alcove in the wall to collect a LEGO canister.

INTRODUCTION

GALAXY BASICS

STAR WARS CHARACTERS

TRANSPORTATION

MOS EISLEY CANTINA

WALKTHROUGH INTRODUCTION

iv EPISODE IV: A NEW HOPE

v EPISODE V: THE EMPIRE STRIKES BACK

vi EPISODE VI: RETURN OF THE JEDI

BONUS FEATURES

Move to the stairs to the south of the throne room. On either side of the stairs are some tables with lots of blue lights. Smash each table and collect the studs that spill out. Collect the rest of the goodies and then fight off any Imperial guards that rush in to put you down. When the upper throne room is treasure free, head down the stairs to the area's lower level.

Jump on the large step you created at the side of the room to get those canisters.

On the bottom level, run underneath the upper throne room and gather all valuables on the ground, including the blue studs. While you're under there, smash the blue pillars on both sides of the stairs to find even more goodies. Explore the rest of the lower throne room and smash all the equipment you see. Collect the studs that litter the ground.

Run to the room's left side and use the dark side of the Force to break the grate in the wall. Assemble the little pieces that fall to the floor into a red fan. Assemble a pile of gray LEGOs on the right. After you have built them, use the Force to put the two pieces together to create a large fan on the ground. A path leads from the south of the throne room, but skip that area for now. Jump on the fan so you can ride the breeze it creates into the air and over to a narrow walkway against the left wall.

Put the fan together so you can ride the air currents to the walkway above.

FREEPLAY AREA

When you get to the throne room's lower level, switch to a bounty hunter and throw a thermal detonator at the equipment along the right wall. Assemble the loose LEGOs on the ground, which remain after the explosion, to create a red circle swirl pad. Use your ascension gun while standing on the pad to grapple to a ledge above. Grab the studs you find, as well as a LEGO canister.

Follow the trail of studs along the walkway until you get to a platform over the next room. Across the way, the Emperor is electrifying the five rows of floor panels to prevent you from crossing. The good news is that he can't cover the whole floor at once. Some panels constantly flicker with electrical energy, some flicker in and out, and some never become electrified at all. Run to the back wall and jump to the two panels that are closest to the wall in the second row—they are safe. Wait for the current to stop flowing to the rest of the second row, then run to the other end and jump on the first panel in the third row.

That one is a safe panel because it never becomes electrified. Step on the first panel in the fourth row next to find another safe spot. Wait for the electricity in the floor panels to die out again and then follow the safe panels all the way to the left.

You finally reach the Emperor again, so let him have it with your lightsaber. When he tries to blast you with energy, switch to your partner to continue the attack. Keep hitting Palpatine until he takes enough damage and flies across the room to escape his fate.

Jump only to the unelectrified gray floor panels so you don't get electrocuted.

You're almost to that evil Palpatine.

CAUTION

Don't try to jump the panels, because the charge they create will knock you off the platform.

NOTE

Make sure you have your friend with you when you fight the Emperor the second time—you'll need backup. If your partner falls off the upper walkway at some point, you'll have to jump down, find him, and then return to the fan to get back up to the upper walkway.

EPISODE VI
RETURN OF THE JEDI

INTRODUCTION

GALAXY BASICS

STAR WARS CHARACTERS

TRANSPORTATION

MOS EISLEY CANTINA

WALKTHROUGH INTRODUCTION

iv EPISODE IV: A NEW HOPE

v EPISODE V: THE EMPIRE STRIKES BACK

vi EPISODE VI: RETURN OF THE JEDI

BONUS FEATURES

When the area is secure and floor panels are safe to walk across, smash all the equipment to find hidden treasure. Then use the dark side of the Force to turn off the red lights in the back of the room. After the lights are stud free, head to the room's right side and wait for the red lights to come on again. Run along the back wall and, as you do so, quickly use the Force to turn off each of the red lights. If you are quick enough and turn off all ten lights at once, a door in the back wall will open and you can grab a LEGO canister that was previously obscured from view.

Run to the south and drop from the upper walkway down to the room below. Smash the equipment lying around the room, then pick up any loose studs that you see. Assemble some loose LEGOs on the room's right side to create an activation panel that only a bounty hunter can use. Use the dark side of the Force to pull a metal grate off the wall, then assemble the pieces that fall out. This creates a large step on the ground. There's nothing you can do with it now, so move through the open doorway in the north wall.

Step on all the green lights to find a hidden canister.

Run along the back wall and use the dark side of the Force to turn off those lights.

FREEPLAY AREA

Switch to a bounty hunter when you're on the circular platform in the center of the room and access the activation panel on the wall. This opens a door to the right of the panel, so go inside the alcove beyond and grab some studs for your collection. Along the same circular wall as the bounty hunter activation panel are two long, gray, rectangular LEGO pieces. Use a thermal detonator to blow apart both pieces. One hides a LEGO canister for your collection and the other has more studs.

While you're on the circular platform in the center of the building, switch to a stormtrooper. Use him to access the activation panel on the same wall as the other panel. A door opens to the right, so run into the alcove beyond to add some more studs to your stash. Move around the short, circular platform until you see some loose LEGOs across from the bounty hunter activation panel. Put the pieces together and then switch to C-3PO; have him access the activation panel you just created. This extends a walkway to the left. Run into the little room at the end of the walkway and add some more goodies to your stash. Construct the loose LEGOs on the floor to collect another LEGO canister.

FREEPLAY AREA

Use your bounty hunter to access the activation panel on the room's right side. This lowers a walkway against the back wall. Jump on the platform you created and from there, jump to the new walkway. Run to the left, and when the walkway ends, switch to R2-D2 and fly to the left. You land on a ledge where you can add a LEGO canister to your stash.

When you get to the back room, you see many green lights on the floor. Quickly run over every green light to turn them all off. A LEGO canister appears at the center of the room, in the center of the ring of lights. The area under the canister is bottomless and you'll die if you fall in, so double jump over the opening to grab the canister and land safely on the other side of the lights.

Exit through the same door you entered and follow the walkway to the south. This takes you to a circular platform in the center of the building. Run around the pillar in the center of the circular platform and use the Force on the lights to uncover hidden goods. After you turn on all the lights, follow the walkway around until you see the room where Palpatine waits for you.

When you get to the next room, the Emperor tries to blast you with his electrical attacks. Use the same switching-characters technique to get an uncontested hit on him. After taking a couple of hits, he flies to a walkway high above the room. Before you go after him, collect the valuable blue studs around the room, then smash all the equipment for even more goodies. Smash the blinking wall panels on the right wall to find some more studs and a small travel chute.

Now move to the room's left side and assemble the LEGOs on the ground to fix the elevator on the wall. Jump on the elevator and use the Force on the controls. Your partner does the same, and together you rise into the air. When you get to the walkway above, jump off and slash at Emperor Palpatine, who has been waiting for you. He doesn't like getting hurt and flies to the right side of the room.

Use the Force to move the elevator to the upper walkway.

FREEPLAY AREA

Switch to a small character and jump into the small travel chute in the right wall. This takes you to a ledge above the room where you can push a box over the edge. When the box hits the floor, it leaves behind a pile of debris. Use your lightsaber on the pile of debris to blast open the door behind you.

Head through the open door. Knock out the Imperial guards in this large Imperial palace room and collect the studs on the ground. Smash the box to the left of the door you came through, then create an activation panel on the wall from the loose LEGOs on the ground. Have C-3PO use the panel to lower a platform along the back right wall. Then throw a thermal detonator at the shiny metal LEGOs to the right of the entrance doorway; afterwards, you find a red circle swirl on the ground. Throw another thermal detonator at the shiny metal grate on the back wall to grab a hidden LEGO canister behind the grate.

Get to the ledge above by using the red circle swirl, then pull the lever on the wall. Some debris falls in the center of the room; go over to the debris and turn it into a movable box. Afterwards, destroy the chairs in the center of the room for some hidden LEGOs. Assemble the pieces into a turnstile. Now push the box along the path on the floor and onto the green circle nearby, then push the green side of the turnstile to turn the green circle and the box on top of it. Keep turning it until the green arrow on the top of the box points to the right.

Push the box off the green circle and along the rest of the path. When you get to the right side of the room, you can see some green arrows on the ground, pointing to the right. Push the box along the arrows and into the wall; this activates an elevator nearby that starts moving up and down. Ride the elevator to the ledges above the room.

Follow the ledge to the left. Make the force fields below you disappear by pulling the lever on the wall, then following the ledges to the right and pulling on another lever.

Drop to the ground and use the dark side of the Force on the black grates on the wall. When they shatter, collect the loot that spills out, then use the dark side of the Force again to turn the fans that were behind the grates. Jump in the alcove over each fan, where the force fields used to be, to collect studs from the right alcove and a LEGO canister from the left one.

Make your way to the back of the room and use the Force to stack the large red chairs against the wall. Double jump your way to the top, where you can switch to a small character and enter the travel chute on the wall. The chute takes you to a small chamber to the right. Destroy the gate inside and collect the LEGO canister behind it, then head back to the main room. Before you leave, smash all the destructible chairs and use the Force on all the wall light fixtures to uncover more hidden studs.

Smash all the containers you find on the walkway and grab what spills out. Then, use the Force on the lights on the back wall to find even more hidden treasure. Double jump across the gap in the walkway on the right to get to the Emperor on the other side of the room. As soon as you land, jump at Palpatine and whack him with your weapon. If you hit him, he flies away in fear to the room below. Use the Force again on the lights on the wall to find some hidden goods, and smash the containers you find.

Drop to the room below, where you fight a barely alive Palpatine some more. Switch characters when you start to get shocked and then cut him down. After suffering a few hits, the Emperor retreats to the circular walkway in the center of the building. With one more direct hit, the Emperor is all out of health and his evil rule comes to an end.

Double jump to the walkway on the right to fight the Emperor some more.

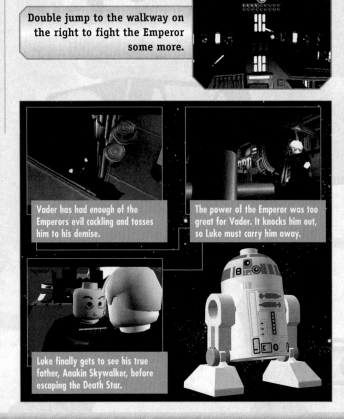

Vader has had enough of the Emperors evil cackling and tosses him to his demise.

The power of the Emperor was too great for Vader. It knocks him out, so Luke must carry him away.

Luke finally gets to see his true father, Anakin Skywalker, before escaping the Death Star.

EPISODE VI
RETURN OF THE JEDI

INTRODUCTION

GALAXY BASICS

STAR WARS CHARACTERS

TRANSPORTATION

MOS EISLEY CANTINA

WALKTHROUGH INTRODUCTION

EPISODE IV: A NEW HOPE

EPISODE V: THE EMPIRE STRIKES BACK

EPISODE VI: RETURN OF THE JEDI

BONUS FEATURES

Chapter 6: Into the Death Star

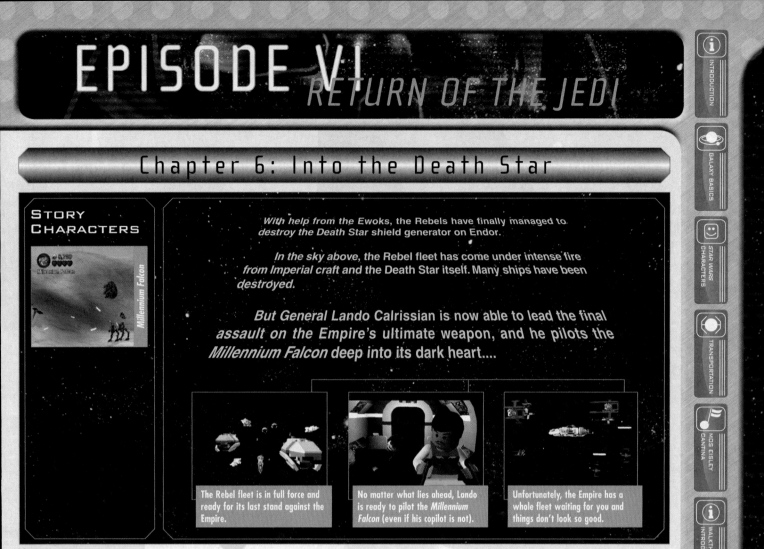

STORY CHARACTERS

Millennium Falcon

With help from the Ewoks, the Rebels have finally managed to destroy the Death Star shield generator on Endor.

In the sky above, the Rebel fleet has come under intense fire from Imperial craft and the Death Star itself. Many ships have been destroyed.

But General Lando Calrissian is now able to lead the final assault on the Empire's ultimate weapon, and he pilots the *Millennium Falcon* deep into its dark heart....

The Rebel fleet is in full force and ready for its last stand against the Empire.

No matter what lies ahead, Lando is ready to pilot the *Millennium Falcon* (even if his copilot is not).

Unfortunately, the Empire has a whole fleet waiting for you and things don't look so good.

This is it—the final confrontation, for better or for worse. With the help of Admiral Ackbar, the Rebels have amassed a mighty force to take on the Death Star. Unfortunately, the Empire is well prepared for the assault. But now that Han Solo and his team have taken out the field generator supporting the Death Star, those brave Rebels have a fighting chance to save the day and bring peace back to the galaxy.

When you start this mission, the large Imperial fleet is in front of you. Not only do you have to take out four large Star Destroyers, but you also have to deal with the TIE interceptors buzzing around the area trying to shoot you down. As soon as the mission starts, fly toward the large Star Destroyer in front of you. Fly over the top of the ship and blast the small gray satellite you see to add a LEGO canister to your collection.

Those gray satellites floating in space hold LEGO canisters, so nab them.

After you acquire the canister, go to work destroying that craft. On either side of the ship are deadly turret guns. Fly in loops in front of the guns and keep blasting. Those strong guns take a lot of shots before they blow up. Every time you destroy a turret gun, be sure to fly over where the gun was and collect the studs floating

in space above that location. After you destroy all the turret guns on the large craft, you can concentrate on taking out the whole Destroyer.

Fly into space and target the TIE bombers buzzing around. They are the ships carrying the purple torpedoes behind them. Break the bombers apart. Now fly through the debris they leave behind and pick up their bombs. Fly over the large Star Destroyer and head for the tall observation deck. When you get close, a purple reticle appears over the ship, so fire your torpedo. Each observation deck has two targets for you to fire at and destroy. After you destroy the second target on the ship, the craft goes down for the count. Fly over the area where the Star Destroyer was and collect the loose studs that remain floating in space.

Fire your torpedoes at the large reticle covering the observation deck of each Star Destroyer.

TIP

If you start to get low on health, fly out into space and knock out a couple of the TIE fighters that are buzzing about. Most of the time they leave behind a heart for you to replenish the hearts you might be missing.

After you take out that first large Imperial craft, you still have three more to go: one to the right, one straight ahead, and one to the left. Fly for the one on the right first and destroy all the turret guns on its surface. Collect the studs that are released after each gun is destroyed. After the last gun is gone, fire some purple torpedoes at the two reticles on the Destroyer's observation deck. After both reticles have been hit, the Star Destroyer drops out of space to its demise.

Next, fly to the Destroyer that was in the middle of the other two Star Destroyers. Fly across its bow and shoot the gray satellite you see to add another LEGO canister to your stash. Next, take out the turret guns, then fire some torpedoes at the control tower to turn that Star Destroyer into scrap metal.

Finally, fly to the left and engage the fourth (and final) Star Destroyer. Take out all the turret guns so that you can collect more studs, then fire two purple torpedoes at the reticles over the observation deck. As the last ship drops out of space, grab the studs it leaves behind.

Take out those turret guns, because they leave behind valuable studs.

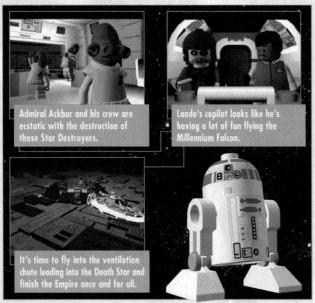

Admiral Ackbar and his crew are ecstatic with the destruction of those Star Destroyers.

Lando's copilot looks like he's having a lot of fun flying the Millennium Falcon.

It's time to fly into the ventilation chute leading into the Death Star and finish the Empire once and for all.

When you approach the Death Star, fly straight into the ventilation shaft ahead of you. As you fly, keep blasting your guns. Destructible wall and floor panels that release studs when they are destroyed line the shaft. Also, be sure to destroy the brown pipes hanging from the ceiling and collect what they leave behind. You'll also find along the wall some turret guns that can be destroyed for more studs, but they are more trouble than they are worth, so speed past them. As you fly through the shaft, enemy TIE fighters swarm around you and try to take you out. Keep moving and blast them before they can blast you.

Farther down the shaft, you eventually get to a purple torpedo dispenser. Fly over the dispenser and collect three torpedoes, then continue moving down the shaft. When you see three purple reticles in the shaft ahead, fire your torpedoes until all three targets are history. Collect the loot that floats in the air after each one is hit. After you destroy the third target, a LEGO canister appears in the shaft ahead. Add it to your stash.

Hit the wall and floor panels to find some hidden loot.

Get some torpedoes so that you can fire at the purple targets in the distance.

CAUTION

The ventilation shaft is narrow and many enemies are buzzing around. If you get shot to pieces, be sure to quickly collect any studs that you've left floating in space after you respawn.

A little farther down, the shaft is blocked by an impenetrable force field. Surrounding the barrier are four more purple targets that you need to destroy. Return to the torpedo dispenser and load up on bombs, then head back to targets and fire away. When you need more torpedoes, just return to the dispenser and repeat. After the fourth and final purple target has been destroyed, the force field disappears and you can continue flying down the shaft.

The next part of the shaft bends to the right, where you find a torpedo dispenser. Load up, then follow the shaft as it bends to the north. As you fly along this new passage, shoot the orange wall panels and snatch the loot that comes out. The shaft leads you to a room where the door to the next area is locked. On both sides of the door are hidden missile launchers. When you get close, the launchers come out and fire their payloads at you. Move to the launcher on the right; when it opens up, fire your purple torpedoes at it until the missile launcher explodes. Do the same thing to the launcher on the left. With both launchers destroyed, the door in the back wall unlocks and opens.

Fire your torpedoes at the missile launchers and destroy them so that you can get into the next shaft.

FREEPLAY AREA

On the wall to the right of the four purple targets is a door that only TIE fighters can enter. Change your ship to a TIE fighter and open the door to reveal a small alcove behind it. Grab the hidden Lego canister inside for your collection.

FREEPLAY AREA

At the end of the long shaft heading north is a door in the left wall that only TIE fighters can open. Switch to a TIE fighter to make the door open. This reveals a small alcove. Shoot the LEGO canister inside to add it to your collection.

Fly through the opening between the two destroyed missile launchers. You're now in a circular room with the Death Star's reactor core in the center. Fly around the room and shoot the gray satellite to add another LEGO canister to your collection. Now fly along the outer wall. You find two purple targets over which a purple reticle appears when you get close. Fire purple torpedoes at both targets to destroy them and open an alcove between them. Fly into the alcove and grab a red power brick for your collection.

Also along the outer wall are some red and white panels. Each panel hides a wall socket that's connected to the reactor core at the center of the room. Slowly fly toward a panel and it opens up to reveal a socket in the wall. Quickly fire your blasters to destroy the socket—if you get too close, the socket zaps you and renders you helpless for a few seconds.

Blast the wall sockets hidden behind each red and white panel.

NOTE

If you need more torpedoes to hit the targets on the wall, just return to the shaft you were in a moment ago. Find the dispenser that you passed earlier.

Continue to fly around the circular room and take out all the electrical sockets in the wall. After you destroy the last one, the protective force field around the reactor core at the room's center disappears. Fly toward the core to see it spinning. Wait until you see the blue part of the core, then fire your blasters at it until the casing around the core is destroyed. Pick up the purple torpedo that is left behind after the explosion, and fire it at the remainder of the core.

You did it! The Death Star is going to blow. Unfortunately, you're still in it! Follow the shaft you're in to get to safety. Keep your foot on the pedal because the fire from the core explosion is following right behind you. If it catches up to you, you'll crash and burn. As you fly, keep shooting your blasters. This not only destroys any objects that could get in your way and slow you down, but also gives you some extra studs. If you continuously fire your guns, you can also destroy three LEGO canisters located in the shaft on the way out. If you happen to miss one, you can go back and get it in Freeplay mode.

Blast the blue panels of the inner core to destroy the whole thing.

Now's no time to stop because the fire is right behind you. Keep those guns blazing to knock out any obstructions in your path.

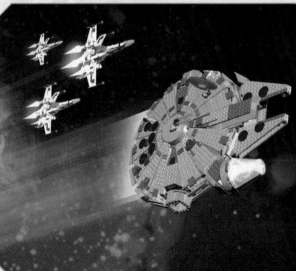

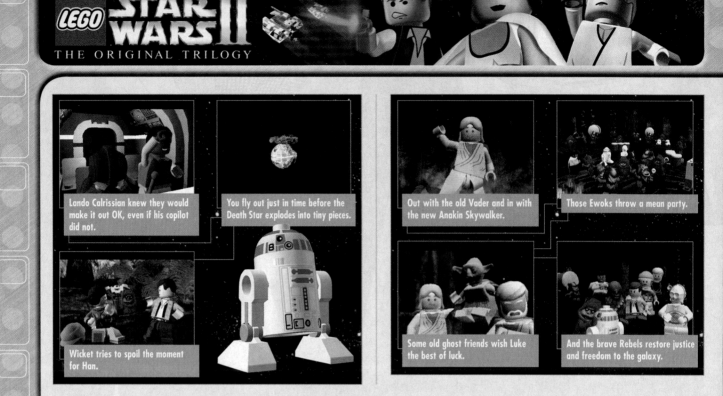

Lando Calrissian knew they would make it out OK, even if his copilot did not.

You fly out just in time before the Death Star explodes into tiny pieces.

Wicket tries to spoil the moment for Han.

Out with the old Vader and in with the new Anakin Skywalker.

Those Ewoks throw a mean party.

Some old ghost friends wish Luke the best of luck.

And the brave Rebels restore justice and freedom to the galaxy.

Chapter 7: Episode VI Bonus

The bonus section contains three parts. The first part requires you to play through all the chapters of Episode VI *Return of the Jedi* in less than one hour while collecting 100,000 studs. The second part has you fighting on the planet of Endor against the worst scoundrels in the galaxy in order to collect one million studs in less than five minutes. And the third part has you flying through the forest of Endor in search of one million studs in less than five minutes. After you successfully complete each part, you get a gold brick for your collection. If you don't complete a mission in the allotted time, you just have to play again until you do, if you want to earn that brick.

SUPER STORY

The Super Story part of this bonus mission requires you to play through all the missions of *Return of the Jedi* again. Those missions are: "Jabba's Palace," "The Great Pit of Carkoon," "Speeder Showdown," "The Battle of Endor," "Jedi Destiny," and "Into the Death Star." The challenge this time is that you have to play thorough all six chapters consecutively while grabbing 100,000 studs in less than an hour. These missions are exactly the same as the first time you played them, except this time you have a time constraint.

Since you don't have any time to lose, don't waste time in areas where you aren't going to find many studs or that are way off the beaten path. Try to hit the areas that had the blue studs or many studs in a centralized location. "Jabba's Palace," which hold loads of studs to add to your total, features many things you can destroy along your way. "Jedi Destiny" has many valuable blue studs that are easy to get to, especially under the Emperor's throne room. Make sure you spend a good chunk of time on this mission to get more studs. After you reach your goal of 100,000 studs, you can then concentrate on getting through the levels quicker so that you can finish in under an hour. If you finish in less than an hour and with 100,000 studs, you get a gold brick.

Jabba is rich and has lots of wealth hidden in items around his palace.

The Emperor's throne room is a treasure trove of valuable studs.

CHARACTER BONUS (ENDOR)

While the Rebel Alliance struggles heroically with the oppressive Empire, and as Luke Skywalker moves closer to his epic destiny, daily life goes on across the galaxy.

In the battle-torn forest of Endor, intrepid adventurers compete to collect one million LEGO studs in the fastest time possible.

It's the desperate, ruthless life of a world in turmoil....

EPISODE VI
RETURN OF THE JEDI

You start this mission high above the forest of Endor in the Ewok village. There, you have only five minutes to collect one million LEGO studs. This mission is played in a Freeplay mode style, so you can choose who you want to play, and the game will pick the rest of your playable characters, all of whom have different abilities. Play this mission after you have completed the game so that you can use one of the ghost characters such as Anakin Skywalker (Ghost) or Obi-Wan Kenobi (Ghost). Ghost characters are impervious to damage, which comes in handy since everyone is gunning for you. Get Boba Fett as your second character (as described in the beginning of the character section) for his powerful gun and his thermal detonators.

This mission is played in the Ewok village in the trees high above the forest floor of Endor. The village consists of large platforms that can be connected by narrow wooden bridges. Scattered all over the place are large orange and blue pots that have many studs inside. On certain platforms, you'll also find shiny metal objects that can be blown open using thermal detonators. These shiny pieces of equipment hold the most valuable studs.

Break the large pots to get a payday of studs.

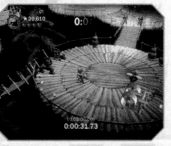

The shiny metal equipment pieces hold valuable purple and blue studs for you to collect.

As soon as the mission starts, move to the back-left platform of the village you're on. Assemble the two piles of LEGOs on the ground to fix the gears of the nearby bridge. Once fixed, the bridge rises up and connects the platform you're standing on to the large platform to the left. Now that the bridge is fixed, walk through the village to the right until you find a bridge leading south. Cross the bridge to another large platform, where you find pots and shiny equipment to destroy.

Move to the gears on the left of the platform to make a bridge rise up to connect the area you're on to the platform on the left. Cross the bridge, and you'll find a collection of small platforms. Smash all the pots and then use a thermal detonator to destroy a piece of shiny equipment to the far left. Follow a ramp in the area to get to the top of one of the small platforms. Run to the gears on the left side. A bridge rises up, connecting your platform to the one in the distance. The next area has more pots and more shiny equipment to destroy.

Fix the gears of the bridge so you can cross later.

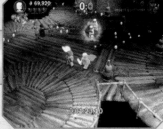

Switch to your ghost character when the going gets tough.

The platforms along the south side of the village are where you want to spend the majority of your time. Move back and forth across those platforms, blasting pots with your blaster and using your thermal detonators on the shiny equipment. Everything respawns after a while, so you can go back and shoot everything again and again. When enemies approach, switch to your ghost character to avoid taking damage. Keep blasting everything in sight until you reach the million-stud mark in less than five minutes to earn a gold brick. If you fail to reach a million studs in less than five minutes, you have to repeat the mission.

Stay to the south of the Ewok village, where you can concentrate on taking out all the shiny pieces of equipment.

MINIKIT BONUS (ENDOR)

While the Rebel Alliance struggles heroically with the oppressive Empire, and as Luke Skywalker moves closer to his epic destiny, daily life goes on across the galaxy.

In the battle-torn forest of Endor, intrepid adventurers compete to collect one million LEGO studs in the fastest time possible.

It's the desperate, ruthless life of a world in turmoil....

INTRODUCTION
GALAXY BASICS
STAR WARS CHARACTERS
TRANSPORTATION
MOS EISLEY CANTINA
WALKTHROUGH INTRODUCTION
EPISODE IV: A NEW HOPE
EPISODE V: THE EMPIRE STRIKES BACK
EPISODE VI: RETURN OF THE JEDI
BONUS FEATURES

You start this mission flying above the forest floor of Endor, where you have only five minutes to collect one million LEGO studs. This mission is played in a Freeplay mode style, so you can choose the vehicle you want to use, and the game will pick the rest of your playable vehicles for the mission. It is a good idea to use a vehicle that is quick, such as a TIE fighter, on this level because enemies hound you during the entire mission.

The forest floor is covered with lush vegetation that you can blast to pieces. All the plants that can be destroyed hold valuable studs to add to your total. You'll also find lots of enemies in the area. Enemy TIE fighters buzz about the skies and AT-AT and AT-ST walkers stalk the ground. As you go about looking for studs, be sure to take out these servants of the Empire whenever you need hearts to replenish your health.

Blast the vegetation to find hidden studs.

Destroy those walkers on the ground when you need to find some hearts.

The lush vegetation is a good source for studs, but a much better source should be at the top of your priority list: Three purple target stations are on the forest floor and each one holds many purple and blue studs. All you need to do is fire a purple torpedo at each station to cause the target to explode and litter the ground with loot. Eventually the targets respawn and you can repeat the process. As you fly from station to station, shoot plants and enemies to collect studs and hearts.

You start in one of three clearings on the forest floor. Each clearing contains a purple target station, but in order to get any studs from the stations, you must blast each one with a torpedo. Fly to the right of the clearing you start in and follow the narrow trail you find as it connects to the next clearing. When you get to the clearing on the far right, you find the dispenser. Collect three torpedoes from the dispenser and fly to the southeast, where you find the first purple target station. Fire your torpedo when you get close, and a purple reticle appears over your target.

Grab torpedoes from the dispenser in the far-right clearing.

There's one of the purple target stations you must destroy to find hidden goods.

Now that you've destroyed the first station, fly to the left and follow the trail that leads to the next clearing. Fire a torpedo at the next purple target station in the second clearing to find more loot. Now, fly to the left again and make your way to the third and final clearing. When you get there, blast the last purple target station to get those valuable studs. You've destroyed all three stations. Go back to the torpedo dispenser and restock with three torpedoes. By this time, the purple target stations have regenerated, so you can go blast them again. Keep doing this until you collect one million studs in under five minutes and earn a gold brick.

Collect all the valuable studs that spill out of the stations.

BONUS FEATURES
Bounty Hunter Missions

A small alcove in the Mos Eisley cantina has a locked door with a small picture of Jabba the Hutt above it. After you complete all the episodes, the door opens. Go inside; you find Jabba himself behind a counter where you can get bounty hunter missions. For all ten of these missions, you have the choice of playing as any of the professional bounty hunters in the game: Boba Fett, 4-LOM, IG-88, Bossk, Dengar, and Greedo. You can switch to any one of them at any time during the mission. Everyone has the same set of skills, except for Boba Fett, who has the added bonus of being able to fly for short periods of time.

Every mission takes place in a small area from one of the game's chapters. Since you already played through every level at least once, you should know exactly where you're going. You have five minutes to find your bounty located somewhere in the area. If you fail to find your mark in less than the time allowed, you must start over again. Scour the galaxy in search of all ten of your famous targets, from Han Solo to Admiral Ackbar, and earn a valuable gold brick after each successful mission.

> The vile gangster Jabba the Hutt plans to kidnap leading figures in the Rebel Alliance. He is threatening to hand them over to Imperial forces unless a ransom is paid.
>
> Naturally, the evil Hutt intends to take the ransom money, trade his prisoners to the Imperials regardless, and pocket a double bounty.
>
> A band of vicious bounty hunters has come together to execute Jabba's scheme.

Mission 1: R2-D2
There's R2-D2 hiding behind the secret door you put together while on Princess Leia's starship, from the chapter "Secret Plans."

Mission 2: Ben Kenobi
Ben Kenobi tries to hide in a doorway near the exit to the Jawas' sandcrawler from "Through the Jundland Wastes."

Mission 3: Chewbacca
To find Chewbacca in the area from the "Mos Eisley Spaceport" chapter, blast the large doors near the movie theater.

Mission 4: Princess Leia
Princess Leia seems to like being a prisoner, as she hides out in the cell across from the one she was in during the "Rescue the Princess" chapter.

INTRODUCTION

GALAXY BASICS

STAR WARS CHARACTERS

TRANSPORTATION

MOS EISLEY CANTINA

WALKTHROUGH INTRODUCTION

iv EPISODE IV: A NEW HOPE

v EPISODE V: THE EMPIRE STRIKES BACK

vi EPISODE VI: RETURN OF THE JEDI

BONUS FEATURES

Mission 5: Admiral Ackbar

While hunting for Admiral Ackbar, put together the controls near the water tank from the chapter "Escape from Echo Base."

Mission 6: Yoda

This area is from "The Battle of Endor." Follow the Ewok village to the left until you find Yoda on a platform in the trees.

Mission 7: C-3PO

Take the elevator to the roof in the area from "Betrayal over Bespin" to find C-3PO, just waiting to be captured.

Mission 8: Lando Calrissian

Run to the landing pad controls from "Betrayal over Bespin" and you'll find Lando Calrissian. He knows that his time is up.

Mission 9: Luke Skywalker

Use an ascension gun when you're standing on the red circle swirl in "Mos Eisley Spaceport" to find Luke hiding on a ledge above the town.

Mission 10: Han Solo

To find Han Solo in "Escape from Echo Base," follow the frozen tunnels until you can jump from the moving cart to an alcove in the frozen wall.

Gold Brick Bonuses

Collecting gold bricks along your adventure can be very profitable and can get you into secret locations. As you collect them during your adventures, they begin to pile outside the cantina. Collect 60 gold bricks and you can put together a large golden question mark on the wall outside the cantina. When the question mark is complete, a doorway forms underneath it, allowing you to enter LEGO City. On the other side of the Mos Eisley cantina parking lot, you'll find another pile of gold bricks. After you find all 99 gold bricks in the game, you can assemble them into a giant golden fountain that spews valuable studs in the air, making you a very rich player.

LEGO City

> *In an infinite universe, all things are possible.*
>
> *As the second Death Star explodes beside an Endor moon, Anakin Skywalker's epic journey is complete. With his final sacrifice, balance has returned to the Force.*
>
> *But in another galaxy far, far away, though, echoes of this drama live on, and a new world awakens....*

LEGO City is a city built from, you guessed it, LEGOs! The goal in LEGO City is to find one million studs hidden around town. Because almost everything is built from LEGOs, much of the city can be knocked apart. Destroying things is one way to find many studs. Other ways to find valuables include assembling loose LEGOs, using thermal detonators on shiny metal LEGOs, and taking local vehicles for quick drives around town. There is no time limit on this mission, so take your time and explore everywhere. After you find the exactly one million studs hidden in the city, you've successfully completed the mission.

Here are some tips and areas of interest to check out as you go about tearing up the city to find all the studs.

Destroy all the trees, light posts, and fences that cover the city.

Some buildings can also be destroyed with a weapon or by using the Force.

Use the Force on all the windows of any building that you can't destroy to find more goodies.

Assemble everything in the city, including bouncing seeds on the ground that sprout into flowers and studs.

Take a ride on all vehicles and beasts you find, because sometimes a trail of blue studs appears on the ground for you to follow.

Jump on the giant lizard to get to the roof of the tall tower, where you can use the Force to assemble a nearby vehicle.

The AT-ST is great for quickly destroying things around the city.

Use the Force to stack the large, brightly colored LEGO bricks until you spell the word *LEGO*.

Run over the ground until all the flowers sprout from the ground. Collect the studs that come out.

INTRODUCTION

GALAXY BASICS

STAR WARS CHARACTERS

TRANSPORTATION

MOS EISLEY CANTINA

WALKTHROUGH INTRODUCTION

EPISODE IV: A NEW HOPE

EPISODE V: THE EMPIRE STRIKES BACK

EPISODE VI: RETURN OF THE JEDI

BONUS FEATURES

Bonus LEGO Fun

There are many fun and exciting things you can do with your LEGO *Star Wars* friends. Story mode might show what happened in the real episodes of the *Star Wars* trilogy, but in Freeplay mode you can create your own story line. Now you can have Luke and Anakin fighting side by side, or see the Emperor on the far-away, frozen planet of Hoth. Play the game over and over again to collect more studs and unlock more characters and extras for you to use any way you like!

Leia really knows how to shake it!

Look, young Luke, you're a Jedi Master in the future. Don't worry. Having your hand cut off won't be that painful...you hope.

Lando is so smooth with the ladies it doesn't matter what type of chaos happens around him.

Aw!...It's family reunion time!

Nobody rocks out on the air guitar like the Gamorrean guards.

Looks like someone got a little too fresh with Princess Leia and is going to feel the awful sting of rejection—also known as a slap.

That bounty hunter looks familiar....

Never upset a Wookiee if you value your arms!

Someone should get the Emperor a sweater—he's old and might catch a chill on the icy planet of Hoth.